INTERNATIONAL HANDBOOK of COMMUNITY SERVICES for the MENTALLY RETARDED

SCHOOL PSYCHOLOGY

A Series of Volumes edited by
Thomas R. Kratochwill and James E. Ysseldyke

Stark, McGee, and Menolascino • International Handbook of Community
Services for the Mentally Retarded

INTERNATIONAL HANDBOOK of COMMUNITY SERVICES for the MENTALLY RETARDED

Jack A. Stark
John J. McGee
Frank J. Menolascino
Nebraska Psychiatric Institute
University of Nebraska Medical Center

 LAWRENCE ERLBAUM ASSOCIATES, PUBLISHERS
1984   Hillsdale, New Jersey   London

Lawrence Erlbaum Associates, Inc., Publishers
365 Broadway
Hillsdale, New Jersey 07642

Library of Congress Cataloging in Publication Data

Stark, Jack A.,
    International handbook of community services
for the mentally retarded.

    (School psychology series)
    Bibliography: p.
    Includes indexes.
    1. Mentally handicapped--Services for--Handbooks,
manuals, etc.   2. Mentally handicapped--Services for--
United States--Case studies.   3. Mentally handicapped--
Care and treatment--United States--Case studies.
I. McGee, John J.   II. Menolascino, Frank J.,
             III. Title.   IV. Series.
HV3004.S82 1984   362.3'58   84-15432
ISBN 0-89859-385-9

Printed in the United States of America
10 9 8 7 6 5 4 3 2 1

To Donna, Shelly, Cindy, Michael, Scott, Mark and Amy; Zailde, Mona, and Maria; Shirley, John, Nicholas, and Suzanne.

Contents

Preface

Communities around the world have embarked on an irreversible trend toward the development of community-based service systems for all mentally retarded persons. Today it is clear that even the most severe mentally retarded, multiply handicapped person can and should remain in their home communities receiving whatever supports they might need across their lifespan. In this book we:

1. Describe the foundational and ideological constructs that have brought about this international movement—the principle of normalization, the developmental model, and the recognition of the full citizenship of all mentally retarded persons—and the role of parent associations in bringing about this social change.
2. Outline the general settings that comprise community-based programs as well as point out the types of programmatic options that are evolving around the world.
3. Analyze the application of these ideological constructs and programmatic innovations in a comprehensive, community-based program called the Eastern Nebraska Community Office of Retardation (USA).
4. Present a systems model on how to establish and maintain a community-based system as well as overcome the major barriers that all community-based systems are faced with.
5. Provide a blueprint for the delivery of community-based services in rural settings with an acknowledgment of critical factors that have contributed to successful rural services in other countries.

6. Define the last ideological and programmatic frontiers that confront community programs—serving the severely mentally retarded/medically fragile and the mentally retarded/mentally ill.
7. Analyze cost-benefit and cost-efficiency issues in the development and management of community-based mental retardation service systems.
8. Finally, we attempt to forecast the issues that parents and professionals will likely encounter over the next two decades in this quest for community integration and interdependence.

ACKNOWLEDGMENTS

During the last 15 years the authors have been closely involved with the development and growth of community-based service systems for the mentally retarded. Our efforts have been rewarded many times over. The culmination of this book and the current and future directions of community-based services are the result of hundreds of clients, families, and staff who have dedicated themselves to establishing and maintaining an excellent array of services for our mentally retarded citizens. We are, therefore, greatly indebted to all the clients, families, and staff with whom we have been privileged to know, serve, and work with.

We are also appreciative of the manuscript preparation efforts extended by Vicki Strampe and Alan Toulouse.

Jack A. Stark
John J. McGee
Frank J. Menolascino

About the Authors

Jack A. Stark, Ph.D. Dr. Stark is currently an Associate Professor of Medical Psychology in the departments of Pediatrics and Psychiatry at the University of Nebraska Medical Center. He is director of Adult Services at Meyer Children's Rehabilitation Institute and has some 15 years of experience in the field, specializing in the vocational needs of mentally retarded individuals. He has authored or co-authored numerous books, chapters, and articles, and conducted hundreds of presentations. His more recent efforts have focused on the "curative" aspects of mental retardation.

John J. McGee, Ph.D. Dr. McGee has some 15 years of experience in working with mentally retarded individuals, particularly persons with severe and profound mental retardation. He was one of the first individuals to be hired by the Eastern Nebraska Community Office of Retardation, having served as a workshop director in one of its first program components. He received his Ph.D. in education and is currently an Associate Professor of Medical Psychology at the University of Nebraska Medical Center where he directs programs for severely mentally retarded/mentally ill individuals at the Nebraska Psychiatric Institute and Meyer Children's Rehabilitation Institute. He is the author of numerous articles, books, and films, and has gained an international reputation among Third World countries for his work with mentally retarded individuals.

Frank J. Menolascino, M.D. Dr. Menolascino is currently the Associate Director of the Nebraska Psychiatric Institute and Vice-Chairman of the Department of Psychiatry. He is a Professor in Psychiatry and Pediatrics at the University of Nebraska Medical Center and is one of the leading figures, both nationally and internationally, for his work with the mentally retarded. He is the author of 12 books and 150 articles; he has received numerous national/international awards for his work with the mentally retarded. He has served on the President's Committee on Mental Retardation and as national president of the Association for Retarded Citizens of the United States. He was recognized by the American Psychiatric Association with the Strecker Award as the outstanding young psychiatrist for his work on behalf of the mentally retarded. Recently he was elected chairperson of the Mental Retardation Committee of the World Psychiatric Association. Dr. Menolascino served as a major architect in the development and growth of the Eastern Nebraska Community Office of Mental Retardation as well as consulting to other community-based programs at the international level.

INTERNATIONAL HANDBOOK of COMMUNITY SERVICES for the MENTALLY RETARDED

IDEOLOGY AND FOUNDATIONAL PRINCIPLES

1 Major Factors Promoting Changes in Community Services

During the last three decades, the Western World has witnessed a revolution in the treatment of mentally retarded children and adults. There has been a rapid swing away from the segregation practices of the past, especially in regard to the institutionalization of mentally retarded children and adults (Scheerenberger, 1983). There has been a move toward supporting retarded children and adults in the mainstream of family and community life. This revolution has primarily come about, not because of financial or technological causes, but rather because of the development of a new ideological construct that has substantially redirected our perception of the value of mentally retarded persons and our expectations relative to their role in society. This new ideological construct consists of four major factors:

1. The recognition of the inherent worth and dignity of the mentally retarded person as equal to that of any other person as stated in the United Nations Declaration on the Rights of Mentally Retarded Persons (United Nations, 1971); yet, because of the nature of their very special needs, there is the concurrent recognition of society's responsibility to provide the types of programs and services needed to support and maintain the person in family and social life. The United Nation's affirmation of the rights of mentally retarded persons is reflected in a myriad of evolving laws in every nation — laws that reaffirm the rights of retarded persons as the same as all other persons.
2. The recognition of the developmental potential of all mentally retarded persons, regardless of the severity and complexity of the handicap and other allied health and/or developmental problems (Berkson &

Landesman-Dwyer, 1977; Menolascino, 1977; Roos, 1979). The developmental model assumes that all persons learn in their own unique way, at different rates, and in different manners. It is presumed that even the most severely retarded person is capable of development.

3. The recognition of the principle of normalization (Bank-Mikkelsen, 1976; Gunzberg, 1970; Kugel & Wolfensberger, 1969; Nirje, 1969; Wolfensberger, 1972; Zarfas, 1970), which assumes that all mentally retarded persons develop best in interpersonal and physical settings that are as normal as possible. Parents and professionals will need to help establish and maintain the types of programs, services, and environments which allow the mentally retarded individual to stay in the mainstream of society.

4. The emergent consolidation of the above three ideological constructs into the belief that all persons are independent; that each depends on the other; that persons with severe disabilities should be supported where necessary and taught where possible so that all are present and able to participate in community life as much as possible.

These four factors began to emerge in Sweden and Denmark in the 1950's. Like most other nations, these countries had passed through a long period of institutionalization as the only option for most mentally retarded persons, especially the severely retarded and multiply handicapped. In both of these nations, as eventually in all nations, parent associations began to form and to question the institutional option with its overcrowding, protectionism and, at times, dehumanizing conditions. In Denmark, for example, in 1953 the newly formed National Association of Parents requested the Minister of Social Affairs to form a committee to study the needs of all mentally retarded citizens. By 1969, Denmark passed landmark legislation expressing the need "to create an existence for the mentally retarded as close to normal living conditions as possible" (Bank-Mikkelsen, 1976). This phrase was the basis for what has become known as the principle of normalization. Likewise, in Sweden by 1968 there was legislation created to cover all the needs of the mentally retarded within the normal framework of social services (Grunewald, 1976).

As a result of these trends in the Scandanavian countries, other countries began to develop normalizing services and alternatives to institutionalization. Today, nations around the world are translating and interpreting these ideological constructs according to particular cultures and customs. Most industrialized nations are confronted with the problem of dismantling large institutions. For example, in 1969 there were over 225,000 retarded persons in state institutions in the United States (Wolfensberger, 1969). It has taken over a decade to decrease this number to 125,000. Third World nations, on the other hand, often do not have this problem. Instead, they are confronted with the challenge of developing an infrastructure of nutritional services, health care, schools, and other human services. The purpose of this book is to review these trends, to highlight practical ways that communities can develop integrative options to institutions, and to focus on specific issues that parents and professionals need to confront in serving all retarded persons in the mainstreams of family and community life.

2 The Challenges Facing Community Services

In this chapter we trace the underlying issues for parents and professionals who are moving toward the development of community-based programs and services for mentally retarded persons. The development of community-based programs requires significant social change. This change starts with a small group of parents and professionals raising their consciousness of the needs of mentally retarded persons in the community, and typically is achieved through a parent association. We offer some examples from around the world of parents and professionals initiating significant social change. Whether parents are struggling in the United States, the Third World countries, or Europe makes no difference if there is a solidarity between parents and professionals. Finally, in this chapter we outline the basic planning factors that parent associations need to deal with as they plan for comprehensive, integrated, community-based programs.

The trends analyzed in this book raise a number of challenges for parents, professionals, and society itself. Indeed, the resolution of one challenge often gives birth to several new ones. The major challenge confronting parents and professionals is how to move toward decent, loving, and integrative options for the mentally retarded and their families. This challenge is evolving existentially in various communities throughout the world — in some communities we see vibrant examples of integrated pre-schools and schools; in other communities we see severely mentally retarded adults working side by side with non-handicapped adults; and in some communities we see little change, indeed, at times we see the replication of old institutional models that have long proved valueless.

There are no easy answers to the questions that parents and professionals must deal with over the next two decades. The common bond that unites parents, professionals, and the mentally retarded themselves is the quest for maximum interdependence among all. Interdependence is the culmination of the ideological constructs that have been the foundation of services for retarded persons — human rights, the developmental assumption, and the principle of normalization, and signifies community presence and participation, the mutual bond between all people. It focuses on people learning to live, work, and play together — the bonding of people living in a community. Hopefully, this bond will be strong enough to help parents and professionals seek out answers to questions such as those that have been raised by the Association for Retarded Citizens-United States (1981) in its ongoing commitment to meet future challenges:

1. Is the developmental model appropriate for all mentally retarded persons, including the most profoundly retarded, multiply handicapped children and adults?
2. To what degree should the normalization principle be applied? Does it mean independence for all persons?
3. Is integration an appropriate goal for all mentally retarded persons? How can a severely retarded person have his needs met in an integrated setting?
4. What relative weight should be given to parents vis-a-vis the rights of their mentally retarded children?

All parent associations must confront these questions as they embark on the development of quality programs for the mentally retarded persons in their community and nation. These questions center around the concept of interdependence. The integration of retarded persons signifies the responsibility of communities to accept their members; to teach all persons a variety of skills and competencies, while at the same time, when recognizing this is not possible, to provide support to retarded persons, where necessary, in order to maintain each person in the mainstream of community life.

PARENT-PROFESSIONAL SOLIDARITY

The primary issue for the next two decades is not based on technological issues or economic factors. The evolution of integrative, community-based services over the last three decades has invariably been born out of a solidarity between parents and professionals. In those communities where integration works, whether they are rich or poor, the moving force behind the movement has been a strong, articulate, and constructive parent association (Perske, 1973). These associations perform three basic functions: (1) They recognize the needs of retarded persons with a hopeful and perservering vision; (2) they judge and select their alternatives from the ideological posture described in Chapter 1 — the equality of all persons, the developmental assumption, the principle of normalization, and the movement toward interdependence; (3) they act on their beliefs. Thus, the first issue communities and nations must resolve is to develop strong, change-oriented parent associations — associations that unite parents and professionals on the journey toward the interdependence of all people — retarded or not.

This issue, however, breeds other issues such as: (1) How do parents develop such groups? (2) How do these associations reach consensus on all of the ideological and technical issues which inevitably confront them? (3) What is the role of the professional within the parent movement? (4) How does a parent association bring about social change and deal with attitudinal barriers? (5) How does a fledgling parent association expand its advocacy efforts from the needs of the fledgling group to the needs of all children and families? There are universal principles upon which parents and professionals can base their advocacy. Each nation and each culture has unique ways of envisioning and implementing programs and services for the mentally retarded. Parent associations are small communities composed of people united together within the context of cultural-political-economic reality.

The first step in the formation of a parent association is to develop a shared ideological posture. As this evolving posture becomes clarified, the next step involves an analysis of the needs of all mentally retarded children within the community. An important step in this recognition of reality is to analyze the residential, educational, and vocational needs of all mentally retarded children and adults within the particular community. Through this needs-based approach a parent association unites into an advocacy-oriented association. It is obvious that the movement toward comprehensive, community-based services for all mentally retarded persons and their integration into community life will take a decade or more to develop. The secret is to begin. Parent associations often have to initiate demonstrative models that prove the feasibility of the ultimate goal — integrated pre-schools, a group home, mainstreamed classrooms, sheltered workshops, integrated industries, etc. These models then become the basis for the evolution of a comprehensive service system. The primary roles of a parent association are: (1) To recognize basic human needs; (2) to envision alternatives that nurture development, stability, integration, and interdependence; (3) to advocate for this vision; (4) to demonstrate this vision where there is societal reluctance; and (5) to monitor the quality of services.

For example, in Chapter 5 we describe a comprehensive community-based mental retardation program (The Eastern Nebraska Community Office of

Retardation — ENCOR) that was created by a local parent association and is now a quasi-government serving over 1,000 mentally retarded children and adults in a range of educational, vocational, and residential alternatives throughout the community. In the late 1960's the Greater Omaha Association for Retarded Citizens (GOARC) — a local parent association — became alarmed at the lack of community services and at the deplorable conditions of retarded persons who had been placed in the state institution. A small group of parents and professionals envisioned all retarded persons living in the community in a network of community-based alternatives. The parent association developed a plan, publicly advocated for their plan, and finally won governmental approval. Ten years later ENCOR serves over 1,000 retarded persons. GOARC initiated the first programs. It no longer runs any direct services. It services new roles — monitoring the quality of programs and providing support to families. The parent association has been struggling for ten years. Its vision remains the same — to strive for the integration of all retarded persons. The parent association has had its problems: (1) the tendency of professionals to take over the association because they "know best"; (2) staff turn-over; and (3) the re-definition of its role across the years — from planning, to demonstrating services, to spinning them off, to externally monitoring the quality of programs. The key to GOARC, and other parent associations, is to maintain and deepen its focus on and commitment to serving the most severely retarded in the mainstream of community life.

Parent associations must begin to define more clearly the realtionship between parents of the mentally retarded and the mentally retarded themselves, between parents and professionals, as well as the relationship of the community at large with retarded persons. Professionals need to learn to provide support to parent associations, to develop parent leadership, to maintain a focus on the long-term needs of retarded persons, and to avoid the trap of taking over the parent association. Parents need to learn to expand their focus to all retarded persons and to reach solutions leading to the interdependence of all retarded persons. The issue should not be one of dependence versus independence, but rather how much "protection" and support does the individual mentally retarded person require in a given situation? There must be a recognition of lifelong, often improving, sometimes worsening, but ever-changing needs. Parents, professionals, and mentally retarded persons need to focus on making decisions in a "best-fit" manner depending upon the situation, always taking into consideration a number of factors such as: the needs of the mentally retarded person, the relationship of the parent to the child across time, the need for programmatic stability, and the pursuit of the maximum degree of interdependence. The final result in the resolution of this existential problem should be the clarification of the concept of interdependence. All people depend upon one another. The question is how much support does a person need at any given point in time? The end result of normalization and the developmental assumption should not be the independence of the mentally retarded person in society, but the maximum degree of interdependence for all persons — mentally retarded or not.

INTERDEPENDENCE

Parents and professionals need to adopt the fundamental principle that all persons — disabled or not — are interdependent; that we all depend on mutual support. Some require more support than others. It is the parent association's responsibility to define the "best-fit" of interdependence each person requires. Perhaps it would be better to define guidelines for this "best-fit" and use the most severely involved mentally retarded child or adult as a reference point:

1. Regardless of the severity of the handicapping condition, all mentally retarded persons should be ensured of programmatic support to gain maximum presence and participation in community life. The retarded person and his parents have the right to be concerned about the stability of any placement decision. Often — in the name of deinstitutionalization — mentally retarded persons are not placed in normalizing environments, rather they are uncerimoniously dumped into the mainstream of community life with no support. Some survive. Many, however, require ongoing supports and services. Dumping often destroys the person. In industrialized nations, it results in the virtual institutionalization of the person in the back-streets of "psychiatric ghettoes." Many parents and professionals have seen this happen and have become legitimately concerned about this pseudo-integration. This is less of a problem in non-industrialized nations, for there still exists the extended-family network in which "weaker" members of the community tend to receive the support they need. However, in economically poorer nations the lack of necessary services can also result in abandonment and decay if the necessary services are not provided. The issue of interdependence revolves around supporting, not supplanting, the family, the school, and the work place.
2. The more severely disabled should have their needs met in settings that ensure whatever specialization and "protection" is necessary. The challenge is to bring about maximum integration even for the severely and profoundly retarded person.
3. The less severely disabled should be ensured of maximum independence, while at the same time they should not be lost in the community. An important factor in any community delivery system should be the ongoing support of all mentally retarded persons. For the severely re-

tarded the provision of support need not mean segregation; rather it should challenge professionals to disperse resources throughout the community.

These are but a few of the concerns that must be dealt with by all active parent groups as they seek to define interdependence. It appears that there is inevitably an existential struggle between those who advocate for independence and those who advocate for dependence. The next two decades should define more clearly the concept of interdependence.

ROLE OF THE PROFESSIONAL

A major issue to be dealt with is the role of the professional in parent associations. The purpose of parent associations is to create the types of programs and services needed by mentally retarded persons. Parent associations are the political support system for the development of programs and services for the retarded. These services are based on the ever-evolving philosophical principles discussed earlier. It is absolutely necessary to ensure that parents maintain a leadership role in program development. Parents have the most to be concerned with — their own children. They bear a lifelong responsibility. They bear the anxiety of their son/daughter's future after their own death. This is no easy responsibility. No matter how independent a son/daughter might become, it is still natural for parents to preoccupy themselves with their child's lifelong well-being. Yet, there does arise the problem wherein professionals push for ever-increasing independence and individual rights. Indeed, parents at times are overly protective. This dialectic is good and can be constructive; yet professionals and parents must come to consensus regarding the primacy of the parents. This does not mean that parents are always correct in their decisions. However, over the long term, the primacy of the parents will create the stability and quality needed to ensure stable, loving, and caring environments.

A corollary issue is the deepening recognition of the individual and class rights of the mentally retarded themselves. In many communities across the world the mentally retarded themselves are forming self-advocacy groups and are demonstrating that much advocacy is able to be done on their own. Most often these self-advocacy groups are encouraged and supported by parents and professionals. These groups demonstrate that many mentally retarded persons are capable of speaking for themselves. This movement has to be dealt with gently for there is the ongoing danger of the mentally retarded being taken advantage of, by professionals who wish to circumvent parental desires. Likewise, there is the danger of forgetting about more severely retarded persons who are voiceless.

The next two decades should bring together a clearer picture of the role of parents, professionals, and the mentally retarded themselves. In order to synthesize this evolving triad we must define the concept of interdependence. Interdependence can best be summed up, not by the degree of independence that a mentally retarded person can attain, but by the process in which parent associations (parents, professionals, and the mentally retarded) band together in community life. This banding together has nothing to do with the delivery of services, but with how we all grow in relationship to one another. The principal goal of community-based programs is the responsibility of their community members in supporting one another and fostering independent growth. This interdependence can best be pictured as the on-going definition of the degree of support that one person needs from others around him or her. The degree of interdependence must be constantly redefined with respect to myriad personal, family, political, economic, and social factors.

SOCIAL POLICIES

A constant issue is the cost of the integration of mentally retarded persons into normalizing environments. In most countries it generally costs more to institutionalize a mentally retarded person than to place the person in a community-based setting (Menolascino & McGee, 1981). Yet, it is difficult to free institutional money for community-based alternatives. Money is available to segregate; it is not available to integrate. This appears to be a generally global phenomenon. Much of the advocacy efforts of the next two decades will involve the redefinition of the political and economic variables which impact on decision making. Public policy must be reformed to support normalizing services for the mentally retarded.

Concern about the availability of money is only a symptom of the need to redefine social policies. All normalizing service systems that have evolved over the last three decades started at the grass-roots level (Biklen, 1980). Only after several years of grass-roots struggle can any nation redefine its national policies. Thus, parents and professionals should not wait for national policies or mandates. They cannot wait for financial support. For example, in Agueda, Portugal a small group of parents and professionals with few financial supports and little political power (see page 17) developed an integrated pre-school. "It costs too much to provide an education to the severely mentally retarded" was the typical response that this group heard. This lament was quickly followed by the position that it would be impossible to integrate these children. It was more costly to educate the severely retarded for they were not in school at all. The parent association, therefore, raised the consciousness of the public that these children had a right to a public education by gradually demonstrating that all children are capable of human development. They then demonstrated that the mildly mentally retarded children who were in a "special" school were in programs with a 3:1 child-teacher ratio and that the severely mentally retarded children in the integrated pre-school required less support than the segregated situation. The Agueda experience will result in the formulation of national policy, not vice versa. This experience is repeating itself in community after community around the world.

SPECIALIZATION

Another basic issue relates to the type and quality of manpower needed to support mentally retarded persons in community-based settings. Many hold that community-based programs are impossible because there is no mechanism to ensure that all mentally retarded persons receive the specialized manpower they require, and that such specialization can be managed only in an institutional setting. It is a false assumption that all mentally retarded persons require highly specialized manpower either in institutional settings or in the community. There are a small percentage who require specialized medical and/or psychiatric back-up support, generally on an acute-care basis. These needs should be met in mainstream hospital settings just as for any other citizen. The National Institute on Mental Retardation in Canada (NIMR) estimates that 80% of all persons who work with the mentally retarded, either in institutional or community settings, are paraprofessionals (NIMR, 1972). This issue, therefore, is one of training parents, professionals, paraprofessionals, and volunteers, and then providing the back-up support and supervision necessary.

COMMUNITY-BASED PROGRAMS

Comprehensive, dispersed, and integrative programs and services in the community are the embodiment of the ideological factors we have described. The most critical factor in the development of these services for mentally retarded children and adults is the role of the parent association as the catalyst for such development. The parent association has the primary responsibility of envisioning the types of programs and services that all mentally retarded persons need, planning for those programs and services, overseeing their development, and eventually monitoring their quality. The initial stage of this process oftentimes involves a smaller core group of parents and professionals who are concerned about the community services for mentally retarded individuals. This group generally is concerned in the beginning only with an existential need: to start a school program, a vocational training program, a group home. Many associations, however, soon transcend this initial need

and begin to critically question the basic human needs of all mentally retarded persons in their community. This is the first step in the development of
a comprehensive community-based service system.

The parent association needs to take a much more change-oriented role,
not only offering support and encouragement to parents and families of the
mentally retarded, but also focusing on the development of comprehensive
services for all mentally retarded persons. The parent association assumes a
three stage, change-oriented posture (see Figure 1).

In all communities the first stage that parent associations must contend
with is the provision of services where few or none exist. This provision begins with the association envisioning the type of programs and services all
mentally retarded persons in the community need and translating this vision
into a long range plan. Typically, the association has the foundation on
which it can demonstrate the feasibility of its vision. This demonstration
gradually results in a parent, professional, and community acceptance of the
mentally retarded in community-based settings. From this base the association can then spin its demonstration services into generic services. It can then
focus on advocating for increased quantity of services for other types of services. For example, if the association has demonstrated that some severely
mentally retarded children can successfully participate in integrated pre-
school services, then it is logical to conclude that all retarded children can
participate in and benefit from such services. The parent association can then
begin to integrate more severely disabled children in the demonstration pre-
school. As these children reach school age it can then focus on their integration into regular schools.

After these initial stages, the parent association begins to focus on increasingly more challenging populations within special sub-groups of the mentally
retarded. For example, it will likely be necessary to prove through demon-

FIGURE 1
STAGES IN THE EVOLUTION OF A PARENT ASSOCIATION

Activity	Stage
— Envision — Plan — Demonstrate	Provide Services
— Advocate increased acceptance — Transform into generic service system — Advocate for increased quantity of services	Obtain Services
— Demonstrate model services for special sub-groups — Advocate for increased quality of services — Encourage self-advocacy	Monitor Services

stration programs that mentally retarded persons with severe behavioral problems and with allied medical problems are capable of human development within the community. As this demonstration occurs, the association concurrently advocates for increased quality of services. Generally, parent associations establish external monitoring committees. These committees periodically survey the quality of services provided by community-based agencies and make recommendations for improved services. Eventually the parent association gives birth to self-advocacy — mentally retarded persons advocating for themselves.

There are several factors that parent associations must deal with in the development of a comprehensive community-based program. The association's envisioning process must not remain abstract, but must deal with the myriad of political, economic, and financial issues that make up the local reality.

The parent association, once committed to a vision, enters into a planning process whose basic goal is to develop a long range roadmap (5 years) leading to an array of residential, educational, vocational, and supportive services for all mentally retarded persons in the community (McGee & deLorenzo, 1976). This plan, based on the philosophical principles described earlier in this chapter, needs to take into consideration a number of basic planning factors as shown in Figure 2.

Figure 2 summarizes all the major service areas the parent association needs to consider as it plans for social change. Every community should have access to a range of educational, residential, vocational, and support services capable of meeting the needs of all retarded persons across their lifespan, including the needs of the most medically fragile and behaviorally impaired persons. The parent association then analyzes current programs and services available, the approximate number of persons in need of specific services, the manpower needed and cost of new services, and what their priorities are over a five-year period of time. With a small group of articulate parents and professionals, this planning can be accomplished in a matter of weeks. Governmental mandates are not necessary. Community-based parent associations can proceed to shape their own future.

PARENT ASSOCIATIONS AROUND THE WORLD

The merger of these philosophical postures with the development of community-based alternatives is occurring around the world — from the villages of Brazil to the towns of Portugal. The process requires strong change-oriented parent associations which embark on the process of envisioning the integration of all mentally retarded persons in the mainstream of community life.

FIGURE 2
AN INSTRUMENT FOR ENVISIONING CHANGE

	Service Area	Current Programs	# Served	# In Need	Manpower Needed	Cost	Priority Date
EDUCATION	Infant Development						
	Pre-School						
	Residential						
RESIDENTIAL	Parent Support						
	Respite						
	Group Home						
	Supervised Living						
VOCATIONAL	Pre-Vocational						
	Workshop						
	Supervised Work						
SUPPORT	Medical						
	Behavioral						

Northeastern Brazil

The development of community-based services — rooted in the advocacy of parent associations — in Third World countries provides an excellent example of the power of the philosophical factors described earlier as the foundation upon which all programs and services for the mentally retarded are built. In these countries the needs of mentally retarded children and adults can be clearly seen within the context of general community development. The majority of the earth's inhabitants suffer from: (1) poor sanitary conditions, crowding, and insufficient medical care; (2) undernourishment and malnutrition; and (3) deprivation of education and work (Stenner, 1976). Yet, in spite of widespread abject poverty, illiteracy, and political oppression, thousands of villages and neighborhoods throughout South America and the Third World countries are gathering together in "base communities" (Conferencia Episcopal de Latina America, 1978) in which local people recognize and resolve their own basic human needs. These base communities are similar to parent associations in that they serve as the vehicle for mobilizing small groups of people to understand and resolve shared problems. In these communities children with special needs are naturally embraced in the quest for community interdependence, and there is often an inherent predisposition to accept those who have special needs in the process of forming base communities. Perhaps because of the lack of material goods, there inherently exists interdependent family and community structures and a valuing of all members of the community. The highly praised service systems in industrialized nations pale in significance when compared to these base communities. For example, in Northeastern Brazil many villages have no teachers or schools. Yet, this does not prohibit the provision of education nor the integration of mentally retarded children by community volunteers. For example, Salinas is a small village in the interior of Northeastern Brazil — 600 inhabitants, 15 hours by car and 8 hours by boat from the nearest city, no electricity, no sewers, no schools, no formal health care. Yet, in spite of these problems, the villagers of Salinas have included all chilren in literacy programs. As children and adults gather under a tree to learn from a volunteer, handicapped children are included with no thought as to their handicap. Acceptance of all community members is a natural phenomenon. Living, working, playing together is the rule.

Agueda, Portugal

An example of social change inspired by a parent association has occurred in a town in Portugal. Agueda, Portugal is a region in central Portugal with a population base of 65,000 located in a main town (Agueda) and several nearby villages. It is economically poor: Many houses have no electricity or running water, unemployment is high (over 35%), and no children with moderate to severe retardation were in school in 1976. They simply remained at home. There was no right to an education. There were no special resources. There was no financing available to educate these children. The people of Agueda, like the people of Salinas, had to make a choice to teach all children to live together or apart from one another. A small group of parents and professionals banded together based on a desire to educate Agueda's moderately and severely retarded children. Finding that no local schools would accept these children, this group resolved to start their own pre-school in which retarded children would learn to live together with their non-disabled peers and vice versa. Perhaps with no high technology resources there was no other option, but it has turned out to be a happy phenomenon.

Seven years of integration efforts have resulted in total educational integration of all disabled children in Agueda. As the integrated pre-school (Escola Bela Vista) "graduated" its students, staff began to convince regular school teachers one-by-one to integrate each graduate into regular schools. At first there was opposition to this integration on the part of regular school teachers. As in North America, this initial opposition had to be overcome (Hoben, 1980). In Agueda, this was accomplished through the demonstration of the effectiveness of the pre-school teachers and the regular primary school teachers. Opposition turned to reluctance as a handful of children was successfully placed. Reluctance turned to enthusiasm as it was clearly demonstrated that mainstreaming was beneficial for all children.

Today there are no children in Agueda who are not in regular classrooms. Two types of support were needed. Those children who presented difficult learning or behavioral problems attend the regular classroom settings with a teacher aide. The regular teacher was free to use the aide as he/she saw fit — for the particular child or for general classroom management. Those children who require special therapeutic services, such as physical or speech therapy, are supported by itinerant specialists.

The Agueda experience began with the awakening of the consciousness of a small group of parents and professionals relative to the right of all disabled children to a free public education, and beyond this the right of all children to learn together. This consciousness was initially challenged by the lack of any governmental support as well as a general attitudinal belief that severely retarded and multiply handicapped children could not learn. It was generally held that these children were not developmental in nature. This non-developmental posture toward the severely profoundly handicapped child is similarly a major barrier in North America (Ellis, Balla, Estes, Hollis, Isaacson, Orlando, Palk, Warren, & Siegel, 1978) as well as in most other nations. To overcome these first two barriers the parent and professional group initiated their own pre-school and within a year clearly demonstrated that the integrated children were capable of growth and development. In this first integrated pre-school, where the large majority of the children were not disabled, 15 severely disabled children were integrated into the pre-school. The teachers enthusiastically began to re-define the goal of education as being *to teach all children to learn to live together.*

They proceeded with newspaper coverage of their pre-school in order to begin to awaken the consciousness of the community at large. They conducted tours. They conducted awareness workshops. They invited teachers from other pre-schools and regular elementary schools to visit their classrooms. They began to network these newly developed friendships with the pre-school teachers and regular school teachers as a foundation for the eventual integration of their pre-school graduates into other pre-schools and regular school classrooms.

By the second year, when some of the more severely disabled children were ready to move onto elementary school, the next barrier was to find a small number of regular classroom teachers and regular school principals who were willing to take the "risk" of integrating these children into the regular classrooms. They found schools willing to do this by constantly emphasizing the general philosophy of their educational program: to teach all children to learn to live together. As the second year passed, a small number of severely retarded and multiply handicapped children were placed in several regular schools, other teachers from other regular schools in the community were invited to visit these integrated elementary school classrooms. By the third year every graduate of the pre-school was accepted into regular schools. Concurrent with these graduations into regular schools, the Agueda Pre-school also began to place other severely retarded and multiply handicapped children into other community pre-schools serving non-disabled children. This then resulted in an educational foundation in which by the fourth and fifth year all disabled children were in regular pre-schools and were able to graduate into regular classrooms in regular schools.

The next barrier was more technological in nature. That is, a small percentage of the severely retarded children presented either severe behavioral problems and/or severe medical problems. Because the community offered no degree of specialization relative to the psychiatric or medical needs of disabled children, the pre-school teachers called upon local physicians, psychologists, and therapists from a nearby major city (Coimbra). These professionals volunteered to orient the Agueda Pre-school staff in the general specialty areas — physical therapy, occupational therapy, behavioral analysis, infant development, etc. In this instruction, these professionals voluntarily accompanied the pre-school staff on site visits to the other pre-schools and regular school classrooms in order to offer the minimal support and guidance which regular classroom teachers required to provide the special service to the children. It was noted that "untrained" regular classroom teachers were quite adept at adapting their classroom teaching style to meet the needs of multiply handicapped children. It was further noted that many of the identified problems found in behaviorally impaired children dissipated dramatically once placed in an integrated setting. Therefore, the demand for specialized services was not as great as had previously been anticipated.

The last issue to be confronted was to provide extra in-the-classroom supports to those teachers who required special supports due to the severity or multiplicity of the handicapping conditions in the one or two disabled children in their classroom. Regular classroom teachers with children with these special needs were given teacher aides to use at their discretion to meet these needs.

After seven years, all severely handicapped children are in integrated pre-schools and schools in Agueda. The process toward the establishment of this total integration coincides with Biklen's (1982) findings of the factors associated with successful educational mainstreaming in the United States:

1. Emerging support on the part of local educational leadership. In the case of Agueda this meant that it was necessary to demonstrate the possibility of mainstreaming at the pre-school level and then to convince local educational leaders to integrate one child into one classroom.
2. Valuing all children as developmental beings. In the case of Agueda it was necessary to redefine the goal of education as *all* children learning to live together.

3. Structuring the mainstreaming so as to result in age-appropriate class-room integration. In the case of Agueda it was necessary to incorporate a personalized, prescriptive teaching approach for all children so that all children would learn at their own pace.
4. Raising the awareness of non-disabled school peers and the awareness of all parents as to the inherent value of all children. In the case of Agueda, community-wide campaigns were held through the media and on-going training. The acceptance of and value of all children was built into the curriculum.
5. Adequate staffing. In the case of Agueda, where necessary, regular classroom teachers were provided with teacher aides, class size reduc-tion, and on-going in-service training. The "specialness" of special edu-cation was demystified.

The Agueda experience demonstrates that the total integration of severely handicapped children with their non-disabled peers is possible, even given the types of barriers frequently mentioned in North American culture. North American literature reports splinter attempts at total mainstreaming; the Agueda experience demonstrates community-wide mainstreaming can be brought about through active parent associations.

The following letter from a regular classroom teacher in Agueda who has integrated a profoundly mentally retarded child into her classroom speaks el-oquently of an integration experience:

> When we were first approached with a request to integrate Guida in a normal classroom, we accepted Guida on the condition that we would need a teacher aide, since we had never seen a child with so many special needs.
>
> This was a new experience. Although the regular teacher admitted her lack of expertise, she dedicated herself to the integration of Guida.
>
> Today we are happy with the results of this integration of Guida as well as the integration of other severely handicapped children whom we now have in our school. Both the mentally retarded children and the non-retarded children are richer human beings. The children have learned to help each other. This is learning to live! This is the purpose of education. It has been an emotional expe-rience. Whenever a retarded child makes the smallest gain, the whole class rejoices — teachers and children.
>
> We do not suppose that we have made a perfect effort but we have given tender-ness, understanding and love. And with this posture our work will not fail.

Mentally Retarded Children in Italy

Italy is a nation that has a national policy of complete school integration — a national policy that came about due to a decade of grass-roots work by parents and professionals. In a recent report (1981) of the Italian Ministry of Education, school integration of all mentally retarded children is termed an "irreversible trend." In Parma, Italy, for example, there has been an integration movement since 1969. Currently, 96% of all mentally retarded children in Parma are in regular classrooms (Cavara, 1979). The Parma schools have divided their mentally retarded children into two groups in order to achieve integration:

1. Mildly and moderately mentally retarded children with or without motor or sensory handicaps.
2. Severely and profoundly retarded children with or without allied handicaps.

All children in the first group have been placed in regular classrooms with a part-time support aide who assists the teacher. All children in the second group have been placed in the regular school with a resource room and a full-time teacher aide. This aide is responsible for toileting, feeding, and transportation. The resource room has two purposes: (1) a quiet room for special individualized learning, and (2) a room wherein non-handicapped children participate with the handicapped children in creative activities such as painting, crafts, and games.

The Parma schools report that in their experience they have not seen any child who could not be integrated. Furthermore, they report that the success of integration does not depend on the level of handicap. The Italian Ministry of Education reports that: "According to our studies integration gives more than the opportunity for the socialization of the mentally retarded students. Integration has also resulted in improved learning. For teachers our national integration policy has resulted in a stimulation for the advancement of teaching methodologies for the entire school population" (Voces, 1981).

The key point in each of these examples of social change is that each was inspired by grass-root efforts. Parents and professionals at the community level identified needs because of their ideological vision to integrate all children into the mainstreams of family and community life. They saw their role as being to advocate for interdependence. They did not wait for governmental mandates or financial support. They brought about social changes.

FACTORS IN THE CHANGE PROCESS

We have described the role of the parent association as being one of envisioning and have made reference to economically rich and poor communities around the world that have embarked on just this venture. Figure 2 outlined the general format a parent association needs to follow in the envisioning process. The development of community alternatives begins with an acceptance of a variety of rights, beliefs, and common feelings. It is crucial that parents and professionals understand and accept the foundation principles. Without this acceptance, the parent association might make a few changes in its community, but it will not substantially alter it. Figure 2 outlined the planning process that parent associations need to undertake to bring about social change in their communities. The development of community alternatives requires the analysis and synthesis of a number of planning factors. The grassroots examples of community change cited in the foregoing came about through parents and professionals at the local level working together. Besides the process indicated in Figure 2, parent associations should be aware of and take into account the following twelve planning factors.

PLANNING FACTORS IN DEVELOPING COMMUNITY SERVICES

1. General Understanding of and Commitment to the Principle of Normalization. Normalization is usually defined as, "The utilization of means which are culturally as normative as possible, in order to establish and/or maintain personal behaviors and characteristics which are as culturally normative as possible" (Wolfensberger, 1972). Normalization does not mean that there are certain behaviors and environments which are acceptable for and desired by the majority of the people in any given culture. It does not mean that all people in a given culture should have the same opportunity to live, work, and play as any other citizen of that particular culture. In relation to planning, normalization means that decisions and actions must tend to integrate people with special needs. They should provide the opportunity for people to be served in their own community and live among their own natural family and friends. Normalization means that retarded persons should be able to be present and participate in the fullness of community life with whatever supports they might need to any point in their life.

If a typical community group involved in planning were to look around at the community, they would see many deviations from the principle of normalization. They would see that a substantial number of disabled citizens have been sent to institutions. They would see a large number of disabled individuals in the community, but typically living or being served in segregated environments. They would see many unemployed, disabled men and women. They would see disabled infants and children not in any school or service. An affirmation of the principle of normalization in any planning process serves to focus efforts on the integration of all disabled persons.

The principle of normalization in practice is exquisite and simple. It means treating the retarded person as a person while at the same time ensuring that the person's developmental needs are met. It means offering normal routines to all children and adults regardless of the severity of their handicap. It is best expressed in the integration of all persons into the mainstream of family and community life. It is on-going interdependence.

2. Physical Integration.   A pre-requisite to disabled individuals' participation in community life is the necessity to be physically integrated into the community. An integrated program should be:

a. in a normal population center, i.e., preferably the person's home community — urban or rural;
b. accessible, i.e., persons should, in general, be able to quickly and conveniently gain access to the program;
c. it should be located near other generic resources and services; for example, the program should be located near schools, churches, shopping, work, etc.;
d. the number of persons served by the program should be small enough to be assimilated by the surrounding community.

In summary, physical integration means a small percentage of retarded children in a regular pre-school; retarded children in regular schools with whatever special services they might require; retarded adults working in industries.

3. Social Integration.   It is possible that a program could be physically integrated, yet persons could still be socially segregated. For example, placing a number of retarded children in a separate classroom in a regular school building would give physical presence, but little social participation. If the mentally retarded are to be socially integrated, it is necessary to establish appropriate communnity attitudes and perceptions towards disabled people and the programs that serve them. It is not fair to assume that by placing developmentally disabled people into the community (physical integration) that they will be socially integrated into the community. The community planning group must find ways to disperse the people throughout the community whether it be where they live, where they go to school, or where they work. The primary goal should be to develop a service system that will facilitate social integration. The planning group should attempt to develop a system that will, from the very beginning, place individuals in socially integrative settings with the necessary supports that each person will need to live, work, play, etc. in that particular environment. Group homes, sheltered workshops, segregated pre-schools, segregated recreational programs, etc., are not socially integrative. The community planning *group*, therefore, must focus on this as a major issue and develop physically and socially integrative alternatives across time for all retarded persons. The aforementioned example of Agueda — the integration of all retarded children in regular classrooms – took the parent association seven years to achieve. Parent associations need to develop this type of patience if integration is to be achieved.

Social integration means learning to live with others. Once physically integrated, parents and professionals need to continually focus on bringing about social integration. For example, to integrate a pre-school, teachers, children, and parents need to be prepared to accept the concept of integration. On an ongoing basis, children should be helped to interact and learn to live together.

4. Comprehensiveness of Services.   If a local parent association is to plan to meet the needs of all of its mentally retarded citizens, then it must develop a system of services that can meet the needs of any given individual at any given point in time in that person's life. Frequently, communities develop fragmented service systems, which can only serve part of a person's needs at any given point in time. For example, if a community develops two group homes and calls that a residential service system, it is necessary to recognize that those two facilities can serve only a portion of the community's needs. The community must strive to look at the total needs of the total disabled population and design a system of services that can meet those needs from birth to death. Such a system must involve both *direct* services as well as those indirect supportive services which disabled individuals may intermittently require.

Comprehensiveness means that programs and services evolve across time. Parent associations begin to question the lack of developmental opportunities for their children. They begin to envision a better future for their children – the right to education, to work, to health care, to live in the community. From these visions arise the seedlings of eventual comprehensive services.

5. Continuity of Services.   The planned service system should enable any disabled person to enter into it at any point and time in that person's life. Ranging from prevention of disabilities to early diagnosis and screening, to infant development programs, to vocational training programs, to residential alternatives, the system must be responsive across the entire lifespan of its disabled citizens.

The community planning group should especially focus on the needs of currently institutionalized persons and the types of structures necessary to be developed in order to reintegrate those persons back in the community. The group should look at the service needs both of its citizens who live in institutions and those at home with no services. Neither group should be forgotten.

The necessary planning to bring about community alternatives should not be reduced to developing a continuum of alternatives; that is, planning must take a strong position related to developing a community service system that will serve all disabled citizens, regardless of degree of handicap in the most integrative manner possible.

In Nebraska, U.S.A., the primary factor that awoke the consciousness of the local parent association was that the families of retarded children had no option for their sons and daughters other than institutionalization. In 1968 there were over 2,400 retarded persons in the state institution. During the last decade of evolution this has been reduced to less than 500 persons. It continues to decrease. Today no children need to be institutionalized. This has been possible due to the development of community alternatives across the state.

6. *Population.*   The population base optimal for a service system is to some extent contingent on the type of service. For human services providing a range of specialty to generic-type program options (e.g., in mental health, mental retardation, special education, etc.), optimal size is in the 50,000 to 150,000 range (regional population). Population size must be large enough to enable efficient services to persons with infrequently occurring needs, such as medical or psychiatric needs. Minimal acceptable size is about 50,000. The upper limits to size are determined by breakdowns in management, which seem to occur as systems approach 500,000 persons. This size necessitates small communities joining together with large communities and urban areas being subdivided into more manageable neighborhood groupings.

Requirements for regional geographical size arise from the need to have services easily accessible to any resident who would use them. The physical size of the region should be such that any service may be reached by an hour's travel or less. Determination of regional boundaries should include consideration of the inclusion of at least one urban area so that the people living in rural areas will be able to take advantage of the services likely to be found in urban areas. Service region boundaries should be drawn to coincide with other relevant boundaries, such as health service regions, political subdivisions such as school districts, etc.

The Eastern Nebraska Community Office of Retardation, highlighted in Chapter 5, serves a population base of 500,000 in an urban-rural area. It is divided into five smaller geographical areas in order to be more responsive to local needs. Yet, the larger population base enables the service system to meet the needs of *all* retarded children and adults.

7. *Client Needs Analysis.*   The community planning group should develop information about the numbers of developmentally disabled citizens in the particular region and their current status. This analysis should be a breakdown of the number of persons living in the region or those who are from the region but are currently institutionalized elsewhere. Groups can be broken down in various ways, for example, into infancy (such as 0–2), early childhood (such as 3–5), school age (6–10, 11–14, 15–20), early adulthood (21–34), and adulthood (35–54) and aged 55 and above. Similarly, it is important to know especially the numbers of developmentally disabled people according to degree of handicap. This analysis need not be time consuming. It should be

recognized that it is simply a means to get a picture of the extent and types of services needed. It should also be noted that any labeling that might occur in this needs analysis should not stigmatize the person in such a way that the person is categorized as needing a particular type of environment.

The community planning group must also analyze current resources available in the community. Such an analysis should include such generic agencies as public schools, community recreation programs, foster placements, transportation, etc. It is important to plan to utilize all current generic services. At times many of the services may not have a history of serving developmentally disabled citizens; however, the planning group should strive to include such persons in the planning process so that as people move into integrative services in the community they will be assimilated into as many generic services as possible.

A key factor that a community planning group must take into consideration is the fact that the design and implementation of the plan to serve all developmentally disabled citizens in a normalizing way in a community will only occur across time. In envisioning the development of appropriate services for all developmentally disabled citizens within the community, the group must understand that the implementation of the plan could easily take four to six years. The group must also understand that many of the structures and resources necessary to integrate all developmentally disabled citizens into the community currently exist, but that the community will have to be shown *how* to make its resources work. The group must also recognize that there will be many barriers toward implementing their long-range plan. It must be clearly understood that the plan involves very substantial social change agentry. The group, therefore, must be ready to meet head-on a long-term struggle to implement its plan. It is necessary that the group develop a very concrete and time lined long-range plan. This plan must then be capable of being broken down in discrete steps that will be carried out on a year-to-year basis.

> To analyze the needs of retarded citizens in Nebraska, it was discovered that four factors are relevant to their community integration: ambulation needs, behavioral needs, medical needs, and self-care needs. Rather than diagnostic labels, it is these four areas which determine the extent and types of resources needed to support a person in the community.

8. Governmental Mandates and Controls. The community planning group, having selected an appropriately populated service area by dividing up a large metropolitan area to sub-areas or by adding on a number of communities in sparsely populated rural areas, should acquire a mandate from local government(s). The group must recognize that, even though there are strong philosophical and legal reasons for developmentally disabled citizens being integrated into community life, this will not come about until local communities develop a mandate from local government(s) and eventually national mandates. It must be recognized that institutions, if doing nothing else, have restricted the development of the kinds of services necessary to maintain or support all developmentally disabled citizens in community life. Any community planning to return all developmentally disabled citizens to community life must recognize that these citizens will require innovative human service delivery systems. It is important that local government takes a firm posture in developing, maintaining, and monitoring services.

> A danger in the development of community programs is when a parent association waits for local or national government to mandate change. This seldom happens. In the example of GOARC, the parents developed a plan that embodied their vision. The association then politicized the situation through press conferences, newspaper, and television coverage, etc., until government responded. Change occurs from the bottom upward.

9. Community Receptivity/Public Education.   Generally, there is a lack of consciousness in communities regarding the needs of disabled citizens. Few communities are aware of the blatant abuses occurring in institutions. Few communities are aware of the human loss that occurs by simply placing people in institutions or not educating children in local schools. Often the community planning group itself is not consciously aware of what needs to be done. It is crucial that the community planning group be intensely aware of the needs of the disabled people in or from their community and develop ways to convey the needs and alternatives to the community. The group should use local media and professional groups for this. At times it is necessary to awaken the people through exposés. The group must understand, however, that the awakening of the community must be on-going and should alert the community to positive solutions. Otherwise an exposé can backfire and result in more resources pouring into the institution.

The community planning group with its local legal mandate will then analyze and develop the kinds and numbers of services necessary to serve all the developmentally disabled citizens in the community. Beyond such a mandate, it is crucial that local governmental bodies participate in the planning process. It is important to receive written resolutions of support from as many governmental and private agencies as possible. It is also important that such commitments be publicly acknowledged in as many ways as possible through the local media.

The community planning group will also have to involve, as much as possible, various professional groups in the community — teachers, doctors, lawyers, social workers, etc. Often these groups, although responsible for the development and implementation of quality services, do not do so. We should not presume that professionals embrace the kinds of values or technology necessary to bring about community-based services for developmentally disabled citizens.

There are many ways to educate the public. In Chapter 3 we cite the example of a parent association in Portugal that wanted to integrate all handicapped preschools. It discovered that the most powerful tool in educating the public was the establishment of its own integrated pre-school. From this small beginning, all handicapped children in the community are now in regular pre-schools and primary schools.

10. Management Systems.   In the past, in developing community-based service systems, a local professional or consumer group would see a need for a certain service or services to be developed in their community. This would result in a group home, a sheltered workshop, or other services being developed in a particular community. At the very best, the local community group would assume a certain power based on the tremendous needs of certain developmentally disabled citizens and would proceed to develop at least a partial service system. This group will need to develop and implement a comprehensive plan as quickly and effectively as possible.

Little is known about the kinds of management systems that will enable the local community or consortium of communities to manage (on-going planning, implementation, and monitoring) comprehensive, community-based systems for retarded persons. However, there are three broad types of management systems (Figure 3) which have evolved in various communities across the world.

A. *Mandated Monolithic:*   A mandated monolithic management system results from a local governmental or inter-governmental mandate to bring about comprehensive services through one government-sponsored agency. Such an agency is mandated by local government to implement and manage a community-based service system. It has direct authority over the development, maintenance, and evaluation of the service system. Such an agency has virtual control over all local services for developmentally disabled citizens, as well as the mandate to return all currently institutionalized persons to the community and to prevent any further institutionalization. It basically has the authority to develop and implement the total range of services for all developmentally disabled citizens in a particular region.

B. *Mandated Brokered Agency:*   The mandated brokered agency also is formed by local government. It differs from the monolithic agency in that it only develops services when it cannot get other agencies to develop such services. In general, it oversees and sets standards for the necessary services for all developmentally disabled citizens. It has the power to control all funding

FIGURE 3
MANAGEMENT SYSTEMS

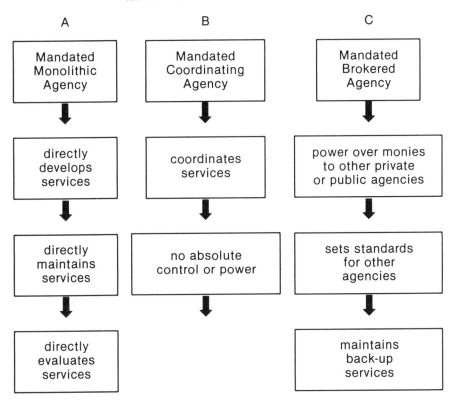

A	B	C
Mandated Monolithic Agency	Mandated Coordinating Agency	Mandated Brokered Agency
directly develops services	coordinates services	power over monies to other private or public agencies
directly maintains services	no absolute control or power	sets standards for other agencies
directly evaluates services		maintains back-up services

going to these brokered services, as well as the power to evaluate all local plans for the development of services. It also serves as a back-up support to the brokered programs.

C. *Coordinating Agency:*   A coordinating agency has much less power than the other two types of management systems. It would typically, however, have a mandate from local government to coordinate, without direct authority, other agencies serving developmentally disabled citizens in the particular region. Often the type of management system selected depends, to a large degree, on the local political and professional make-up. The standard should be that the stronger the mandate the agency has in the control of the development and management of services, the better the service delivery system will be to developmentally disabled citizens.

11. Direct Services.   The agency that is developed should be able to embrace the major areas of direct services necessary to maintain, establish, or support the developmentally disabled citizen in community life. Each of these direct services is a sub-system in itself:

a. Residential Services — There should be a sub-system for residential services, allowing for the development of a range of individualized living arrangements, from minimum supervision to maximum direct services, depending on the needs of each person served.
b. Developmental Services — There should be a range of infant, early educational, and educational services which allow for the individual child to grow and develop in the most normalizing way possible.
c. Vocational Services — There should be a range of vocational opportunities, from pre-vocational training to the mobilization of services that will maintain even the most severely disabled person in a productive work environment.

12. Personnel Development.　A major safeguard of program quality is the development of personnel competent to bring about integrative human services. There should be included within the plan the training necessary for volunteers, direct service personnel, administrators, and the community at large. Training should include an ongoing analysis of the ideological and technological principles upon which the system is based as well as the technological requisites necessary to work with retarded persons, such as applied behavioral analysis, curriculum planning, prescriptive teaching, etc. (In Chapter 12 we examine the issue of manpower development.)

A practical way to ensure manpower development is to serve a mix of mildly to severely retarded persons in the community program from the start. This enables paraprofessional to professional staff to develop practical skills in serving the entire range of retarded children and adults. If programs exclude the more severely retarded, it becomes difficult to serve them as time goes by.

CONCLUSION

As parent associations emerge across the world, community-based alternatives will evolve and envision the integration of all retarded persons into the mainstream of community and family life. The planning factors we have reviewed can serve as practical guidelines for such associations in shaping their visions into action-oriented plans. These plans, based on the twelve planning factors described herein, then evolve into reality through the ongoing public advocacy of the parent association.

The issues are complex. For this reason we have stressed the need to build strong, articulate, politically active parent associations. The move toward serving all retarded persons in the community depends upon a solidarity between parents and professionals. Technological breakthroughs will not integrate retarded persons in the community. Only a firm commitment to the vision of all persons living together will bring this about.

3 Foundational Principles Essential to Successful Community-Based Services

We have emphasized the need to make a clear, ideological commitment to integrate all retarded persons in the community. This commitment requires the establishment of an array of concrete and functioning programs and services in the community. The mentally retarded, like all other persons, have a range of residential, educational, vocational, and recreational needs. Each person needs a place to live, learn, work, and play. Thus, parents and professionals need to envision the placement and support of each retarded person in these environments: family settings, regular schools, and business and industries.

It is important that the ideological foundations of normalization and the developmental model be translated into concrete, environmental options for all mentally retarded persons. Residential, educational, vocational, and leisure-time settings make up community-based service systems. There cannot be normalization, nor maximum human development for mentally retarded persons, without the establishment of community-based service systems that nurture the retarded persons' integration. They result in interdependence. They provide the framework for the support needed by retarded persons across their lifespan.

Modern community-based programs are the embodiment of the recognition of the developmental potential of all mentally retarded persons — as well as the recognition of the principle of normalization. These programs are comprehensive in that they serve all mentally retarded persons in the community, regardless of the severity or complexity of the handicapping condition. They are community-based in that they provide the programs, services, and supports that the individual needs in the mainstream of family and community life. They are specialized in that they meet the needs of the individual in normalizing settings but at the same time bring together whatever technological supports the individual might require (Gilhool, 1978; Gollay, Friedman, Wyngardner, & Kurtz, 1978; Menolascino, 1977).

There are four major environmental dimensions (McGee & Menolascino, 1981) involved in community-based mental retardation programs: residential, educational, vocational, and leisure time (Figure 4). Community-based programs recognize these environmental structures as encompassing the basic human needs of all mentally retarded persons — living, learning, working, and playing. They focus on establishing programs and services that support mentally retarded persons within these major environmental dimensions. These dimensions run counter to institutionalization, which tends to congregate large numbers of developmentally disabled persons under one roof and protects them from society. Institutions gradually lose sight of the developmental potential of their residents and often evolve into human warehouses (Blatt, 1963; Blatt & Kaplan, 1966; Flint, 1966; Taylor, 1977; Wolfensberger, 1969). Community-based programs, on the other hand, focus on supporting the needs of individuals who are dispersed in normalizing settings throughout their community.

ROOTS COMING TO FRUITION

In the 1980s, the ideological roots reviewed in Chapter 1 have come to fruition in scores of communities around the world. Community-based programs demonstrate that they are capable of serving all mentally retarded per-

FIGURE 4
ENVIRONMENTAL DIMENSIONS

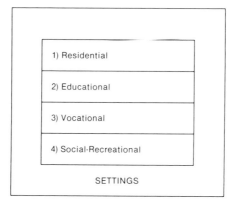

sons, even the severely and profoundly mentally retarded, in the mainstream of community life, given appropriate supports and services. Berkson and Landesman-Dwyer (1977) concluded that a mere 20 years ago most severely and profoundly retarded persons were isolated at home or spent the day in a ward doing little. Most professionals felt no services were possible beyond custodial care. The community integration movement is resulting in the placement of severely and profoundly retarded persons in small group living situations in their communities and in developmentally-oriented day programs. The severely and profoundly retarded are now considered and recognized as sentient humans who can learn and are social beings. New methods for assessing the needs of previously "untestable" individuals have been developed. The importance of integrative environments and of adequate stimulation has been confirmed repeatedly. Basic principles of learning have been used to increase self-help, social, academic, and vocational skills of severely and profoundly retarded persons.

For the severely and profoundly mentally retarded population, the developmental model signifies the maximizing of the human qualities of each individual while at the same time adapting environments to meet their needs. Such maximizing of the human qualities of persons with very special needs can be understood as "normalizing" them; that is, normalization signifies decreasing a person's deviancy or better increasing the person's potential to be in the mainstream of community life. For the most profoundly retarded persons, in certain rare instances (for example, cases involving gross neurological deterioration), the goal of the principles of normalization and the developmental model (that is, increased responsiveness, control over the environment and increased complexity of behavior) may at times appear to be unattainable in view of technological limitations. In these instances, it may be appropriate to design programs with primary intervention goals that maximize the individual's quality of existence while remaining sensitive to future developmental and normalizing possibilities (Roos, 1979). The concepts of normalization and the developmental model embody a philosophical position concerning the personal dignity and human rights of any individual, including the most severely and profoundly mentally retarded. They refer to an attitude and an approach to the most severely retarded individual which stress the opportunity to live a life as close to normal as possible.

Modern programs serving the mentally retarded in normalizing and developmental settings emphasize: (1) programs and environments that physically and socially integrate the mentally retarded into the community; (2) the attainment of integration through comprehensive, dispersed, community services based on population density and distribution patterns; (3) the activation of these persons in daily routines comparable to those of non-retarded persons of the same age.

RESIDENTIAL SERVICES

In relation to residential needs, community-based programs should support, wherever possible, the natural family rather than supplant it (International League of Societies for the Mentally Handicapped, 1979; Skarnulis, 1976). An array of supportive services should be available to each family, providing a comprehensive service system for all mentally retarded citizens. For retarded children, the services needed are noted in Figure 5 (McGee & Hitzing, 1978):

This array includes services such as: (1) Parent training and support. For example, the Pilot Parent program is a volunteer service provided by many parent associations in the United States in which experienced parents are trained to counsel new parents of disabled children. They are then matched with these new parents and provide on-going support. This has proven to be a relatively simple and effective way to support parents of newly identified retarded children (Menolascino, 1977). (2) Respite care. In this service, parents of disabled children have the opportunity to take a break from their disabled child. Some communities have a small group home for such short-term, out-of-the-home residential care. Other communities have an "extend-a-family" program. In this program volunteer families are identified, trained, and matched with families needing respite care. Through respite care many families receive the support necessary to maintain a healthy family unit. Without such support, some retarded children would likely be institutionalized. (3) Out-of-the-home residential care. When the disabled child is not able to re-

FIGURE 5
ARRAY OF RESIDENTIAL SERVICES

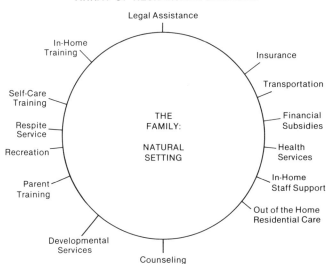

main at home or as retarded children reach adulthood, communities need to provide an array of residential options (Figure 6).

Community-based programs need to provide an array of residential alternatives such as foster homes and small group homes. The key factor in any residential placement is to maintain the person in the community, as close to the family as possible. Residential alternatives are characterized by their smallness (usually three to six persons maximum) and the provision of individualized support services. The need for community-based residential services becomes especially critical for mentally retarded adults around the world (Stenner, 1976). The most common residential alternative is the group home in which a small number of mentally retarded adults live together in a home-like, interdependent community, sometimes with house-parents living with them, sometimes with small teams of staff working on shifts. Within the group home setting there are two general purposes: (1) to create a stable, loving, nurturing environment, and (2) to provide the types of support and developmental training that the residents require.

The group home can be a permanent residence for those who are unable to live more independently or it can be a springboard toward more independent residential alternatives. Indeed, the large percentage of mentally retarded adults can move into less structured and protected environments. There is a smaller percentage, however, who require the stability, structure, and support of a small group home – generally those with severe and chronic medical

FIGURE 6
ARRAY OF RESIDENTIAL ALTERNATIVES

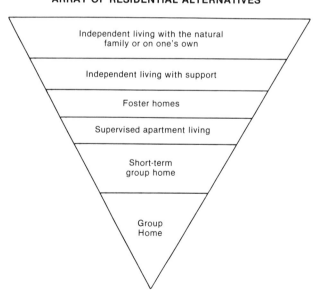

Independent living with the natural family or on one's own

Independent living with support

Foster homes

Supervised apartment living

Short-term group home

Group Home

problems and/or behavioral problems (Menolascino & McGee, 1981). It should be noted that in many communities across the world there are many such persons living in foster homes and other less restrictive alternatives. Nevertheless, there are some mentally retarded adults and children who require the group home model in order to have their needs met in a stable, consistent manner. Parents and professionals must always keep in mind that our ultimate responsibility is the paradoxical goal of the promotion of community integration while at the same time ensuring stability and support.

Typically, as community-based services begin to evolve in communities across the world, parent associations need to seek a range of options supportive of community integration. The development of community-based residential alternatives does not really depend on any one service model. First, no residential service can ever duplicate all a young person's family home can give him when it is functioning as a healthy family system. So, when analyzing the needs for alternatives outside of the natural family, we must respond to three basic pressures that might cause a person to move from the home before the usual age: the existence of a stress-causing problem originating within the person, the family, or the community (Skarnulis, 1976). It is important to preserve the bond between the person and his family for as long as possible for once severed it becomes increasingly difficult to mend or create new ones. It is important to support the mentally retarded child within the family network because the greater the distance from the family, the longer the time spent apart from the family, and the larger the number of unrelated persons living together, the broader the gap becomes in the relationship between the mentally retarded person and his or her family.

The key residential formula that should guide us in the development of community-based alternatives is to support, not supplant the natural home (Skarnulis, 1976). With children, this means supporting the family as early and for as long as possible. Rather than taking a child from the family because he is mentally retarded, it is more important to ask, "What do you need in order that your child can grow and develop in his home?" When that question is asked, parents are encouraged to express what they really need. We often hear responses such as: (1) a request for periods of relief or respite, (2) a request for counseling and support, (3) a request for in-home training, (4) a request for short-term crisis assistance, (5) a request for special appliances for adapting the home to become barrier-free. For mentally retarded adults, the concept of supporting-not-supplanting means assisting the mentally retarded adult toward achieving a status as independent as possible in the living situation. If a child or adult, in spite of all supportive attempts must leave the natural home, every effort should be taken to develop an alternative residence that is as close to the home as possible in the smallest group setting possible. If a child or adult must leave the home permanently, great care should be given so that the person is not placed in an institution, but rather in a community-based alternative. (In Chapter 4 we describe more fully how to develop residential alternatives.)

EDUCATIONAL SERVICES

In relation to educational alternatives, community-based programs need to provide a range of services designed to meet the educational and developmental needs of all disabled children from birth to an upper age limit consistent with national customs. These educational services are provided in the least restrictive, most normalizing setting possible and are based on the needs of each individual. Educational services should include: (1) early identification, (2) parent training, (3) infant development, (4) pre-school services, and (5) general school services. Early identification is a critical element in the provision of developmental services. Many nations (such as Italy) maintain a registry of all handicapped children and monitor infant progress in local "well-baby" clinics. It is obvious that early identification is the first step toward the provision of adequate and appropriate services and a basic tool in the prevention of secondary disabilities.

Infant development services should be provided from the early months of infancy through the 30th to 36th month. These services should focus primarily on the teaching of basic developmental skills to the parents who in turn teach the infant in the home environment. These services are generally provided in one of two ways:

1. Through infant development centers wherein parents bring their disabled children one or two days per week for two to four hours. During this time an interdisciplinary team of specialists demonstrate and teach the parents basic infant development techniques. Such centers can also serve nondevelopmentally disabled infants through the teaching of basic parenting techniques.
2. Through in-home-based infant development programs itinerant specialists provide the same services, but in the home.

Integrated pre-schools, such as the previously mentioned Agueda preschool, are the next component in the continuum of educational services. For most handicapped children this is their first structured exposure to their nonhandicapped peers and vice versa. Communities around the world are beginning to offer this first integrative opportunity. Typically, the same resources that would have been used in a segregated pre-school are transferred to an integrated pre-school setting. Through this transfer of resources, even the most severely and multiply handicapped children can be physically and socially integrated with their non-disabled peers. Such early integration is not a matter of resources or technology, but rather it is a matter of parent and professional willingness to integrate rising out of the community's awareness — what Freire calls "conscientization" — of the ideological factors described earlier in this chapter (1970).

Educational services for school-age children are a continuation of the integrated pre-school experience. Indeed, some communities have almost completely eliminated the concept of special schools and special classrooms by integrating both handicapped children and specialized personnel into regular classrooms. Parma and Florence, Italy, are two such communities (Cavara, 1981).

Typically, communities develop a cascade system of ever-increasing normalizing environments within their schools. In this system there is a series of educational alternatives (see Figure 7) (Dupont, 1968).

Mainstreaming children with disabilities in regular education is an emerging world-wide phenomenon. Mainstreaming must not be equated with the random, non-planned placement of children within the regular school; rather it is the careful, planned placement of disabled children in educational settings which are as normal as possible with all of the special supports which a child might require.

In the United States, several factors are used to determine the degree of integration (see Figure 8) (Alioa, 1979):

FIGURE 7:
ARRAY OF EDUCATIONAL ALTERNATIVES

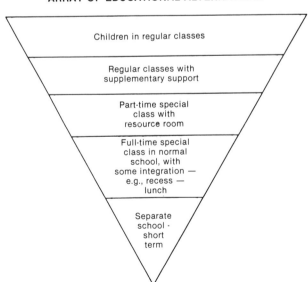

Children in regular classes

Regular classes with supplementary support

Part-time special class with resource room

Full-time special class in normal school, with some integration — e.g., recess — lunch

Separate school - short term

FIGURE 8
PLACEMENT FACTORS

Child Parameters	Placement Situation	Family Parameters
Learning rate	Size of class	Healthy home environment
Ability to follow oral instruction	Desire of teacher	Parents' desire
Capacity to work independently	Location of room	Acceptance of disability
Age similarities	Individualized teaching style	Involvement
Receptive language	Support teachers	
Expressive communications	Supportive aides	
Social development	Supportive administration	
Self-control	Resource specialists	
Interpersonal relationships	Preferential seating Modified materials	
Emotional development	Parental involvement	

There is no easy solution to the issue of educational integration. There is a myriad of factors to consider as indicated earlier. It must be remembered, as Taylor (1981) points out, that the question is not whether educational integration can work, but how to make it work. In his review of mainstreaming in the United States, Taylor points out a number of instrumentalities in use in the United States as initial attempts of educational mainstreaming:

Physical Integration.   Various communities have closed segregated facilities for the severely handicapped. At the very least, classrooms for children with severe disabilities are dispersed throughout regular schools. Such minimal physical integration affords opportunities for social integration.

Integration in Extracurricular Activities.   Activities such as mealtimes, recreation, field trips, library, homeroom, music, art, and physical education afford multiple opportunities for integration.

Reverse Mainstreaming.   Many schools involve normal students in special activities in segregated classrooms. These students can play a number of roles—helpers, tutors, companions, advocates.

Schools-Without-Walls.   Central to current educational approaches for severely handicapped children is an emphasis on teaching students functional living skills (Brown, Branston, Hamre-Nietupski, Johnson, Wilcox, & Grunewald, 1979). Thus, many schools use the community as a "classroom."

Classroom Integration.   Taylor reports several schools in the United States are completely integrated. In reviewing these, he states, "Each of these integrated classes is a warm, happy setting. The severely handicapped students blend well into the classes. Children interact freely with one another. Distinctions between 'handicapped' and 'non-handicapped' seem irrelevant."

VOCATIONAL ALTERNATIVES

Just as there has evolved a range of educational and residential alternatives for mentally retarded persons, there is also a range of community-based vocational training options for mentally retarded adults.

Like the other developmental and environmental options we have examined, there is a vocational continuum ranging from low to high integration (see Figure 9).

Some examples of the options evolving in various countries are (Galloway, 1979):

FIGURE 9:
ARRAY OF VOCATIONAL ALTERNATIVES

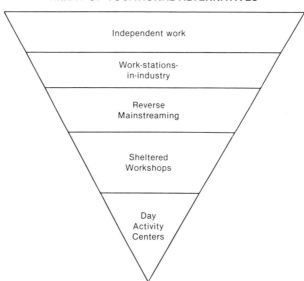

Integrated "Sheltered" Work Settings. This type of setting is characterized as a rehabilitation-oriented business that employs both handicapped and non-handicapped line workers and trainees. The best known American example of this type is Minnesota Diversified Industries, located in St. Paul. This model is characterized as "the affirmative industry" by its developers. The developers attest to the (re)habilitative importance of built-in, normal setting expectations, the passive (but crucial) role of non-handicapped, "model workers," and the availability of powerful training technology for workers who find learning job tasks more difficult. Another example is Cabra, a small village in Spain, which has two such industries in which 20 to 30 severely mentally retarded adults work side-by-side with 40 to 60 non-handicapped workers. One integrated shop is a furniture factory. The other is a chicken farm (Toledo, 1981).

Machine Intensive Training. Another example of an integrated "sheltered" setting is Center Industries in Wichita, Kansas, an independent non-profit industry, employing handicapped and non-handicapped workers. It especially focuses on adapting machine intensive work to the needs of physically handicapped persons through the use of creative machine adaptations. This alternative originated in Australia.

Workshops Without Walls. This work training arrangement is a fluid setting. Crews of supervised trainees perform a wide variety of contracted work in varying community settings such as janitorial work, landscaping, etc.

Workstations in Industry (WSI). This term was coined to describe a range of training settings managed by the Eastern Nebraska Community Office of Retardation (ENCOR). Essentially, a (re)habilitation agency contracts with an established local business that has its own work force to provide additional on-site labor. Small crews of handicapped workers, along with a trainer supervisor, fulfill the contract demands and learn "real" skills in a normal business setting. The ENCOR work-station experience has been that: (1) the client costs of operating this program are a small proportion of that required for agency-operated sheltered workshops; (2) the rate of successful movement to competitive employment exceeds the comparable rate for segregated sheltered workshops; and (3) over time, increasingly more handicapped persons can be trained in work-stations as staff competency (and expectations) increase and as the industry involved sees the partnership as manageable and in their mutual interests.

Specialized On-The-Job Training. Industries provide the setting for training. However, the training provided is personalized, short-term, and very intensive. A good example of this model is Ahead, Inc., a non-profit corporation that operates in Harrisburg, PA, and serves severely and multiply handicapped adults.

Core Training Centers. In direct partnership with a consortium of business/industry advisors, a (re)habilitation agency provides training delineated by the consortium; provides a trained workforce; and adapts the particular industry to meet the needs of the client. The Training Alternatives in Living and Learning (TALL) project in Kansas City (USA) is an example of such a partnership (President's Committee on Mental Retardation, 1978).

Centers for Independent Living. In Berkeley, California, disabled persons themselves have banded together to advocate for their own rights and human needs. It is much more than a training program, rather it focuses on self-advocacy and social change brought about by adults with disabilities themselves.

SOCIAL-RECREATIONAL ALTERNATIVES

An equally important factor in meeting the basic human needs of mentally retarded persons is the social-recreational dimension of human life. This dimension, although it is not related to any specific environment, is nevertheless crucial to the social integration of the mentally retarded person into the mainstream of community life. This dimension relates to the total person and how the person regards himself or herself and interacts with the world around. It has to do with self-image, human interactions, human sexuality, and the mentally retarded person's integration into community living.

Like other service dimensions that we have analyzed, social-recreational services can be described in a continuum of alternatives ranging from minimally integrative to maximally integrative (see Figure 10).

For the more severely mentally retarded it may be necessary to provide highly structured social-recreational activities as an integral part of the person's individualized services. Likewise, parents and professionals might utilize social-recreational services as a teaching mechanism to help the person acquire basic interactional skills in a more relaxed manner. Structured recreational activities can take the form of representational play for the more severely involved, giving the person a multitude of opportunities to acquire basic interactional skills through the constructive use of play (Fletcher, 1982).

As retarded persons acquire interactional skills, many communities and parent associations assist them in forming social clubs such as the Gateway Clubs in England. This provides socializing opportunities to many mentally retarded adults.

FIGURE 10
SOCIAL-RECREATIONAL SERVICES

Another form of social-recreational activity can be found in citizen advocacy programs. In these programs parent associations train and match laypersons to become "advocates" for individual mentally retarded persons. These advocates form enduring, personal relationships with the mentally retarded "protege," offering a variety of personal supports just as in any enduring friendship.

In the United States a more recent form of social-recreational service has been initiated by the mentally retarded themselves in the People First movement, in which they organize themselves as their own advocates. These groups generally receive support from the parent association in their initial stages of development, but gradually become their own spokespersons.

Eventually, communities begin to offer the same social-recreational opportunities as are available to any other citizen. That is, the mentally retarded person becomes physically and socially integrated into the mainstream of community life, taking advantage of the generic social-recreational activities that are available to any other person — parks, clubs, churches, etc.

CONCLUSION

In previous chapters we have reviewed the ideological foundations that have helped parents and professionals around the world reconsider the very nature, meaning, and potential of persons with mental retardation. We further emphasized the need to create local parent associations to serve as the force behind the birth of community-based service systems — associations that envision, provide, and finally monitor the establishment of developmentally intensive and normalizing services for all mentally retarded persons regardless of the severity of handicapping conditions. We also indicated the primary factors that parents and professionals must confront in the envisioning, change-oriented process. In this chapter we have summarized the range of services and types of options that various communities around the world are developing to serve retarded persons across their lives in the mainstream of community life. Some of these options are traditional; others are at the cutting edge of community integration. All are helping to shape a world where retarded and non-retarded persons can learn to live, work, and play together.

Advocates for community-based integration need to understand the range of options that need to be made available to all mentally retarded persons. The key rule is to discover mechanisms to support, not supplant, each person in natural environments — in families, schools, and factories. In the next chapter we cite several mechanisms for such integration.

4 The Four Basic Program Components in a Community-Based System

To create the types of programs and services needed to serve all mentally retarded persons in the mainstream of community life, it is important to recognize the programmatic trends reviewed in the previous chapter. Beyond these general trends there are four key instrumentalities or programmatic components that have been adopted in communities around the world to initiate the development of community-based service systems: integrated pre-schools, group homes, sheltered workshops, and work-stations-in-industry. These four programmatic components serve as the starting point in the development of community alternatives. In this chapter we outline the steps involved in the establishment of each of these components.

COMPONENT 1: INTEGRATED PRE-SCHOOLS

Introduction

It is common that, as parent associations focus on the development of community-based programs, the association selects pre-school services as a top priority. We have cited the Agueda experience in Chapter 2 as an example of an integrated pre-school.

The development and management of an integrated pre-school is an excellent initial step in the development of community-based service systems. A parent association advocating for the development of integrated pre-school services can either start its own pre-school for the handicapped and non-handicapped children or it can negotiate to integrate handicapped children

46

into existing pre-schools. Figure 11 shows how a community group initiated an integrated pre-school service. The group was already running a segregated pre-school and wanted to disperse its children throughout regular community pre-schools.

The integration process involves the public education of parents, teaching personnel, and program managers. In pre-schools this is an easier task than in primary schools for there is less bureaucracy and more accessibility to decision-makers. Perhaps the best way to educate the regular pre-schools is

FIGURE 11
PLAN FOR PRE-SCHOOL INTEGRATION

WITH THIS	DO THIS	SO THAT
Director	Develop a program to disperse children and staff into community pre-schools that will be integrated	Children who are developmentally disabled will receive their pre-school education in the same setting and manner as all other children
Child Service Coordinator Family Service Coordinator	Contact community pre-schools	A relationship will be established between the special pre-school and other pre-schools
Child Service Coordinator	Invite staff from other pre-schools to participate in joint in-service training	Community pre-school teachers develop an awareness of the needs of developmentally disabled children and how to plan to meet those needs
All Staff of Pre-schools	Set up joint planning meetings	Various pre-schools can develop a plan to disperse, integrate, and serve developmentally disabled children
Child Service Coordinator	Determine which community pre-schools could best meet the needs of developmentally disabled children	Appropriate settings might be selected
Child Service Coordinator Family Service Coordinator	Make agreement with selected community pre-schools to serve currently segregated children	Gradual placement into integrated settings takes place
All Staff	Continue to provide and strengthen the above relationships	Complete integration will occur
Executive Director	Provide services of itinerant specialists and resource teachers	Individualized and developmental services will continue to be provided to the children in integrated settings
Child Service Coordinator	Help pre-schools develop individualized program plan	All children will receive optimal developmental services
Director	Develop and implement a management system	All children with special needs in integrated settings will be ensured quality, developmental services

to demonstrate that integrated education is possible, as the parent association in Agueda, Portugal did.

The general strategies in the development of an integrated pre-school system involve:

1. Needs Assessment.   The barriers to social integration are not within the child with special needs; rather they are within the surrounding environment. There are several needs that must be looked at and considered:

- population to be served,
- legal mandates,
- demographic and political make-up of the locale,
- qualitative assessment of local resources: community pre-schools, support services, public school system, etc., the types of needs that the children who are disabled will have in terms of social integration.

It is necessary to implement needs assessment as quickly and as effectively as possible, with a minimum of time and money being spent. If there is a strong commitment to social integration, this will lead the community to define *all* children with special needs as having the right to maximum social integration, not only children who are currently being served in special community pre-schools, but also those who are hidden in the community and those who are in institutions. Such a broad-based commitment eventually must lead to the development of a local or state provincial mandate to serve all children with special needs in integrated pre-schools. At this point social integration becomes an economic and political issue.

Few admit that the teaching of children with special needs has both economic and political bases. Teachers, parents, and consumer representatives must recognize this. To actually bring about socially integrative pre-school services for all children, the parent association must recognize itself as a political movement. Through petitions, public hearings, and political and bureaucratic pressuring, parent associations create the necessary economic and political structures for social integration.

2. Planning.   Having internalized a commitment to integrate children with special needs into community pre-schools and having stated the educational, economic, and political needs, the next strategy is to develop a specific plan.

The group that develops this plan will make it happen. They are committed to the social integration of children with special needs. In the day-to-day struggle of bringing about long-term change, there will be many variations to planned objectives. The key to implementing an action is to be action-oriented and performance-oriented. Once objectives are set, it becomes a matter of flexibly moving toward the objectives, developing the necessary social alliances to meet the objective, and not being satisfied with something only good on the way to something better. The people involved in the Agueda plan — parents, teachers, consumer representatives — had good pre-schools. But they refused to accept them. They are now moving on to something better. Such is the evolution of social change.

Serving the Child with Special Needs

How can children with special needs be educated once they have been socially integrated? The key to such educational management is the individual program plan.

Today, the concept of individual program plans for children in integrated educational settings is becoming recognized as a key management tool. An individualized program plan is a social contract with and for the child and his or her family. It indicates the services the child will receive, the quality of those services, and the efficiency of their delivery. It is a validation of the services that are being delivered. It is a way to monitor the growth across time of the child.

Individualized program plans are divided into two parts: (1) a long-range plan, and (2) a short-range plan. The former is based on the initial screening or assessment of the needs of the child. It projects into the future how those needs will be met or how the child will be able to adapt his needs to those of the community. The latter is based on the day-to-day educational services rendered to the child building up to the fulfillment of the long-range plan.

How to Write an Individualized Plan

It is obvious that human service systems invest a lot of time and effort in diagnosing and evaluating children. All too often, after a child is labeled, little happens. Integrated pre-schools need to develop action-oriented program plans for each child. These plans should pinpoint the child's broad needs in each major developmental area:

- self-care
- language and motor development
- personal relationship
- cognitive skills
- inner feelings
- supportive needs

The long-range goals point the child in an appropriate direction. However, it is necessary to be much more specific: The short-range plans takes the broad goals and states specifically what will be done with and for the child in relation to each need.

When and Where.   Focus on when and where learning occurs. Can a child learn to feel values when all those around are also devalued? Does it do any good to teach a child self-care skills in a "greenhouse" environment? Select the most normative time and place for learning to occur.

Materials and Instructions.   Focus on how the child learns. An adult should learn in an adult environment and atmosphere: A child should learn in a child's environment and atmosphere. The learning should occur with materials, instructions, and feelings appropriate to the person's age, culture, and needs.

Behavior to be Increased/Decreased.   Once the broad goals have been described, it is necessary to take each goal and make concrete pinpoints. A broad goal might be acquiring appropriate self-care skills. A specific pinpoint might be toilet training.

When a specific pinpoint has been described, it is then important to recognize the concept of competing behaviors. For every behavior a child needs to acquire, there is generally a competing non-desirable behavior, sometimes in opposition, sometimes appropriate, and sometimes not.

Measurement.   The measurement of individual program plans refers to the need to validate the growth of the person who is developmentally disabled, as well as the services provided to him. Quite frequently, individualized program plans are measured at too infrequent an interval to be useful. If individual program plans are measured only quarterly, for example, decisions as to whether or not the plan is valid occur only four times a year. It is important to have a frequent way to validate the quality and effect of individualized program plans.

Sequencing vs. Redundancy.   A popular phenomenon in teaching preschool children with special needs is to break down behaviors into very minute learning ladders. Although it is extremely important to understand that learning occurs through a series of progressive steps, it is also important to avoid developing unnecessary numbers of minute steps a child must go through to learn the behavior. The teacher should see where the child is in terms of any special behavioral sequence. The child should be allowed to have the opportunity to develop his/her learning in any appropriate sequence.

Total Child—Total Needs.   It is fairly easy to pinpoint behaviors and personal needs. It is difficult to keep a human perspective while doing this. No matter how we pinpoint and work with a child's needs, it is crucial to always look at and relate to the entire person. The adolescent learning vocational skills must know how to relate those skills to his total being. The child learning to socialize in the classroom must be able to socialize at home. Normalization means the integration and growth of the total person.

Normalization does not imply that all children are nor have to be the same. It does say that all children in a given culture should have the opportunity to live, work, and play as any other citizen in that particular culture. It does not say how to do specific things, but the actions, interactions, and interpretations of a person who is developmentally disabled should be allowed to develop in the least restrictive way.

Teaching Retarded Behaviors—Teaching Adaptive Behaviors.   It should be remembered that all too frequently people working with disabled children have a tendency to teach behaviors retardedly. A skill is taught, but at a rate which hinders the child from functioning in society. For example, a child learning to button his shirt is learning a valuable objective. Many teachers stop there. They teach the person to button the shirt over a period of time that can only be considered retarded; for example, ten minutes. Therefore, the teacher working with a child who is developmentally disabled must realize and demand that behaviors be learned as normally as possible. Where a skill cannot be acquired in this manner, teachers need to find ways to adapt the environment.

The concept of the development and management of integrated pre-school services is both simple and complex. It is simple educationally and ideologically because learning in socially integrated settings is best for all concerned—children, teachers, parents, and community. It is complex in that the dynamics leading to social integration will require the commitment and involvement of many people. Parent associations interested in focusing on pre-school age children have a concrete instrumentality to develop integrated services—the integrated pre-school.

GROUP HOMES

Introduction

For more severely retarded adults and for retarded persons with severe behavioral and medical problems group homes are the cornerstone of community-based programs around the world (Goodfellow, 1974; National Institute on Mental Retardation, 1975; Rosen, 1976; Servicio Internacional del Informacion sobre el Deficiente Subnormales, 1978; Sigelman, 1973). They can provide both structure and integration, stability and, where possible, movement. They prevent the removal of retarded persons from the community. They prevent institutionalization. Figure 12 shows the typical steps required to start a group home (Willowbrook Plan, 1976). The concept is simple: (1) A group of persons in need is identified; (2) a plan for a group home is written based on their needs; (3) various legal-regulatory steps are undertaken; (4) supportive services are identified; (5) funding is arranged; (6) staff is trained; and (7) clients are moved to the residence.

Besides these pre-planning issues, professional staff need to be aware of the more detailed processes in managing a group home. Several factors need to be dealt with in the day-to-day operation of a group home. Figure 13 outlines some of the on-going issues that need to be dealt with to safeguard the appropriate grouping of clients, their individual rights, and their continued learning and integration into the community.

FIGURE 12
FACTORS IN GROUP HOME DEVELOPMENT

- [ ] Identify the persons to be served
- [ ] Provide statistics on the number of people who need the service
- [ ] Obtain letters of support
- [ ] Cite family needs for services
- [ ] Conduct public education campaign
- [ ] Select or develop a sponsoring agency
- [ ] Make a contract for funds to spell out obligations
- [ ] Select a board of directors
- [ ] Include regulatory agents as consultants (e.g., zoning)
- [ ] Be sure funding is available
- [ ] Select possible sites
- [ ] Examine the sites
- [ ] Examine the location
- [ ] Select a facility that fits into a neighborhood
- [ ] Meet with neighborhood leaders to gain support
- [ ] Finalize proposal
- [ ] Select a compatible mix of residents
- [ ] Select staff
- [ ] Train staff

FIGURE 13
THE DEVELOPMENT AND MANAGEMENT
OF A GROUP HOME

_____ 1. What is the age range of clients served in this facility?

_____ 2. What is the range of retardation of the clients served?

_____ 3. What is the range of mobility of the clients served?

_____ 4. In addition to mental retardation, what other disabilities, if any, are present in the current population of this facility?

Yes   No

☐   ☐   5. Are furniture and furnishings safe, appropriate, comfortable, and home-like?

☐   ☐   6. Do multiply handicapped and non-ambulatory residents have planned daily activity and exercise periods?

☐   ☐   7. Do all residents have planned periods out of doors on a year-round basis?

☐   ☐   8. Do residents participate in household responsibilities?

☐   ☐   9. Are residents encouraged to have possessions which are age- and culture-appropriate?

☐   ☐   10. Are residents' birthdays and other special events celebrated individually?

☐   ☐   11. Are the residents' given at least three meals a day?

☐   ☐   12. Are meal times consistent with the cultural norm of the community?

☐   ☐   13. Do all of the residents eat at a table in the dining area?

☐   ☐   14. Does each resident have an adequate allowance of neat, clean, and fashionable clothing?

☐   ☐   15. Is the facility in harmony with the surrounding neighborhood?

☐   ☐   16. Does the exterior of the building blend well with the exterior of other buildings in the neighborhood?

☐   ☐   17. Are opportunities made available for social integration with members of both sexes?

☐   ☐   18. Are opportunities made available for social interaction with non-disabled persons?

☐   ☐   19. Does the building present barriers to any of the clients in terms of access to any part(s) of the facility?

		20.	Do the facility grounds or surrounding areas present any problems in terms of access and/or mobility?
		21.	Is at least one each of the following accessible to and usable by individuals in wheelchairs?
			a) drinking unit or means of obtaining drinking water?
			b) toilet?
			c) telephone?
		22.	Have any of the clients in the facility been denied services of any type (including employment and recreation) because of transportation limitations?
		23.	Is transportation provided during evenings, weekends, and holidays? If yes, what methods are used?
		24.	If necessary, is each resident's clothing properly (and inconspicuously) marked for identification?
		25.	Is clothing kept in good repair?
		26.	Is storage space to which each resident has access provided for his/her clothing?
		27.	Is ample and accessible closet and drawer space provided for each resident?
		28.	Are residents' haircuts and styles age- and culture-appropriate, fashionable, and individualized?
		29.	Are mirrors provided which are accessible to all residents?
		30.	Is regular assistance provided to those individuals who require it for cutting toenails, fingernails, and for shaving?
		31.	Are residents' bathing schedules appropriate and adequate?
		32.	Do residents brush their teeth, or have their teeth brushed daily?
		33.	Are individual toothbrushes properly identified and stored?
		34.	Do toilets, bathtubs, and showers provide for individual privacy?
		35.	Are sleeping rooms arranged so that no person needs to go through another bedroom to gain access to his/her bedroom?
		36.	Are residents allowed free access to all areas within the home (with due regard for privacy and personal possessions of others)?
		37.	Do residents have freedom of movement on the premises of the facility?

		38.	Do residents have freedom of movement off the premises of the facility?
☐	☐	39.	Do residents have access to phones for incoming and local outgoing calls?
☐	☐	40.	Are residents allowed to make long distance calls?
☐	☐	41.	Are residents allowed to open their own mail and packages without direct surveillance?
☐	☐	42.	Are residents allowed to send letters without having them read by staff, unless staff are requested to do so by the resident?
☐	☐	43.	Are the individuals' families and/or friends encouraged to visit the facility?
☐	☐	44.	Are close relatives permitted to visit at any reasonable hour, without prior notice?

The key factor is to create and manage the group home in such a way as to ensure each retarded person that their needs will be met across their lifespan in a small, individualized, loving environment.

Client Groupings

There is no magic answer as to who should live with whom and how many persons should live together. The general rule is, the smaller the better — a grouping small enough to enable the development of a personalized, interdependent community. Current group homes seldom exceed six persons. The mix of clients within the group home also needs to be considered. The general rule is that care should be taken relative to appropriate age groupings and compatible needs groupings. Clients in the residence should be matched so that as much mutual support as possible can occur. For example, a nonverbal, severely retarded adult should be in a group of other adults who could support that person's needs and at the same time serve as appropriate models.

Facility Location

The group home should blend into the neighborhood. For those persons in wheelchairs, it should be barrier-free. It should be near or accessible to grocery stores, department stores, theaters, parks, public transportation, etc., in order to ensure as many opportunities as possible for social integration within the larger community.

Individualization

Consideration needs to be given and safeguards developed for the individual rights of each person in the group home. Personal privacy and possessions should be ensured. The group home should evolve into a community wherein each person has both a community life and a private life. The group needs to learn to share in the responsibilities and joys of living together and at the same time have his/her personal life preserved.

Staffing

A crucial factor is the staffing available for the group home. Staff need to be competent to handle a wide variety of needs. Figure 14 outlines the basic competencies that group home staff should possess.

In most situations staff will consist of paraprofessionals trained in the areas described in Figure 14. Seldom do professional staff need to be involved in the day-to-day staffing of a group home. Professional staff should serve as back-up supports to individuals in group homes. For example, persons with active seizures do not generally require a nurse on-duty. Such a person would require professional support to: (1) identify and diagnose the seizure activity, (2) the prescription of seizure-control medication by a

**FIGURE 14
STAFF COMPETENCIES**

Staffing/Personnel Competencies. Training: Place a checkmark (✓) under each individual's name across from the training subject for which there is documentation that training sessions have been attended and/or a level of competency has been demonstrated.

STAFF								STAFF							
Completing assessments/ evaluations								Individual program planning							
Writing objectives								Seizure disorders							
Detection and prevention of communicable diseases								Proper use and care of prosthetic devices							
Dental and oral hygiene								Nutrition/diet control							
Use of mechanical supports								Proper lifting techniques							
State laws regarding storage and handling of meds								Detection of signs of injury, disease, and abuse							
Administration of medications								Normalization							
Least restrictive alternative								Developmental model							
Human and legal rights								Human sexuality							
Behavior management								Precision teaching/charting							
Sign language								Food storage and handling							
Budgeting								Balancing a checkbook							
Menu planning								Housekeeping							
Laundering/Care of clothing								Physical therapy							
Occupational therapy								Speech therapy							
First aid								Disaster planning							
Safety								Prevention of mental retardation							
Proper feeding techniques								Physical intervention techniques							
Sensitivity to the needs of the handicapped								City, County, or State rules, regulations, laws, and/or codes applicable to the facility							

physician, and (3) the monitoring of the seizure activity and medication regimen by a qualified nurse or physician on a periodic basis. However, the day-to-day support of the person in the group home would not generally require on-site professional staffing. The paraprofessional staff could be trained and supervised on an on-going basis by competent professionals. Likewise, a mentally retarded-mentally ill person would require the back-up support of a psychologist or psychiatrist; but the day-to-day needs of the particular person could be met by trained paraprofessionals.

An allied issue is the level of staffing required by the clients involved. The general rule is that the level of staffing should be sufficient to meet the needs of each client. In a specialized group home for the mentally retarded-mentally ill, for example, this may mean 1:1 staffing for a particular person until the person's high frequency self-abusive or aggressive behaviors are brought under control. Care should be taken to reduce the staffing levels as soon as possible to avoid excessive costs. The average staffing pattern in a group home is 3:1 for moderately to severely retarded persons.

SHELTERED WORKSHOPS

Sheltered workshops serve as the most common instrumentality for the training of the majority of mentally retarded adults. In most communities as parent associations begin to focus on the needs of mentally retarded adults, they typically embark on the development of a sheltered workshop. Often these workshops have the initial purpose of only providing day activities for retarded adults. Eventually, however, it becomes clear that mentally retarded adults can learn vocational skills and that those skills should be relevant to the needs of the surrounding community. Sheltered workshops must evolve into vocational training centers designed to prepare mentally retarded adults to participate in the world of work (Chemarin & Desroy, 1980; Lynch, Kiernan, & Stark, 1982; Olshansky, 1972; Seminario Internacional sobre Empleo Protegido, 1980; Wehman, 1981). The basic steps in the development and management of a sheltered workshop can be seen in Figure 15.

There are two types of sheltered workshops: (1) the transitional shop, preparing retarded adults for the actual world of work, and (2) the extended care shop, wherein clients who are inconsequential "producers" are given work activities. Sheltered workshops also differ from one another in their approach toward the meaning of work. The sheltered workshop can regard work training as only an activity to fill the day or it can regard it as specific training relevant to a person's vocational development.

In a modern sheltered workshop, work is used as the primary vehicle for client development. Thus, workshop contracts need to be selected on the basis of their habilitative value. According to Gold (1979), the ideal work con-

FIGURE 15
SHELTERED WORKSHOP ISSUES

1. Identify vocational needs of retarded adults.
2. Identify number requiring vocational training.
3. Select work-oriented training location.
4. Identify relevant contracts for work production.
5. Develop policies and practices to encourage: appropriate training, valued work, integration opportunities, options for training,
   machine intensive work, movement into independent employment, pay commensurate with work production.
6. Acquire location and equipment.
7. Select and train staff.
8. Analyze and resolve safety concerns and production concerns.
9. Provide specific skill training.
10. Provide normal work expectations.
11. Provide social adjustment training.
12. Ensure that all retarded persons, regardless of the severity of
    their handicaps, can receive vocational training.

tract has the following characteristics: (1) It requires skills that must be taught rather than skills that the client already has. (2) Client training considerations are as important as production considerations. (3) Contracts should be both labor-intensive and machine-intensive, with an emphasis on machine-intensive contracts. (4) Contracts should involve complex operations to afford a variety of skills and sub-skills. (5) It should be profitable to the workshop and to the clients. (6) Wherever possible, the acquisition of the skills in the contract should lead to opportunities for work in the community.

Sheltered workshops, as mentioned in Chapter 3, can provide integration experiences through reverse mainstreaming — that is, employing non-handicapped workers to work side-by-side with retarded trainees. These people simply serve as passive role models to the retarded trainees. For example, a small town of 5,000 inhabitants in Spain has a furniture factory that serves as a sheltered workshop of retarded persons in the community and at the same time employs non-retarded workers. In Cabra, Spain's factory-workshop, many of the issues discussed thus far disappear because both work and integration have occurred.

WORK-STATIONS-IN-INDUSTRY

Another instrumentality to meet the vocational-developmental needs of mentally retarded adults is the work-stations-in-industry. The work station is essentially a sheltered workshop within a regular factory or industry. It is sheltered from the perspective that it provides the necessary support and supervision a retarded person might need through trained work supervisors. It is integrated because the work experience occurs in the mainstream of a regular factory.

Work-stations-in-industry offer a more normalizng pattern of work training. Often work shop personnel say that they have a normalized setting.

However, in observing many "sheltered workshops" it becomes obvious that most of these programs fail to provide a high degree of physical or social integration into the community. People defend "sheltered workshops" saying that they are needed for various kinds of specific training of adaptive skills. This may be so for some people who are retarded. Most communities that have "sheltered workshops" easily find ways to defend the existence of these workshops. Although there may be a need for them to exist, it is also becoming more and more obvious that if services to citizens who are mentally retarded are to become individualized, then other alternatives should be established that will fit their needs.

Many of the typical learning activities involved in work training can be carried out in a work-station-in-industry, in a normal routine of work, with normal workers. In a real place of work there are a myriad of learning opportunities that naturally occur at normal times and routines. The work schedule is normal. People clock in and clock out. A certain kind of dress is automatically required. Industries are generally located in accessible areas. Buses come and go with workers or else workers share transportation. Industries are located among other industries. There is accepted structure in the interpersonal relations that exist between workers: Workers are expected to treat their supervisors in certain ways. Work supervisors are expected to play a particular role in relation to their work crew. Many workers take pride in the work that they do. Workers learn to use a vast array of tools and machinery. Workers learn to work an eight-hour-day for a just pay.

Often workshops purport to be involved in such kinds of training. No matter how much they try, however, it is often quite apparent that the routines and activities in a workshop are far from normal: Indeed, they are often make-believe. They often bear little resemblance to actual work-routine conditions.

Work-stations-in-industry are for small groups of people with trained supervisors from the world of work. These work crews are dispersed in small groups — approximately eight people — in various industries in a community. The age of the people makes no difference as long as they are adults. The only applicable criteria is what is normally acceptable in the particular industry. It is crucial to have an industry whose size enables the integration of the work crew into the industry. It is important to avoid overcrowding an industry with workers who are mentally retarded. Such a move would eliminate many of the benefits that accrue from social integration.

Setting up a work-station-in-industry depends upon the specific industry involved. There are some common steps that should be taken: (1) contact industries that are potentially receptive to the idea, (2) demonstrate that a work crew is available and capable of doing a particular type of work, (3) demonstrate that trained supervisors from the world of work will be able to manage this particular work crew, (4) proceed with the normal sub-contract bidding process, (5) determine if space is available to do the sub-contract work in the industry itself, (6) demonstrate the cost benefits of doing the sub-contract work in the industry — transportation expenses, quality control, time-saving, etc., (7) demonstrate the wage and hour prerequisites, (8) state that work trainees are paid based on work produced, plus bonuses, (9) attempt to attain a contract sufficient to cover supervisors and work trainees' wages, and (10) select the work station supervisor and work trainees.

One argument that employers might raise is that if there are handicapped workers on the premises, insurance rates will automatically increase. This is not necessarily so. However, if the particular industry uses this argument, the service agency can guarantee within the contract negotiation that it will purchase liability insurance on the premise for the handicapped workers. This is a very low cost insurance. If this is what is necessary for the establishment of a socially integrating work-station-in-industry, it is of very little cost to the program.

It is necessary to avoid establishing work-stations-in-industries in places not valued by society itself. For example, it might be tempting to set up a work-station-in-industry in a nursing home doing maintenance work, or in many of the typical places where professionals have sought job placements for workers who are mentally retarded. In developing work-stations-in-industry, it is important to remember that their major purpose is to socially integrate the retarded person into the world of work. This world has a myriad of options in each and every community across the country. Therefore, it is good to remember and to challenge ourselves to find those places which are valued by workers themselves.

Similarly it is necessary to avoid developing work stations in just one or two types of industry in any community. Each work station must be able to profitably employ eight work trainees and one supervisor. The contract volume must be such that the work station will pay the wages of the eight people and the supervisor.

The way in which the agency manages the work-station-in-industry is extremely important. The agency serving people who are retarded should not interfere with the internal operation of the industry itself, beyond the training of the work supervisor, the entry of the work trainee into the work-station-in-industry into competitive employment, as well as other supportive services. The agency must, however, avoid making the industry itself and the work trainees within the work-station-in-industry an obvious social service program.

The benefits that accrue for the work trainees from work-stations-in-industry are many. One of the most obvious benefits is that the work and the work trainees are considered to be worthwhile. It is necessary to understand that the purpose of work-stations-in-industry is only to train people to work. Often people try to change behaviors of retarded people according to some mythical code. Often the behaviors of normal workers in an industrial setting are not too much different from some of the behaviors which are seen in "sheltered workshops." One major difference is that workers in industry typically have a work ethic that is often absent in a "sheltered workshop."

The work trainee in a work-station-in-industry is inundated with normal work expectations. The whole routine and rhythm of the industry literally forces the work trainee to adapt to that particular environment. In "sheltered workshops" the work supervisors often adapt to the low expectations commonly held of people who are retarded. In industry the expectations flow in the opposite direction. The work trainee is in a world of work. This, therefore, helps him and enables him to adapt to this kind of world.

The typical consequences of a real work setting are much different from those which occur in a "sheltered workshop." They often use reinforcers of hugs, kisses, food, etc. These are ruled out in the real world of work. In a real industrial setting, the consequences for adult workers are those which we would normally expect — an occasional "good work," an occasional yell, an occasional layoff, and, at times even a promotion.

There are also benefits for the community. Public education is a highly touted phrase in professional circles. There is no better public education than demonstrating to the public that people who are mentally retarded can work, can compete in real work settings. In industry, work is what is valued. If it is demonstrated that work trainees in the work-station-in-industry are able to compete, not as retarded people, but as workers, then there could be no better public education.

Example of a Work-Station-in-Industry

A company in Omaha, Nebraska (Lozier Corporation) has had a work-station-in-industry for several years. This large company manufactures store shelving. Unlike most "sheltered workshops" the prerequisites for entering this work-station-in-industry are quite minimal: (1) coming to work on time, (2) coming each day, (3) no unnecessary sick leaves, (4) controllable seizures, (5) operating food and drink machines, (6) counting 0–9, (7) taking the bus in all kinds of weather, (8) wearing work clothes, (9) using a cutting blade, (10) using a hammer, (11) handling self safely around machines, (12) using a phone, and (13) following instructions. Whereas most "sheltered workshops" require sophisticated and esoteric screening devices for admitting people into sheltered workshops, it is obvious from the above behaviors that in the real world of work it is the work itself which is valued along with workers' ability to relate to those around them.

In this particular work-station-in-industry, the work trainee has various tasks to learn: (1) operating an electrical sander, (2) operating a pinning machine, (3) packaging parts, (4) assembling parts, (5) using an electrical grinder, (6) using an electrical hammer, (7) working independently, and (8) working under pressure of quotas and timetables.

Just as the role of the work trainee in a work-station-in-industry is different than that of the "client in the sheltered workshop," so also the role of the work station supervisor is different from that of the "trainer" or "teacher" in a "sheltered workshop." In this particular work-station-in-industry, the work supervisor is involved in the following tasks: (1) assigning tasks and quota to each work trainee, (2) establishing and maintaining the most efficient work flow, (3) checking quality control, (4) maintaining production required by the industry, (5) maintaining records of contracts completed in quantity, (6) informing the service agency placement coordinator about the work trainee's progress and job readiness, (7) bidding all contracts, (8) billing each contract, and (9) determining bonuses for workers based on contract production. It is obvious that this role is quite different from the role of many of the workers in the traditional "sheltered workshop."

FIGURE 16
CHECKLIST FOR WORK-STATIONS-IN-INDUSTRY

1.	Is the industry near a transportation system?	Yes	No
2.	Is the industry accessible to the workers?	Yes	No
3.	Is it large enough to accommodate 6 to 8 work trainees who are retarded?	Yes	No
4.	Is the industry perceived by the community as being valued?	Yes	No
5.	Are the work trainees labeled as such?	Yes	No
6.	Do the work trainees begin and end work at the same time as other employees?	Yes	No
7.	Do the work trainees have the same breaks as the regular employees?	Yes	No
8.	Do the work trainees have the same benefits as the regular employees?	Yes	No
9.	Do the work trainees dress as the other employees?	Yes	No
10.	Do the work trainees take the same risks as the regular employees?	Yes	No
11.	Are the work trainees expected to work as hard as the other employees?	Yes	No
12.	Do the work trainees work side by side with the regular employees?	Yes	No
13.	Do the work trainees develop friendships with the regular employees?	Yes	No
14.	Is there a number of work-stations-in-industry so that training can be individualized?	Yes	No
15.	Do the work trainees participate in union or other activities?	Yes	No
16.	Are the work trainees compatible with the age and sex of other employees?	Yes	No
17.	Is the work supervisor provided sufficient training?	Yes	No
18.	Is the program administered in such a way that it is not obvious that this is a "special" program?	Yes	No
19.	Is the growth and the development of the work trainees individualized and monitored?	Yes	No

Figure 16 contains a checklist of issues related to the development and management of work-stations-in-industry. It becomes obvious that the role and expectations of the work-stations-in-industry can play an important part in developing less restrictive and less costly alternatives to a traditional work training environment. Just as it is necessary to bring all people out of the hell of institutions in this country, so it is also necessary to develop alternatives to the purgatories that are traditionally set up in communities for adults who are mentally retarded. Work-stations-in-industry are one of those alternatives. The form and format of any given work-station-in-industry will depend on the belief that there is a dignity of risk that work is valued by society, and that for the adult who is mentally retarded, one of the best ways to socially integrate a person into the community is through the world of work.

CONCLUSION

In this chapter we have reviewed the four most common program components in the development of community-based service systems. Building upon this concept, in the next chapter we demonstrate how one community has mobilized its resources to develop a community-based service system by utilizing these components as the programmatic foundation for a comprehensive array of residential, educational, and vocational services. We have stressed that our beliefs serve as the basis of all programs and services. We next show how one community has translated these beliefs into actions.

II FROM IDEOLOGY TO PRACTICE

5 Establishing a Community-Based Service System – The Encor Model

INTRODUCTION

In this chapter we focus on the development of the Eastern Nebraska Community Office of Retardation (ENCOR) as an exemplary model of how to establish a community-based service system. This program serves as a symbol of what parent associations and local communities can do in the development of community alternatives. It shows how parents and professionals can work together to bring about change.

In the late 1960s, the citizens of eastern Nebraska made a commitment to the decision that all mentally retarded persons should remain in or return to their communities and be as independent as possible. This commitment was based on the belief that individuals who are mentally retarded have a right to live in the least restrictive environment consistent with their individual needs. It was based on the belief that all mentally retarded persons should have the right to live and grow in their home communities. There had been previous efforts in the United States to make institutions smaller and more responsive, in California and Connecticut (Scheerenberger, 1983), but these attempts fell far short of community integration.

The agency created to meet that challenge was ENCOR. Today, with the support of parents, the community, and elected officials, ENCOR is well on its way to achieving this goal. The concept of community services is an emerging reality in Nebraska.

Since ENCOR's beginning in 1970, services have been provided to over 2,000 mentally retarded persons. A range of residential, vocational, educational, and support services have been developed. All but 228 persons from

Beatrice State Developmental Center (the state institution for the mentally retarded in the State of Nebraska) have been returned to their communities in eastern Nebraska. Beyond ENCOR in eastern Nebraska, a system of community services has been developed across the state through six community-based mental retardation regions. The population at the institution has declined from over 2,400 persons in 1968 to a total of less than 475 in 1983. Only 228 persons from the five counties in the region called ENCOR now reside in the institution. This region encompasses the Greater Omaha metropolitan area and outlying towns in a five county area. The total population base is approximately 500,000 persons. All mentally retarded persons in Nebraska have had a right to a free public education since 1973, including the right for every handicapped child to receive a free public education from the date of diagnosis until age 21. All of these changes have emerged from the original and on-going advocacy of the local parent association.

Today ENCOR serves approximately 1,045 mentally retarded persons in the community in direct day and residential programs and other supportive services, and continues to bring people out of the state institution into community-based programs.

In the 1960s, parents of mentally retarded children in Nebraska, as in most communities around the world, had very limited program choices. They could decide to send their son or daughter away to the state institution for the mentally retarded or remain with their children at home. Local schools would provide some service. More severely retarded persons were not generally

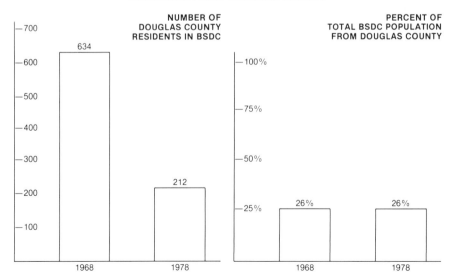

FIGURE 17
TOTAL BEATRICE STATE DEVELOPMENTAL CENTER
RESIDENTS FROM DOUGLAS COUNTY

served at all. At the time, there was a waiting list to enter the institution. If parents had enough money, they could send their child away to a private institution. If parents rejected institutionalization altogether, they were left with virtually no supports in the community to assist them, limited access to education in the public schools, no services or programs such as vocational training, respite care, or residential services in the community.

It was during the 1960s that the parents of mentally retarded individuals banded together in Nebraska to work for changes in the conditions that existed for their mentally retarded children and themselves. Parents began to envision alternatives to institutions.

At that time, the existing conditions were called "the blackest pages in our state's history book." The conditions at the state institution were deplorable. Over 2,400 persons were crowded into the institution; 634 of these people were from the Omaha area. The institution was overcrowded; it was grossly understaffed; the building were old and dangerous; and the residents did not even receive a minimum of care or treatment.

Members of the Nebraska Association for Retarded Children, the statewide parent association, requested a study of the institution in 1968. The Governor of the State appointed a Citizens' Committee to examine conditions at the institution and to give him direction. This committee, composed of parents of mentally retarded persons both in the institution and living at home, several state elected officials, and professionals, provided the Governor with an extensive report of the conditions that needed to be improved at the institution, but their most urgent recommendation was that the population of the institution be reduced from 2,400 to 850 residents in six years.

The committee report, entitled *Into the Light* (Wolfensberger, Clark, & Menolascino, 1969), stated:

> Underfinancing of public institutions is the problem. Public zoos spend more to care for a large animal than is spent to care for the average retarded resident in our institution. While five of the largest zoos spend an average of $7.00 per day to care for their large animals, average expenditures for the mentally retarded in Nebraska institutions is approximately $4.50 per day. The national average is about $7.00. Kansas, a state very similar to Nebraska, spends over $12.00.

> In many ways we treat the retarded like animals. Retarded persons who could be trained to eat independently, to use the bathroom, and to wash, clean, dress, and groom themselves are often sentenced to living in untrained conditions and to waste away without attention. Some Nebraska retardates who could learn self-care and walking, spend most of their days helplessly in bed, naked or crawling hopelessly in their own excrement.

> "Warehousing" residents at the Beatrice State Home is the result of an outdated philosophy that the retardate is something society must be ashamed of, must lock away for life, and ignore. Such a philosophy has no place in modern Nebraska.

The Study Committee attempted to transform its words into action and based its report on five basic principles:

1. No matter how handicapped a retarded person or institution resident is, he is not an animal, vegetable, or object, but a human being and citizen deserving of respect, and in possession of certain human, legal, and social rights. As much as possible, retarded persons, whether institutionalized or not, should be treated as ordinary persons of their age are treated in the community. Every effort should be made to "normalize retardates," that is, to diminish those aspects that differentiate a retardate from a typical citizen of comparable age.
2. There should be a maximal continuity of contact and atmosphere between all phases of service agency (including institution) functioning and the community.
3. Continuity of contact between a retardate and his family should be maximal, limited only by liberally interpreted considerations for the welfare of the retardate, his family, and the agency (for example, institution) serving them.
4. Service agencies (including institutions) should provide an environment conducive to their retarded clients' physical, intellectual, social, and emotional well-beings and growth, with special emphasis on the development, welfare, and happiness of children.
5. Each retarded person, particularly if he resides in an institution, should have a special relationship to a competent individual citizen who will act as his personal advocate, vigorously representing his interests and safeguarding his welfare.

These principles formed the philosophical basis for planning in eastern Nebraska.

THE DOUGLAS COUNTY PLAN

At the same time, a similar study committee was established in the greater Omaha area (Douglas County)—the most densely populated area in the State, located in eastern Nebraska. This committee was again composed of parents and professionals (some of whom had also been on the Governor's Committee). The Committee wrote a plan for services at the local level that would eliminate the need for any mentally retarded person to leave his or her home community to receive necessary services. This county plan was the start of the Eastern Nebraska Community Office of Retardation.

Wolfensberger, Clark, and Menolascino (1969) developed a strong rationale for services in the Douglas County Plan. The report discussed the waste of mentally retarded persons—socially, morally, and economically—through pervasive segregation and isolation in crowded, understaffed, remote institutions. It declared strongly the belief that all persons have an inherent value and a right to develop to their full potential regardless of the severity of their handicap. The report stated that mentally retarded persons were citizens and that their rights were currently being violated in the State of Nebraska. It pointed out that it was very difficult to gain admittance into the Beatrice State Home due to overcrowding, but that it was equally difficult to gain release once admitted. It also stated that all children in the State of Nebraska between the ages of five and 21 were guaranteed a right to a free basic education under the provisions of the state constitution. At the time, however, the state allowed the parents of residents at the Beatrice State Home to be billed for the "free, basic education" they were receiving there. The report concluded that it was reasonable to predict that provision of a wide range of services to retarded persons was inevitable, and that the crucial question was not whether services would be provided, but when and how.

The report summarized the parent association's posture and goals by stating:

> National ideals dictate that a retarded person be perceived not as an object, not as a vegetable, and not as an animal, but as a human being; not as a static organism that cannot change or learn, but as a person capable of growth and development. It follows that attitudes, behaviors, and services should be based on the recognition of human dignity, of constitutionally anchored legal rights, and of pedagogic principles, rather than upon pity. It further follows that society must commit itself to the principle that many human services should be rendered as a matter of right rather than charity, and that adequate tax support is the only realistic and just basis for implementing this principle. While the expenditure of public monies may be a painful thought for many, the consolation comes with the realization that in the long run, the provisions of developmental, rehabilitative, and normalizing services are likely to be less costly than wasted lifetimes of dependency, non-productivity, and dehumanization.

The report provided a plan for the establishment of a comprehensive system of services within the community including residential, vocational, educational, and family support services. The plan proposed that many residents of the Beatrice State Home could be maintained in the community with services provided that would be far less costly and more humanizing than institutionalization, and would enable many retarded persons to stay with their families and become a part of community life.

The plan also proposed that the children labeled "trainable" or "educable" should be enrolled in public school special education classes. It suggested that industrial space could be leased to establish workshops, and recommended that homes and apartments could be rented and used to establish residences for those individuals who could not remain in or return to their natural homes.

The plan also emphasized the use of generic services, based on the belief that mentally retarded persons should be able to experience normal routines and rhythms of life, that they should leave a residence in the morning to attend school or work in a different location, that children and adults should not attend the same "day programs," and that they should be able to utilize existing community resources and settings for recreation, transportation, and health services. It estimated that most mentally retarded persons could attain some degree of self-sufficiency and that many could become competitively employed, tax-paying, independent citizens.

In 1969, the parents presented their plan to local elected officials. The Greater Omaha Association for Retarded Children — the local parent association — was funded to develop services. The intent of the plan was that these services would later be spun off to a governmental agency to deliver comprehensive community services to mentally retarded people.

During the 1969 legislative session, the state legislature passed a bill establishing six mental retardation regions in the State of Nebraska and provisions for state matching funds by the Office of Mental Retardation for local planning (Figure 18).

At that time the Department of Public Institutions was the state agency responsible for the administration of the one state institution. In addition, the

FIGURE 18
THE SIX MENTAL RETARDATION SERVICE REGIONS IN
NEBRASKA
Established by the Nebraska State Legislature in 1969 under LB 855

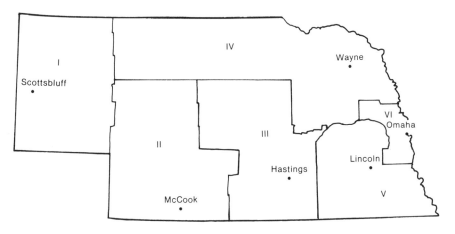

Percentages of Nebraska's Total Population and Area
Region I: 18% of total area; 6% of population
Region II: 20% of total area; 7% of population
Region III: 20% of total area; 15% of population
Region IV: 29% of total area; 15% of population
Region V: 10% of total area; 22% of population
Region VI: 3% of total area; 35% of population

FIGURE 19
STATE INSTITUTIONS

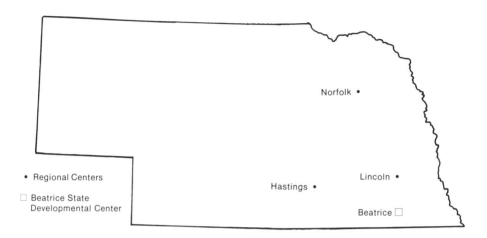

Norfolk •

• Regional Centers

☐ Beatrice State
Developmental Center

Hastings •

Lincoln •

Beatrice ☐

department administered three state Regional Centers – smaller institutions. All of these operated mental retardation units (Figure 19).

The 1969 legislative bill also transferred the Office of Mental Retardation from the Department of Health to the Department of Public Institutions, bringing both community and institutional services to the mentally handicapped under the same department.

The parents and professionals who developed the plan for services also took responsibility for its implementation. In July of 1970, four surrounding rural counties (Cass, Dodge, Sarpy, and Washington) joined together with Douglas County in this planning effort. The Eastern Nebraska Community Office of Retardation (ENCOR) was formed as a local, quasi-governmental agency responsible for the development and management of a community-based services system for all mentally retarded children and adults in the Greater Omaha area.

THE DECADE OF DEVELOPMENT – THE 1970s

The dream of the parent association gradually took shape. In the early 1970s the five counties were able to form a regional administration to provide community-based mental retardation services. At this time, ENCOR took over the educational, vocational, and residential programs while the local parent association changed from provider and demonstrator of services to public advocate and monitor of the quality of services.

One county board member from each of the five participating counties served as a member of the ENCOR Governing Board, responsible for the appointment of the agency's executive director, creation and enforcement of the agency's rules, the adoption of annual budgets, and general policy making for the agency. Funds for the agency were allocated by counties. State and federal dollars were allocated by the State Office of Mental Retardation. These local dollars drew federal matching funds.

ENCOR was designed to provide a continuum of services to meet the individual needs of retarded persons. Programs were located in both urban and rural communities. The agency began to provide services to meet the needs of any mentally retarded person from mildly to profoundly retarded, from infancy through old age.

In 1973 the Nebraska State Legislature passed a law giving all children, regardless of handicapping condition, the right to a free public education. Up until this time, ENCOR provided educational services to school-age retarded children. In 1973 the local school districts in the region took over these duties as mandated by law. By 1977 another state law mandated that local school districts provide a free, public education from the date of diagnosis for all handicapped children until age twenty-one. ENCOR closed its last preschool program at the close of the school year in 1977, turning these services over to local school districts. Thus, educational services were spun off to their rightful agent—local school districts.

From 1970 to 1974 ENCOR rapidly expanded its services to include residential, vocational, educational, guidance, and support services such as transportation, speech, physical and occupational therapy, psychological, medical, and recreational services. ENCOR also began service development in each of the other counties in the region and stopped virtually all admissions into the Beatrice State Home. Half of the residents of the region who had formerly been served at the institution were now being served through ENCOR in their local community.

In July 1974 ENCOR became a part of the newly formed Eastern Nebraska Human Services Agency (ENHSA). The Governing Board of ENCOR became the Governing Board of the newly created human services agency. At that time, ENCOR became a program office under ENHSA. Other ENHSA program offices included the Eastern Nebraska Community Office on Aging and the Eastern Nebraska Community Office on Mental Health. ENHSA was designed to provide administrative and fiscal support to its program offices and provide specialized transportation services to clients of all three program services.

From 1975–1976 there was a slow-down in ENCOR's service development. A serious federal financial crisis in 1975 and 1976 caused ENCOR to close some of its support services. Among those totally eliminated were staff training, social service offices, which had been established in each local community, adult evening educational programs, recreational programs, structured correctional programs for mentally retarded offenders, a crisis assistance unit, public education and information functions, and volunteer coordination. All planning, evaluation, administrative support staff, and an ombudsman were terminated. Other services were drastically reduced, such as counselors, speech therapy, physical therapy, and psychological services. Even with these program cuts the agency was able to maintain its basic services and eventually rebuild its comprehensive services. Through the 1970's ENCOR was still able to virtually halt the institutionalization of retarded persons in spite of this financial crisis (Figure 20).

THE ENCOR SYSTEM

ENCOR has established long-range goals in order to measure its effectiveness as an agency. These goals can serve as the framework for any community-based service program:

1. To obtain or provide community services at the local level which will eliminate the need for any mentally retarded person to be separated from his/her natural family or involvement in community life.
2. To promote the delivery of services for mentally retarded persons through the use of the same resources and settings available to all citizens.

FIGURE 20
REGION VI
ADMISSIONS AND READMISSIONS
TO THE BEATRICE STATE DEVELOPMENTAL CENTER
IN HISTORICAL PERSPECTIVE

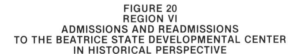
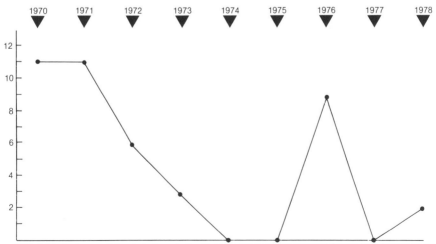

*Total Admissions and Readmissions to the Beatrice State Developmental Center that Region VI was made aware of and had an opportunity to offer alternative services had they been available.

3. To increase the skills of mentally retarded persons so that they may participate in and contribute to the community.
4. To support and assist families in meeting the needs of their mentally retarded family member.
5. To increase the public's understanding of the abilities and needs of mentally retarded persons.
6. To advocate for the realization of full citizenship.

The philosophy of ENCOR has been and is the most important aspect of its service system. It is what gives ENCOR its purpose, its direction, and its meaning. The philosophy shapes the relationships staff have with mentally retarded persons and the development of services. It shapes the system's relationship with the greater community as well. The ENCOR philosophy is based on:

1. The ultimate dignity of each human being and the realization of full citizenship.   Each human being has a basic dignity and rights which cannot be denied by any governmental or societal structure. The agency is committed by this philosophy to treat all individuals with the dignity they deserve as human beings. ENCOR strives to insure that every individual is able to take full advantage of his/her human, legal, and social rights. To further this end, consumer involvement is sought in individual, program, and agency decisions.

2. The developmental model.   Under the developmental model, all mentally retarded persons are considered capable of growth, development, and learning. The image of the mentally retarded person as unable to learn disappears under this model, regardless of the severity or multiplicity of the handicapping condition. This image is replaced with the belief that all individuals can advance through the use of positive programmatic principles. Through this model, the individual needs of each person are analyzed; and the major responsibility for the integration of the retarded person depends on the agency rather than on the individual person.

3. Normalization.   This principle states that ENCOR must provide services to mentally retarded individuals in a way that is typical, normative, and socially valuable in accordance with their individual needs. Individuals who are retarded are valued as peers in their community. This principal further requires the agency to assure that each person lives in as normative a situation as his/her skills allow. ENCOR strives to increase the individual's skills so that he/she is capable of living in a more normal environment and experience integration in the community.

The determination as to whether or not an individual is eligible for ENCOR services is based on two requirements.

1. Mental retardation.   The individual's primary disability must be mental retardation, regardless of secondary disabilities that may be present. The definition of mental retardation accepted is that of the American Association on Mental Deficiency. It states: Mental retardation refers to significantly sub-average general intellectual functioning, existing concurrently with deficits in adaptive behavior.

2. Residency.   The individual must either be living in or a legal resident of one of the five counties in the ENCOR region. The general definition of residency as it pertains to eligibility for ENCOR services is:

a. A minor under the age of 19 shall assume the residency of his/her parents.
b. An individual who has reached the age of majority (age 19) shall be recognized as an adult and he/she is able to establish his/her own residency.

There are no other criteria for services. Level of retardation, lack of self-care skills, behavioral or allied medical needs do not and cannot prevent a person from being served. Indeed, these factors demand more services, not fewer.

In order to provide services consistent with the philosophy of the agency, ENCOR has had to establish priorities for services. They are as follows in order of priority:

1. Emergency referrals (classified as such by the Governing Board or Executive Director) which are generally individuals in a life-threatening situation or individuals who are threatened with institutionalization.
2. Moves from one ENCOR facility to another that are programmatically necessary for a client.
3. Individuals who are institutionalized but are original residents from one of ENCOR's five county service regions.
4. Community clients from ENCOR's five counties.
5. Prevention of persons from going to regional centers, nursing homes, and private institutions.
6. Institutional residents presently in regional centers, nursing homes, and private institutions.

The region is administered by a centralized structure, with five smaller geographic sub-regions, each with an area director. This means that all personnel in the community-based mental retardation region are employees of the region and are directly responsible to the Regional Director and ultimately to the Governing Board.

Encor Administration

The ENCOR Director insures the most effective and efficient manner of coordination of effort in program activities and resource management, through responsible administrative supervision of all ENCOR programs and plans in accordance with the stated purposes and policies formulated by the Governing Board. The duties and responsibilities are as follows:

1. Provide a continuum of services for mentally retarded persons in the region.
2. Provide for public participation at appropriate levels of agency activities.
3. Identify and promote fundamental agency concepts.
4. Provide information to the ENHSA Director and Governing Board to allow them to keep alert to changing community needs and modify policies accordingly.
5. Directly supervise the area directors.
6. Provide the administrative structure for the agency reflecting actual operational patterns of the community-based programs.

ENCOR SERVICES

As a comprehensive, community-based service system, ENCOR provides an array of supportive, residential, educational (up until 1978), and vocational services.

Residential Services

The purpose of residential services is to prepare mentally retarded persons for the use of the same residential and other social environments available to all citizens within a community, independent of ENCOR support. A variety of residential alternatives is available in order to meet the specific individualized need of the person. Many coincide with those cited in Chapter 3. The primary residential alternatives are (see Figure 21):

1. Core Residences.   Core residences are operated and staffed by the agency, designed to provide 24-hour care in a residential setting. Each is capable of various staffing and programming levels, depending on the needs of the clients. Programming in the residence is designed to teach clients basic living skills, as well as social skills necessary to function in the community.

Phillip had spent the last five years in an institution for the retarded. As he entered ENCOR he was placed in a core residence. Because of a history of severely aggressive behaviors he was provided with one-to-one staffing. His needs were assessed. An individual plan was developed to engage Phillip in appropriate social behaviors. As he learned to interact appropriately, he has moved into a smaller, more independent alternative.

2. Alternative Living Units (ALUs).   ALUs are facilities that are structured more individually and provide a more normalized environment for development. Programming is also more individualized and enhances development toward greater independence apart from ENCOR residential services and support. One to three clients may live in an ALU, and supervision of the facility varies according to the needs of the clients.

a. Staff ALUs — full-time live-in staff.

Joe had spent 30 years in a state institution. He is mildly retarded. He spent several months in a core residence in order to adapt to community living. He now lives with one part-time staff person and requires minimal supervision beyond that given by his live-in "friends."

b. Off-site ALUs — staff support from core residence as needed.

Bill and Harry live in an apartment and care for themselves. They socialize in the community. A staff person drops by their apartment for three hours every evening to help them plan their meals, manage their money, and provide companionship.

c. Home Teachers — clients (children) are placed in a family home other than their own; staff support is given to home teachers through a core residence.

Bobby lives with a foster family. He is severely retarded and autistic-like. His foster mother teaches him skills under the supervision of an ENCOR counselor. More importantly, she and her husband provide the love which only a home can provide.

3. In-Home Services.   In-home services are provided by agency staff to families of mentally retarded persons, to prevent removal of persons from their natural homes, to prevent emergencies/crisis situations in their natural homes, to promote growth in the natural home, or to return persons to their natural homes.

Mary is severely retarded and autistic. ENCOR provides respite care periodically as well as parent support and training. This helps Mary to remain with her family.

4. Respite Care.   Respite care services are available on a limited basis through the use of the Crisis Assistance Unit — a respite care, group home.

This residence, along with several crisis homes located throughout the region, provides short-term residential care for retarded persons during times of stress or family need, such as a death or illness in the family, vacations, etc. Arrangements for the use of respite care services is made through each client's counselor.

5. Developmental Maximation Unit (DMU). The DMU, located at a local hospital, is structured to provide 24-hour care to persons who are severely and profoundly multihandicapped and medically involved. The emphasis is to minimize the physical/medical involvement so that the individual can continue towards development of more complex skills and toward a less structured environment. Services are available to children and youth under age 18. Movement from DMU requires a stable medical condition, enrollment in a daytime educational or vocational program, and transfer to a more normal residential program. There are generally eight children in this medical/developmental service.

> The DMU is a living example that even the most multiply handicapped, medically fragile children are capable of community living. In its first five years over 150 medically fragile children graduated from the DMU and moved back to their natural families or substitute family settings.

Through the 1970's ENCOR developed a number of community-based residential services (Figure 22). The key to the development of all residential services has been to focus on the utilization of local community resources, especially the use of small, family-like residential options.

An In-Depth View of Residential Services

With the present level of knowledge and experience in the development of residential alternatives, a number of specific community-based options have evolved within ENCOR, each designed to meet specific needs. Some of these have already been mentioned; each is more fully described in the following.

ENCOR provides a continuum of residential alternatives. The number of alternatives is only dependent on the creativity of staff and the needs of ENCOR clients. Generally, retarded persons served by ENCOR move through this continuum from most structured (core residences) to least structured (alternative living units). The continuum of service is based on each client's age and needs for intensive training directed toward increased independence and integration. The first rule for an individual in need of residential services is that the residence should afford him the greatest degree of independence and socially integrative opportunities possible, with the least structure and controls by the service agency. The provision of a range of residen-

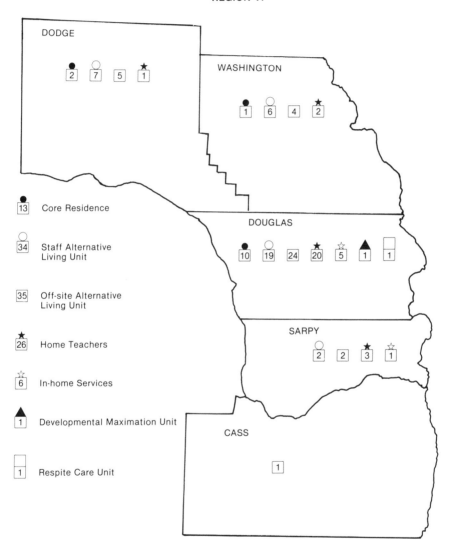

FIGURE 21
RESIDENTIAL FACILITIES
REGION VI

DODGE

● 2   ○ 7   5   ★ 1

WASHINGTON

● 1   ○ 6   4   ★ 2

● 13   Core Residence

○ 34   Staff Alternative
Living Unit

35   Off-site Alternative
Living Unit

★ 26   Home Teachers

☆ 6   In-home Services

▲ 1   Developmental Maximation Unit

□ 1   Respite Care Unit

DOUGLAS

● 10   ○ 19   24   ★ 20   ☆ 5   ▲ 1   □ 1

SARPY

○ 2   2   ★ 3   ☆ 1

CASS

1

81

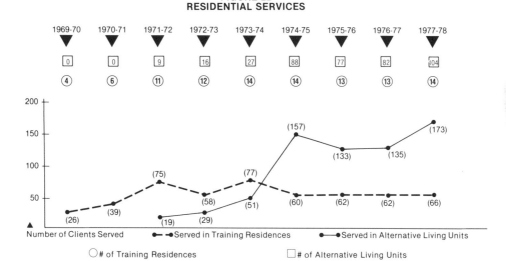

FIGURE 22
RESIDENTIAL SERVICES

1969-70 1970-71 1971-72 1972-73 1973-74 1974-75 1975-76 1976-77 1977-78

Number of Clients Served   ●— —●Served in Training Residences   ●——●Served in Alternative Living Units

○ # of Training Residences   □ # of Alternative Living Units

tial types and backup support services, however, allows for movement back and forth as needed for any one individual.

1. Developmental Homes. A developmental home is very similar to what is commonly known as a foster home, providing a residence for one child in an unrelated family. That family is regarded as a teaching home. It is different from a typical foster home for three reasons:

a. The developmental home's substitute parents are screened and trained extensively by ENCOR, and are considered part of the agency staff, receiving the same training and support that other staff receive.

b. A developmental home is considered a long-term placement for that child, ideally to result in adoption, not a short-term transitional placement.

c. The professional support and backup provided to developmental home parents assist them in the training and care of the child. This includes a counselor assigned to assist the parents with the necessary manipulation of agency and generic red-tape, medical services, etc.

2. Children's Intensive Training Residences. Although first priority for any child in need of residential services is to support, rather than supplant, the natural family, many children, for various family, behavioral, or medical reasons, cannot be placed into developmental homes immediately. These children need varying levels of support, supervision, and assistance. For those who need additional extensive attention and individualized supervision, children's residences are provided to accommodate a small number (three to six) of children. It is important that intense attention and home living skill training be provided while the children attend public schools. Such residences are regular homes in the community, staffed with houseparents and, if necessary, houseparent assistance. Emphasis in this setting is on maintenance of a normal rhythm and routine of life with informal as well as formal training in the development of skills fostering movement into more integrative services such as developmental home or, ideally, back into their own homes.

3. Adolescent Intensive Training Residences. As with children, some adolescents need intensive services to correct behavioral problems or increase self-help skills. It is desirable to serve some of these individuals in a small group (three to six) in local homes staffed with houseparents. These residences, like those for children, maintain a normal rhythm of life, enabling adolescents to attend public schools, agency training programs, or other generic educational or pre-vocational programs.

4. Family Living Residences. When specialized group residences were initially conceived, it was thought best to have separate facilities for children, adolescents, and adults. Experience, however, has shown that this is neither normal nor best for the training of some clients. Except for those individuals requiring intensive training, members from all three groups are placed together to form a more normal family living unit configuration. The goal of this configuration is to place less impaired adults or adolescents with children who are more impaired, with the expectation that the adults or adolescents will be of assistance to the houseparents. These are typical homes in the community with houseparents and normal routines and rhythms of life, with all individuals attending day training and education programs in the community.

5. Intensive Adult Training Residences. An intensive adult training hostel is a short-term residence geared to young adult and adult mentally retarded persons over the age of 18 who are either actively involved in vocational training programs or working in the community, but in need of intensive training in independent living skills. Persons in this type of residence are those who do not have adequate family homes or who have adequate family homes but need training away from the family unit in order to prepare for eventual self-sufficiency as adults. Each such home serves up to six individuals.

6. Adult Minimum Supervision Residences. These homes are for adults over the age of 18 who do not need intensive training and are involved in competitive or semi-competitive employment or in sheltered workshops, although they may still need some supervision and assistance in refining independent living skills or may display periodic adjustment problems in community living. Minimum supervision residences function more like a rooming house with a landlady than a family living model with an intensive training unit.

7. Board and Room Homes. Adults who have completed programs in an intensive adult training residence or an adult minimum supervision residence, or have come directly from their own homes or institution and do not need intensive training, have the same residential options as anyone else in the community. Therefore, the agency provides and/or coordinates and maintains quality control of local board and room homes. These homes provide little training and typically are staffed only with a houseparent whose function is to provide backup support.

8. Adult Developmental Homes. Adult developmental homes are very similar to the children's developmental home concept, with one adult, or possibly two, living in a family home in the community. This family has the backup support system of the agency, providing training and quality control. These homes, unlike children's developmental homes, however, are not considered to be long-term in most instances. Training provided in the home and through the person's day training program lead eventually to a semi-independent or independent living situation.

9. Cluster Apartments. In contrast to residential group homes, apartment living residences provide numerous options for varying the amount of independence and integration for which a particular person may be ready. The apartment cluster is composed of several apartments in physical proximity, functioning to some extent as a unit and supervised by staff members who reside in one of these apartments. The apartment cluster includes one apartment for staff members and one to four apartments for client residences. As the most flexible of the three apartment programs, the cluster-apartment offers many options pertaining to supervision, peer integration, and normal living. The cluster is usually in one apartment building or in neighboring buildings. Supervision of retarded persons varies according to individual needs. Being part of the normal living unit provides the person with numerous opportunities for participating in normal interactions with non-retarded persons.

10. Counseled Apartments. A counseled apartment is a more independent step from a cluster or co-residence apartment because no staff members live in it. A person may live alone in a counseled apartment but usually lives with two to four other retarded adults. These individuals require very minimal supervision (e.g., one night per week or one day of the weekend) in areas such as physical or social skills, personal grooming, budgeting, or increasing confidence in mobility skills. This counseling is provided through the counseling division of the agency. Contact is only as frequent as needed; but an attempt is made not to provide any more assistance or support than is absolutely necessary.

11. Independent Living (Counseling Provided).   Independent living arrangements are almost identical to counseled apartments, except that there is no systematic effort on the agency's part to intervene in the life of the person. Support and assistance are available through the agency, through counselors if requested by the retarded individual.

12. Five Day Residences.   Although some persons live with their own families, some need additional residential facilities during the week due to special training needs or the distance between home and programs. Residences that operate only during the week allow residents to return home on the weekends. In rural areas this is found to be very satisfactory. These residences are for both children or adults.

13. Specialized Residences: Behavioral and Medical Needs.   Behavior shaping residences provide a very intense specialized service needed by individuals who are severely or profoundly retarded with major behavioral problems such as aggression, self-mutilation, and/or low or minimal social or self-help skills. The residences provide a transitional residential and developmental program operated on a strict behavioral management methodology in order to prepare these retarded persons for more normalized day programs and residential settings. In these units a high staff to client ratio on a 24-hour per day program is provided in order to accelerate the individual's development and readiness for a more normalized program. Many of the individuals served in these programs are persons from institutions with severe behavioral problems who would not ordinarily be able to return to the community.

Such services are also available for community persons who, because of severe behavioral problems, would in all likelihood otherwise be placed in an institution or excluded from public school and other community services. For example, a community resident excluded from the public schools for acting-out behaviors could enter a behaviorally oriented residential program for a short time, learn to redirect aggressive behaviors, then return home. Much parent training is involved in order to maintain skill development after the individual leaves the program. One caution for this type of specialized unit is warranted from experience. Many persons within a system may appear to need intensive behavior shaping, but in reality could receive better training in a regular program instead of a specialized unit.

14. Developmental Maximation Unit.   The Developmental Maximation Unit is designed to serve severely and profoundly retarded individuals who are non-ambulatory and have multiple handicaps, including uncontrolled seizures, physical impairments, special sensory handicaps, and a range of highly at-risk medical needs. Since these services are primarily medically oriented, only those who are critically medically fragile are served in this facility. The service provides combined residential and developmental programs for basic stimulation and fosters acquisition of self-help skills, ambulation, social-personal awareness, and small group interaction. These services are provided for those children and adolescents whose complex medical challenges require treatment and/or management models to embellish their developmental potential. The purpose of the unit is to stimulate the client's development and stabilize his medical problems so he can participate in more advanced programs in the future.

15. Crisis Assistance Unit.   One of the major reasons for institutionalization has been the need for residential care during times of crisis either on the part of the family (e.g., illness or death) or because of behavioral or medical problems involving the retarded person. To eliminate the use of a long-term answer (institutions) to short-term problems, crisis assistance homes have been established to provide short-term care for any individual or family who needs special emergency residential services.

Crisis homes are an extension of the crisis assistance unit. Families in the community are recruited to serve as respite providers and the parents are trained to be on standby to provide a home on a short-term basis if the crisis assistance unit is at capacity or the person lives so far away that he could not continue to attend his normal day program.

Vocational Services

The purpose of ENCOR's Vocational Services is to prepare mentally retarded persons for the use of the same vocational environments available to all citizens. ENCOR's vocational programs demonstrate that individuals with any degree of retardation can successfully engage in community-training programs geared toward increasing independence and self-sufficiency. There is a variety of vocational training and placement services (Figures 23 and 24).

Industrialized Training Centers (Sheltered Workshops).   The purpose of these centers is to assist mentally retarded adults in the acquisition of pre-vocational and vocational skills. Any individual, regardless of level of retardation or severity of handicap, who is over the age of 18 and meets ENCOR's eligibility requirements, is eligible to receive vocational services. ENCOR operates five Industrial Training Centers (sheltered workshops) within the region, as well as a pre-vocational training center.

The purpose of these vocational training facilities is to prepare mentally retarded adults for movement toward the same community vocational settings available to all citizens by preparing them to perform work tasks in integrated industrial settings. Their goal is to increase each person's skills and

FIGURE 23
VOCATIONAL FACILITIES
REGION VI

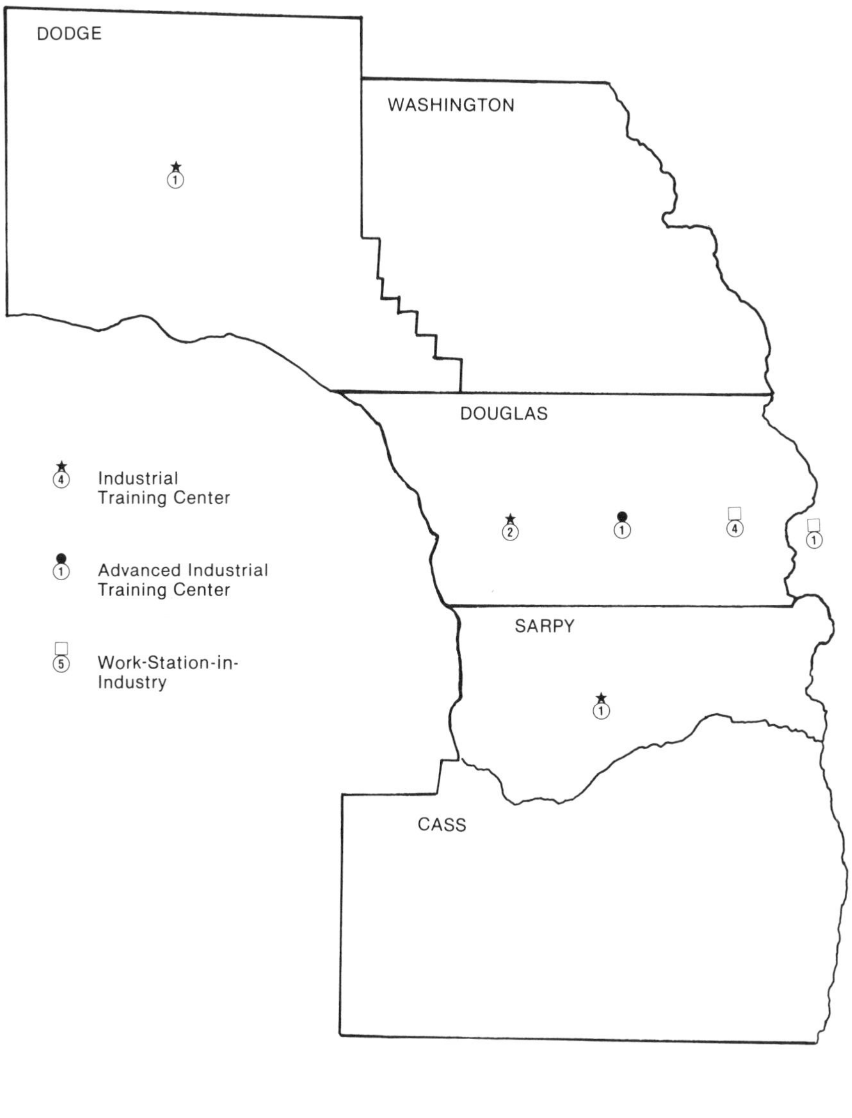

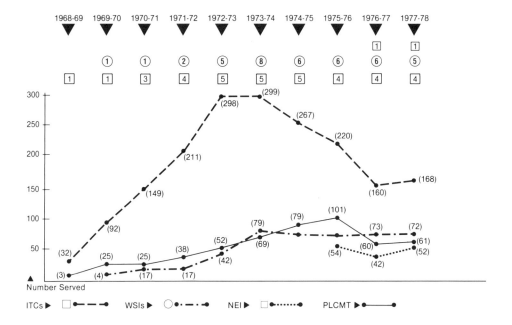

FIGURE 24
VOCATIONAL SERVICES

abilities so that they can successfully participate in local business and industry.

Sub-contract work from local industries and individual program planning are the basic components of training for each individual in the Industrial Training Centers. This training exposes individuals to the expectations of an industrial employer while continuing to provide individualized training support. The areas of training emphasis for each person are centered around the following:

1. job application and interview techniques,
2. personnel policies and employee benefits,
3. production,
4. quality control,
5. industrial safety,
6. equipment operation,
7. supervisor/employee relationships.

Work-Stations-in-Industry.   The purpose of this vocational component is to move mentally retarded individuals to competitive employment through training experiences within the mainstream of businesses and industries in the community. Work-stations-in-industry offer mentally retarded individuals specific skill training in a variety of employment options. This training is conducted on-site in local industries, rather than sheltered workshops. In this vocational option, areas of stress include: productivity, quality control, co-worker relationships, supervisor-worker relationships, industrial safety and general work habits.

Specific requirements for entrance into each work-station differ based on the type of work performed. Evidence of appropriate grooming and hygiene, attendance and promptness, acquisition of production skills, self-help skills, and taking public transportation are generally required. Current work-stations represent a range of work training options; for example:

1. manufacturing of shelving and store fixtures,
2. housekeeping,
3. packaging and assembly, and
4. food service.

Work-stations provide a practical alternative to sheltered workshops. They focus on work training with the necessary support and supervision each person requires. More importantly, they provide a high degree of physical and social integration since they are in the mainstream of industries.

A corollary ENCOR vocational service is to move ENCOR trainees from training programs to the competitive labor market by providing successful employment opportunities with necessary direction and support. Job placement of individuals from Industrial Training Centers or Work-Stations-in-Industry is done by ENCOR staff who provide on-the-job training and follow-along with the employee and employer until the placement is successful.

COMPLEXITY OF PERSONS SERVED

This system of services would have less value if it were not open to and capable of serving all retarded persons, including the most severely retarded and multiply handicapped. An important dimension in the development of community-based alternatives to institutions is to clearly demonstrate that the most severely retarded persons are capable of community integration. The following comparative data (ENCOR, 1979) demonstrates that ENCOR serves as severely retarded and complex a population as the institution.

The majority of persons who are served by ENCOR are in the mild and moderate ranges of retardation; however, ENCOR actually serves more people in the severe range of retardation (127) than the institution (Figures 25 and 26). ENCOR also serves 43 persons in the profound range of retardation.

FIGURE 25
INDIVIDUALS SERVED BY ENCOR
LEVEL OF RETARDATION
BY NUMBER AND PERCENT

(Number served by ENCOR — 784)

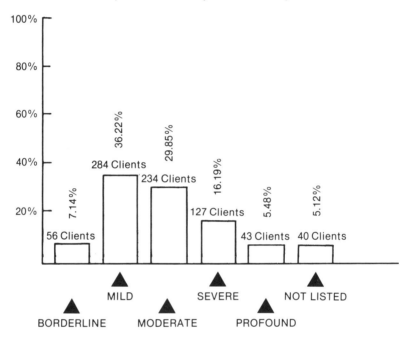

The majority of persons remaining in Nebraska's institution are in the severe and profound range of retardation (77%, or 201 clients), but a significant number of persons from the Omaha area who are mildly and moderately retarded still reside there (22%, or 57 persons).

Many believe that mentally retarded persons will not be able to function in community-based mental retardation programs unless they have certain prerequisite skills such as feeding, dressing, and toileting skills. ENCOR, since its inception in 1968, has based its service delivery on the belief that the client has the right to be served in the least restrictive alternative and that it is the responsibility of the staff to help the client acquire these skills in the most natural and most normalizing setting. It is the philosophy of ENCOR that the system must be flexible enough to meet the special needs of the client and not that the client must change to be served by the system.

The needs study revealed that ENCOR was serving 142 persons who could not eat independently as opposed to 629 persons who had independent feeding skills. ENCOR served 221 persons who were unable to dress themselves and 554 persons who could. In addition, there were 176 clients in ENCOR who were unable to toilet themselves independently, and 600 clients who could. The institutional population data revealed that 184 clients remaining at the institution were capable of feeding themselves and 72 needed assistance; 121 could dress themselves and 132 needed assistance; 131 persons were capable of toileting themselves and 120 needed assistance (Figures 27 and 28).

Based on these comparative population profiles (level of retardation and self-care needs), we can conclude:

1. At the time of the needs study, ENCOR was serving 16 children between 0 and 2 years of age and 84 between the ages of 3 and 5. There were 192 public school aged children between 6 and 18, and 79 young adults between 19 and 21. ENCOR was also serving 408 adults ages 22 to 60 and five persons 61 or older.

FIGURE 26
INDIVIDUALS SERVED BY BSDC
LEVEL OF RETARDATION
BY NUMBER AND PERCENT

(Region VI Population at BSDC assessed was 259)

*Individuals from Region VI who were not diagnosed as retarded were not included in this assessment.

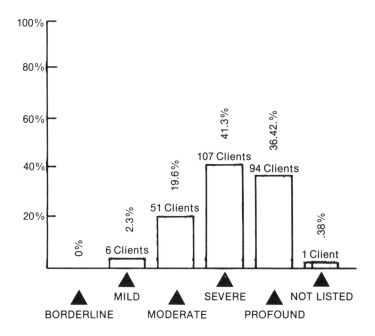

FIGURE 27
SELF-HELP SKILLS — ENCOR
BY NUMBER AND PERCENT FOR
INDIVIDUALS SERVED BY ENCOR

Total = 784

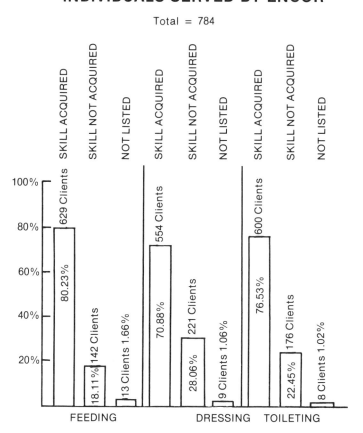

2. The majority of persons were from the larger metropolitan area (611 persons); however, 167 were served in rural communities.
3. Forty-two percent of the clients served by ENCOR were females; 58% were males.
4. The majority of clients served by ENCOR were in the moderate and mild ranges of retardation. However, ENCOR served more persons in the severe range of retardation than the state institution. ENCOR also served 43 clients in the profound range of retardation.
5. The study showed that ENCOR was serving a total of 115 persons who could not ambulate without some kind of assistance. In addition, six persons were deaf and 83 had hearing impairments; 52 persons had im-

paired speech which made communication with others extremely difficult and another 154 clients were listed as being nonverbal.

6. Even though self-care skills are considered by many to be a prerequisite for service in a community-based program, ENCOR served 142 individuals who could not feed themselves; 221 persons who could not dress themselves; and 176 persons who could not toilet themselves. All of these persons were either in residential settings with less than six persons or in their natural homes.

7. One hundred and forty-six of the persons served by ENCOR had a secondary diagnosis of cerebral palsy; 235 has some form of epilepsy; 21 were autistic; and 12 had dyslexia.

FIGURE 28
SELF-HELP SKILLS — BSDC
BY NUMBER AND PERCENT FOR
INDIVIDUALS SERVED BY BSDC

Total = 259

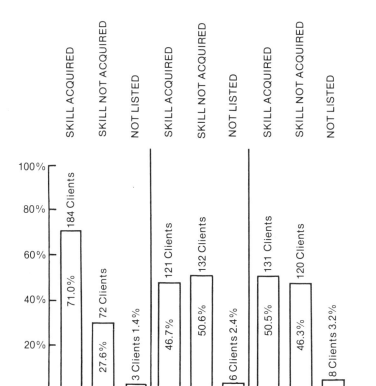

8. Major needs for families included behavior management, parenting education, babysitting, respite care, homemaker services, and information about resources available in the community.

The state institution by the late 1970's was serving a population that was no more complex than those served in community-based programs:

1. No preschool children (0–5 years) from the ENCOR region resided in the institution nor were there any residents over the age of 65. A total of 48 children from the ENCOR region between the ages of six and 18 were in the institution. A total of 35 youths between the ages of 19 and 21 resided in the institution and a total of 170 adults between 22 and 60. There were four persons between 60 and 65 years of age.
2. The majority of the persons from the ENCOR region in the institution were from the larger metropolitan area of Omaha, a total of 221. In addition, there were 38 persons from rural communities in the ENCOR catchment area.
3. Approximately 52% of the persons residing in the institutions were male; 48% were female.
4. The majority of the persons remaining in the institution were in the severe and profound range of retardation. A total of 201 persons fell within that range. Another 57 persons were classified as mildly or moderately retarded. There were more persons served in the ENCOR program who were mildly, moderately, and severely retarded. There were slightly fewer persons served in the ENCOR program that were classified as profoundly retarded.
5. There were a total of 81 persons from the ENCOR area in the institution who were not entirely ambulatory and 171 persons who were. In addition, there were four persons who were deaf, 11 were considered to be legally blind, and 11 had no communicative language.
6. There were 72 ENCOR area residents in the institution who needed help with feeding; 132 who needed assistance dressing, and 120 who needed help with toileting.
7. Of the ENCOR area residents who were in the institution, 74 had some form of epilepsy and one was reported to have autism; 43 persons were reported to have cerebral palsy.
8. All of the individuals from the ENCOR region still residing in the institution were listed as needing residential services upon movement to the community. Only eight individuals were listed as needing intensive, 24-hour medical support such as provided in ENCOR's Developmental Maximation Unit. The rest of the institutionalized population was thought to be able to be served in group homes and alternative living units with variations of support.

These data demonstrate that mentally retarded persons of all levels of disabling conditions can live in the mainstream of community life. There is no clinical reason for the institutionalization of any mentally retarded person. These comparative figures between ENCOR and Nebraska's state institution for the mentally retarded clearly show that all persons can be served in community-based programs regardless of their level of mental retardation and allied medical or psychiatric needs. For example:

1. ENCOR serves 170 severely and profoundly mentally retarded persons, the institution serves 201.
2. ENCOR serves up to 221 persons who do not possess at least some of their basic self-care skills, the institution serves no more than 132 persons lacking such skills.
3. ENCOR serves 115 non-ambulatory persons, the institution serves 81 such persons.

Unfortunately, some mental retardation experts hold that the more severely mentally retarded are "decerebrates" and are, therefore, "subtrainable" (Ellis, et al, 1978). They likewise hold that the potential for growth for the severely mentally retarded is so low that training programs are inappropriate even for living within the sheltered environment of an institution. The comparative data above clearly show the fallacy of such a position. The severely mentally retarded can grow and develop within the mainstream of family and community life if they receive the types of supports, programs, and services they require. The issue of deinstitutionalization is further analyzed in the next chapter.

The two most difficult populations to serve are severely mentally retarded persons with chronic medical needs and with chronic behavioral needs. The question of community-based services for these two populations depends upon the mobilization of the necessary treatment approaches which each individual requires in a dispersed service delivery system. These two populations require structured group homes or developmentally intensive foster homes with paraprofessional staff working under the supervision of appropriate professionals (McGee & Pearson, 1981). For example, a mentally retarded-autistic adult with severe behavior problems (aggressive behaviors, self-mutilation, and head-banging) could live in a group home with three or four other adults. This person would be involved in a structured sheltered workshop setting during the day and in structured developmental programming activities while in the home setting. Paraprofessionals would work with this person in developmental activities that would result in the redirection of the inappropriate behaviors toward appropriate skills and interactions. Likewise, for example, a severely retarded child with cerebral palsy might be in a preschool setting with normal children. This child would have an individualized educational plan. Teachers and teacher aides would receive secondary support from specialists. The environment might have to be adapted—a wooden ramp to the front door, physical therapy in the classroom, etc. Teachers would spend some time teaching the normal children about handicapping conditions. Volunteers might be used in the classroom to give extra support to the teacher. Because extra supports and services might be required, three or four other mentally retarded children could be integrated at the same time into the regular preschool in order to reduce the costs of specialized services for the one child (see Chapters 9 and 10).

ENCOR serves children and adults in community-based residential, educational, and vocational programs who lack basic self-care skills. Toileting, dressing, and feeding are not prerequisite skills for community living. In fact, it is our belief that generally these basic life skills can be best acquired in functional, mainstreamed settings. It is in these settings where the acquisition of appropriate skills and behaviors takes on meaning. For the small percentage of mentally retarded persons who cannot acquire basic skills, community programs have the responsibility of supporting them in the most normalizing way possible. There is no reason, for example, that a child who cannot feed himself should be institutionalized. This type of support can be provided in a group home setting.

6 How to Overcome the Arguments Against Integrated Community Services

INTRODUCTION

In Chapter 5 ENCOR was presented as an example of a community mobilizing its resources to serve its retarded citizens. As has also been indicated around the world, parents and professionals are providing strong leadership in achieving major gains on behalf of retarded people. In this process a high degree of consensus has evolved on the importance of the ideology of normalization and community-based services in enhancing the quality of life and the developmental growth of *all* mentally retarded citizens. The consensus has evolved from the clear-cut demonstration of the art-of-the-possible in agencies such as ENCOR, the integrated schools of Agueda, and the integrated industries in Cabra, Spain.

As communities and nations develop community alternatives to institutions, there remains a small number of opponents to such integrative strategies. These opponents base their arguments on several basic issues which advocates of community alternatives should be prepared to deal with. These reactionary trends are symbolized in the United States by a group of professionals who submitted a report (Ellis et al., 1978) to a federal court designed to halt deinstitutionalization. The report, composed by ten leading mental retardation professionals, purports to explain an institution's failure to meet modern treatment goals.

Their report reached the following conclusions:

1. that the potential for growth in a substantial number of Partlow (an institution in Alabama) residents is so low that training programs seem

97

inappropriate "even for living within the sheltered environment of the institution" (Ellis et al., Memorandum, October 18, 1978, p. 4);

2. that persons who are not "trainable" should be assigned to programs for "enriched daily programs" (idem, p. 7) in the institution;

3. that community living is a "serious injustice" for most institutionalized residents, who are unable to live adequately outside a highly sheltered environment such as the institution (idem, p. 4).

These conclusions focused on the falsely founded assumption that the severely and profoundly retarded with complex medical and behavioral needs are not capable of development. These same conclusions are held around the world all too frequently. There are many objections to these recommendations, which (1) essentially classify most institutionalized persons as "subtrainable," and (2) abandon training and education efforts on their behalf. Some of these objections are:

1. Such classifications generate self-fulfilling prophecies of client failure.
2. Such a grouping violates the long established principle of individualization upon which individualized programming is based.
3. Such an approach facilitates the phenomenon of "blaming the client" as an explanation for poor or inefficient programs.
4. Such a poor prognostication for the residents of Partlow is an opinion, not a research finding. Indeed modern applied research clearly demonstrates this to be false (Berkson & Landesman-Dwyer, 1977).
5. Such predictions ignore the intent of the developmental model as well as new technologies of training for severely and profoundly retarded persons.
6. Such a recommendation runs counter to the constitutional principle that the coercive segregation of individuals from community life is justifiable only on overriding evidence that public safety requires such segregation.

In short, the recommendations of the aforementioned professionals portend not only a lower level of humane and individualized care, but also a stagnation in the technologies and treatments necessary to most effectively enhance the lives of retarded citizens.

Abundant research is now available to support the facts that (1) institutionalization frequently has destructive consequences (Blatt, 1963; Blatt & Kaplan, 1966; Flint, 1966; Goffman, 1961; Halderman v. Pennhurst, 1978; Taylor, 1977); (2) appropriate community-based residential settings are generally more beneficial than institutional placements (Ferleger & Boyd, 1979; Gilhool, 1978; Kushlick, 1976); and (3) mentally retarded people with a wide spectrum of disabilities — including severely and profoundly retarded people—can be successfully served in community-based settings (Biklen, 1979; Bodgan & Taylor, 1976; Dybwad, 1978; Edgerton & Bercovici, 1976; Gollay, Friedman, Wyngardner, & Kurtz, 1978; Menolascino, 1977; Tizard, 1979).

Despite this and other impressive evidence, these professionals, as well as others around the world, conclude that "most residents now [in institutions] will not be able to adequately live outside a highly sheltered environment such as an institution" (Ellis et al., 1978, p. 17).

THE "NEW" INSTITUTION

Institutional proponents have apparently forgotten that regulation, accreditation, and massive amounts of money were supposed to have made the difference between institutions being places of abuse and neglect versus places of growth and development. In most instances this has not occurred. For example, in a recent evaluation of hospital accreditation survey data in the United States from 48 state mental retardation facility surveys performed in 21 states, 35 facilities failed this critical minimal test of treatment quality (Braddock, 1977). Those not accredited failed primarily for the following reasons:

1. the excessive use of chemical restraint and physical seclusion;
2. the impersonal nature of the physical environment;
3. excessive crowding of residents in living space;
4. the failure to provide comprehensive, interdisciplinary initial and periodic evaluation, program planning, follow-up in relation to educational needs or rehabilitative needs, as well as a general lack of developmental services;
5. the lack of the use of direct care personnel in training residents in self-help skills; and
6. the failure to employ sufficient numbers of qualified personnel in direct care service, dentistry, education, nursing, physical and occupational therapy, psychology, recreation, social services, speech pathology and audiology, and vocational training.

These deficiencies are not the result of minor mismanagement that can be eliminated by pouring in more money. Newer buildings and more manpower have not eradicated the elements that make up the very nature of an institution: isolation, removal from ongoing public and professional scrutiny, segregation, depersonalization, and in the worst cases, direct abuse of the residents. Nor should these deficiencies be blamed on the nature of those who reside in today's institutions.

Characteristics of Those Who Are in Institutions

Institutional proponents base their position on the false premise that a sub-stantial number of currently institutionalized mentally retarded persons are "sub-trainable." But what are the needs of those who are housed in today's in-stitutions? Are they "subtrainable" and doomed to lifelong custodial care?

The Partlow report gives a misleading posture relative to who resides in to-day's institutions. The report holds that a substantial number of that institu-tion's residents has such a low potential for growth that training programs seem inappropriate and that those residents should be assigned to enriched daily living programs. This unfortunate view is clearly contradicted by a study of the basic needs of Nebraska's institutionalized mentally retarded population (Horacek v. Exon, 1978). It is important that today's profession-als and advocates understand who resides in today's institutions. The Nebraska data strongly indicate that the mentally retarded persons in its state institutions should not be doomed to life long custodial care, and indeed di-rectly refutes the Partlow report.

The Nebraska study showed that of the state's 873 institutionalized men-tally retarded persons (1978), only 74 had major medical or major behavioral needs. A person with major to moderate medical support needs was defined as requiring immediate medical back-up support. A person with major behavioral needs was defined as generally requiring a very structured, inten-sive, behavior change-oriented environment with a 1:1 staff-to-client ratio. The large majority of institutionalized persons, however, would present no major problems relative to their placement in community-based alternatives given adequate resources and support. Indeed, Nebraska's community-based programs currently serve a population as complex as those found in the insti-tutions. This fact has been clearly demonstrated by the data presented previ-ously (Chapter 5).

Almost two-thirds of these 873 persons come from the *urban* areas of Nebraska, thereby dispelling a corollary myth that the large majority of those with the most special needs were from rural areas. This assumption had led to the incorrect conclusion that large numbers of retarded persons could not be served in communities with few resources. In Nebraska, the institutionalized population is proportionately distributed across the state. There is no validity to the repeated argument that the institutionalized population is skewed to-ward the rural areas of this state and perhaps other states.

The study indicated that over 500 of the 873 institutionalized persons had major self-care needs. Nebraska's institutions house those who need help in toileting, bathing, dressing, feeding, etc. Yet, the large majority of the people could move about; 587 of the 873 persons had minimal mobility needs (i.e., they could walk without any assistance). The large majority had appropriate behaviors: 517 persons required little or no intervention relative to their interpersonal interactions. The large majority were not medically fragile: 597 of the 873 persons had no more than routine medical needs.

Indeed, the medically fragile mentally retarded population is considered to be the group which demands institutional care the most. However, a further refutation of the Partlow argument can be made based on a study of Nebraska's institutional and community-based mentally retaded population. In this study, the accounting firm of Touche-Ross (1983) made the following conclusions:

1. In the opinion of the Nebraska institution's medical staff only *eight* institutionalized mentally retarded persons required medical services not typically provided in Nebraska's community-based mental retardation programs.
2. All other institutionalized persons with special medical needs could be adequately and appropriately served in community-based programs given: a) the proximity of appropriate medical services, b) special training for residential and day program staff, c) barrier-free facilities, and d) additional staffing to assist in self-care, ambulation, and positioning.

It is the areas of behavioral and developmental needs which can generally be surprisingly and favorably dealt with through specific, individualized programming, contrary to the Partlow report. Experience has shown that people with similar needs in community settings typically attain many of these skills after consistent exposure to developmental programming. In fact, the aforementioned Touche-Ross report states that the amount of direct care (developmental) services in community programs in Nebraska for the most severely involved is approximately 42 hours per week as opposed to the institutions, 21 to 32 hours per week. Thus, the highest need mentally retarded persons receive more developmental services in community programs than in the institutions. Even those who do not attain all of these skills can still be supported in community settings in a humane and dignified manner. Confirmation of this goal is the fact that Nebraska has virtually eliminated new admissions of retarded persons into institutions. Today there are only ten children less than six years of age and only 240 school-age children in Nebraska's institutions. Of these, over two-thirds are in their late adolescent years. Early identification, early intervention, in-home supports, parent training, etc. have eliminated the need for institutionalization in all but the rarest instances. In fact, one of the most powerful forces in deinstitutionalization has been the virtual halt of new admissions to the institution.

Those who are institutionalized in Nebraska are the middle-aged mentally retarded persons who had no other alternatives in previous decades. They were placed there when there were no community alternatives, when rights had not yet been articulated, and when families had none of the alternatives that exist in today's community programs. Thus, placement in less restrictive alternatives is mandatory.

These data contrast sharply with the Partlow conclusions and other pro-institutional statistics. The "new" institution is skilled in employing resident data designed to justify the institution's existence. The false assumption is the more severely retarded the population, the greater the need for the institution. To exaggerate needs, the "'new" institution uses monoevaluations, i.e., so many blind, deaf, orthopedically handicapped residents; so many mildly, moderately, severely, and profoundly retarded residents. "New" institution proponents use such lables — rather than describe developmental needs — in an apparent attempt to shock the public into the false conclusion that persons with such labels cannot be served in their families and/or communities.

The fact of the matter is that the institutional population is a complex and challenging population, but it is not the type described by pro-institutional proponents. The large majority are neither medically fragile nor behaviorally violent. The last two decades of applied research clearly demonstrates that all mentally retarded persons are capable of growth and development. All are sentient human beings who can learn (Berkson & Landesman-Dwyer, 1977).

Alternatives to Institutions for Severely Involved Persons

"We cannot make the assumption that by dumping these individuals out of the institutions, the community will somehow assume its responsibility and will begin to treat them like human beings. Communities have herded 'deinstitutionalized' persons into a wide variety of equally restrictive or more restricted environments" (Leland, 1981). There is much ignorance both on the side of pro-institutional advocates and pro-community advocates about the nature of community-based alternatives. Often little more is done than blindly moving persons out of institutions into community housing arrangements regardless of individual needs. Such dumping typically occurs into nursing homes, board and room homes, hotels for transients, etc.

Dumping is deinstitutionalization only in the sense that it reduces the numbers of people in state institutions. However, it is clearly not the placement of mentally retarded persons into less restrictive environments meeting their basic human and developmental needs. True deinstitutionalization is not merely the reduction of the institutional population, rather it is the individualized placement into community-based service delivery systems that ensures the physical, spiritual, and developmental well-being of mentally retarded persons across their lifespan. It is the guarantee of an array of residential, educational, vocational, and leisure time services based on each mentally retarded person's needs.

Our data and experiences indicate that for those with more complex behavioral, medical, and developmental needs the "new" institution is clearly not necessary. Deinstitutionalization is a function of the development of adequate and appropriate community-based services. This does not mean that all institutionalized persons can immediately move directly into their communities. Adequate and appropriate alternatives still must be developed in most communities across the nation. Community-based alternatives must be able to ensure mentally retarded persons and their families that there will be:

1. a variety of community-based less restrictive options which utilize modern treatment and programmatic techniques in small dispersed residential, educational, vocational and leisure-time services;
2. maximum parental input while still ensuring individual client rights;
3. ongoing internal and external monitoring of the quality of services;
4. a realistic cost per person for services, and assurance that program financing will be ensured across time; and
5. prudent risk for all mentally retarded citizens as they live, work and play in communities, while at the same time safe-guarding each person as much as necessary.

Community programs can adequately, appropriately, and developmentally serve even the most severely involved mentally retarded children and adults. The ENCOR program demonstrates this fact (Biklen, 1979; Menolascino, 1977). Services for the most severely involved clients can be characterized as follows:

1. they are concrete, comprehensive, replicable, developmentally-oriented programs;
2. they are ensured across the person's lifespan based on the degree and intensity of services required by each individual;
3. they are small, no more than six to eight persons being housed in any given setting;
4. the various programs and services are dispersed throughout the community and state in a well-managed service delivery system;
5. manpower resources are derived and trained from the local community with adequate medical and psychiatric back-up personnel.

Barriers to Movement

If the vast majority of those who are housed in institutions around the world are not there due to their personal needs, why are they there? There are several barriers that impede the movement of people out of institutions and contribute to their placement into institutions:

1. There are several persistent inter-related misconceptions about who is currently institutionalized. These misconceptions have been examined already. Their effect, if allowed to spread, would be to undermine efforts to create community-based alternatives and to make institutionalization appear as an accepted course of action.
2. There are also related misconceptions about who can be served in community programs. Quality community programs can serve nearly anyone who is currently institutionalized, given redistribution of money, manpower, and management systems and, more importantly, a rebirth of the human and legal rights of all citizens.
3. There are several misconceptions about what community-based alternatives to institutions are. They are not mini-institutions. They cannot be dumping grounds. They must be small dispersed and developmentally-oriented environments that ensure adequate and appropriate services across each person's lifespan.
4. Finally, in nations around the world, there is a myriad of federal and local social policies and funding mechanisms which promote incentives to institutionalization, trans-institutionalization and dumping while at the same time providing disincentives to the development of community alternatives.

The movement of mentally retarded citizens from institutional environments to community-based alternatives requires reallocation of institutional funding. In other words, it costs money to support persons within their family and community. The hundreds of millions of dollars that are expended in today's "new" institutions must be redistributed as the people move into community and family life. This financial reality, the need for money to follow the client from the institution to the community, was underscored as early as 1970 (Cook, 1970). As the retarded are integrated into community systems of care, so too must the financial resources be redistributed. Community-based programs have demonstrated themselves to be cost-effective when compared to institutional costs. For example, in 1978–79 Nebraska's community-based programs, serving a similar population, spent slightly over $8,000 per year per person as compared to $23,500 per year per person in Nebraska's state institutions for the mentally retarded (Horacek v. Exon, 1978). More importantly, our professional and societal postures toward retarded persons must be unified so that the Catch 22 to today's social policies and financial outlays can be resolved in a positive fashion. Society cannot ensure some of its retarded citizens community integration while millions of dollars continue to be spent to institutionalize their mirror images in "enriched" institutions (Rothman, 1979).

CONCLUSION

The overwhelming majority of mentally retarded persons who currently reside in our world's institutions are not there because of some exotic need related to their disability. All retarded persons are capable of growth and development. The professional posture that some retarded citizens are "subtrainable" and hence need to reside in "enriched" institutional settings for the rest of their lives is an archaic one contradicted by the major ideological and programmatic breakthroughs of the last two decades (Menolascino, 1977). Currently institutionalized mentally retarded persons are there because of outdated professional views that persistently support social policies designed to maintain institutions regardless of the demonstrable needs and potential of the mentally retarded who reside therein. The "new" institution has taken on a new language, a new look, and new management neologisms; but it is still a system that generally dehumanizes and depersonalizes its residents in the same procrustean bed. Yet we should take heart that communities across the country are serving mentally retarded persons of all levels of needs in spite of the array of regressive professional postures and social policies noted previously in this chapter. Parents and professionals, as well as the mentally retarded themselves, must push for further public and professional education to help support the rapidly emerging national policies based on the normalization principle, the right to treatment, and the developmental aspects of community-based service systems that enhance the person, the family, and the community.

7

A Systems Model for Overcoming the Barriers to Services

INTRODUCTION

Writing a chapter on the barriers precluding accessibility to services for the mentally retarded is an ambitious project. It is ambitious because of the vast quantity of data available in this area. In this respect, such data are reflective of much of the research of the mentally retarded population. As Wolfensberger (1967) has noted, "The quality of research has been low. What is needed is not more research, but better research." A computer search and review of the literature on barriers to services (Harris & Harris, 1976; Nagi, McBeoom, & Collette, 1972) reveals significant similarities regarding the quantity vs. quality problem. In addition, an analysis of the research on barriers reveals a general trend in which information is presented and described but seldom systematically analyzed in order to recommend "what to do" and "how to do it" in a comprehensive manner.

A great deal of funding, easily in the dozens of millions (Urban Institute, 1975), has been allocated since 1961 by various federal agencies (Department of Labor, Department of Commerce, Housing, and Urban Development, Department of Health, Education, and Welfare) to investigate and report to Congress the barriers to services for handicapped individuals (President's Committee on Mental Retardation, 1976). Unfortunately, many of these barriers still exist for large numbers of the mentally retarded population (National Congress of Organizations of the Physically Handicapped, 1976). The dilemma we faced in writing this chapter was, how does one go about recommending a plan of action to reduce barriers to services and make sound suggestions on "what to do" and "how to do it" for a given country, state,

106

county, or village. In an attempt to resolve this dilemma, five issues are systematically analyzed. These issues are: (1) interrelationships and linkages with other system components; (2) current state of the science findings; (3) model methodology; (4) implementation of a model; and (5) barrier analysis.

INTERRELATIONSHIPS AND LINKAGES WITH OTHER SYSTEM COMPONENTS

The purpose of this section is to briefly illustrate the interrelationships and linkages of this chapter with the other chapters of this book.

The prevention of mental retardation is an exciting topic that has the attention of federal officials, judging by the renewed emphasis and priorities established for this area. The major focus is on primary care prevention. That is, the genetic manipulation and "in utero" intervention thereby affecting the primary prevention of any disabling condition. An even more exciting area of research which has received a great deal of attention lately is secondary prevention, a care level concerned with the complete or partial reversal of developmental disorders. The technological advancement of brain implants for individuals with cerebral palsy and epilepsy, the development of new drugs for seizure control and memory enhancers for the mentally retarded are indicative of the progress being made in this area. It is also significant to note that the National Association for Retarded Citizens has recently made "cure" one of its three major goals (Menolascino, Neman, & Stark, 1983). Tertiary care involves the amelioration of disabling conditions. The rate of improvement in this area is constantly increasing due to powerful learning strategies, bioengineering devices, and technology.

Barriers to health care and residential services can be managed and studied vis a vis a systems analysis approach. The resource input available in a comprehensive and interdisciplinary health care program should significantly contribute to the reduction of the incidence of handicapping conditions. However, we can expect to see a continuing increase in services to the severely, multihandicapped individual because of improved medical technology and the early identification of these individuals and their needs. The development of residential options will facilitate the deinstitutionalization process and enhance the rehabilitation goal to complete independent functioning.

CURRENT STATE OF THE SCIENCE

The current state of the science reveals an abundance of information in books, articles, monographs, and congressional reports containing sections directly or indirectly referring to thousands of barriers limiting the quantity and quality of services to the developmentally disabled. The 1977 *Resources Guide to Literature on Barrier-Free Environments* published by the Architectural and Transportation Barriers Compliance Board reveals that at least 93 periodicals publish information frequently on this area. There are also 140 national or international organizations concerned about barriers that preclude services to handicapped individuals. Over 1,500 citations were listed in this extensive and most comprehensive document on barriers to services for the handicapped.

Similarly, a computer search on such barriers produced 142 citations. However, the overall quality of many of these citationss was disappointing, and it is interesting to note that the six most significant studies on this topic did not appear in the computer search. Each of these six studies was carefully selected for review because of its comprehensiveness and unique ability to penetrate beyond surface issues. Their analysis here provides a clear picture of the current state of the science in this area.

Dybwad (1967) identified a number of roadblocks to the renewal of residential care for the mentally retarded: (a) the medical model with its focus on pathology and the traditional medical diagnostic approach vs. educational programming in the institution; (b) the roadblock of institutional management; (c) professional attitudes toward the dignity of the mentally retarded and their emphasis on administration-orientation rather than client-orientation; and (d) architectural-programmatic roadblocks involving the care and treatment of clients. It is indeed frustrating to see many of the recommendations made by Dybwad more than 15 years ago still not implemented in the manner he suggested.

One example is seen in the 1974 needs assessment survey and conference, which was conducted to develop programs and identify barriers to providing a continuum of services to deaf/blind individuals (Spencer, 1974). Over 190 administrators, educators, and staff of the deaf/blind from the states of Arkansas, Iowa, Louisiana, Missouri, and Oklahoma were surveyed via the Nominal Group Technique. Over 1,000 barrier items were identified and categorized under 15 headings representing problem areas for the developmentally disabled population. These rank-ordered categories of barriers to services among these five states were: (1) agency cooperation and coordination; (2) staff development and staff training; (3) education, training, and programming (4) parental and family support; (5) funding; (6) prevocational/vocational training; (7) identification/diagnosis/evaluation; (8) public awareness; (9) transportation and geographic distribution of programs; (10) residential options; (11) legislation; (12) facilities/equipment; (13) medical; (14) recreational social; and (15) research development. This document also contained excellent solution strategies for overcoming these major barriers.

McGee and Hitzing (1976) identified a number of significant barriers in meeting the residential needs of developmentally disabled individuals in integrated settings. An excellent point is made of the fact that there are *91* separate programs in the Federal Governmemt for retarded citizens – all of which are not unified regarding common goals and are sometimes conflicting. For example, Title XIX monies have been primarily used to support institutions while Title XX monies have been primarily used to support community-based programs. They also note that there is very little data regarding the cost benefit efficacy of integration as well as knowledge about managing community-based services.

Advocacy groups and parents complicate matters by disagreeing on approaches, i.e., institutionalization vs. deinstitutionalization. The most important barrier they pose is attitudinal and conceptual, particularly as it applies to the more severely handicapped.

Skarnulis (1977) listed over a hundred barriers related to community integration of the mentally retarded, delineating specific barriers under the headings of environmental, attitudinal, administrative, legislative and regulatory, and political/programmatic.

A unique and elaborate barrier identification assistance system was developed for the Human Services Coordination Alliance in Louisville, Kentucky (1977). This project involved the linkages between 24 human service agencies to improve the planning, programming, and delivery of services. Some 19 generic problem areas were identified and each cross-referenced with specific information regarding assistance in a United Way services directory. Some of the general areas included: housing, food and clothing, employment, family planning, adoption, consumer protection, transportation, community information and safety.

One of the more elaborate barrier analyses was conducted by Cook, Dahl, and Gale (1977). This research group concentrated on the vocational training and placement of the severely handicapped. Four major areas constituting significant barriers were analyzed, sub-categorized, and specific solution strategies were suggested. These were: (a) Attitudes – low self-esteem of the disabled, low societal expectation, and lack of knowledge over hiring the handicapped; (b) Communication – impaired ability to speak, hear, read, and use communication equipment; (c) Environment – transportation use via ordinary means, difficulty with architectural barriers, perceiving and responding to environmental signals, and use of tools in the work environment; (d) Skills – independent living, basic educational skills, vocational skill development and lack of work adjustment attitude, and skills and capacities.

A listing of all the categories and barriers to services for the mentally retarded is a multi-year task and far beyond the scope of this chapter. Instead, in each of the following sections, the major barriers are analyzed and solution strategies in each of seven categories explored. The following discussion is intended as a starting point that any country, state, community or village could utilize in developing change strategies. The following sections also contain a problem-solving model for this process, which delineates "who" needs to be involved, "what" needs to be done, and "how" it can be accomplished.

MODEL METHODOLOGY

Model Components

The purpose of this section is to provide a conceptual and theoretical framework upon which the model used in this chapter is based. Three criteria were used in the selection of this model: (1) effectiveness; (2) efficiency; and (3) applicability to a variety of complex problems.

Investigation into the most significant human service problems by Stark (1973) reveals seven major areas that an effective and efficient model must address.

These are:

1. too many children, families, and clients to serve;
2. lack of staff and frequent staff burn-out;
3. insufficient financing;
4. lack of adequate time to do what is expected;
5. short-term effects and frequent loss of gains made;
6. lack of generalization of learning across settings;
7. attitudes of society towards mentally retarded individuals.

These problems seem to have no geographic boundaries. The limitations imposed on all of us require a sophisticated model if we are to accomplish our goals and avoid the potential "burn out." It would appear therefore that it's not so much a question of "idealism" or "pie in the sky" but a fundamental issue of survival.

Conceptual Basis

Systems Analysis.   Systems analysis is an approach to viewing problems. A system is defined as having an input, a process, and an output, spanning time, and connoting some change in state occurring between the input and the output (many times referred to as the process).

There are established procedures for doing systems analysis (SA). Used extensively by the Department of Defense, it has been described as "nothing more than quantitative or enlightened common sense aided by modern analytical methods" (Enthoven, 1969). The elements involved in SA are the following:

1. There is a need to examine the entire operation and structure of the system under study. Forrester (1972) states that the "boundary must be established within which the interactions take place that give the system its characteristic behavior."

2. A model of the system should be developed. A model is a representation of reality. It should include only the relevant variables that require study and analysis and should be presented as simply as possible. Figure 29 presents a visual display of the delivery service system. It is not intended to be a final product but a starting point for analysis. This figure illustrates the related systems and resources that provide inputs, the major service-process variables, and outputs described according to outcomes and evaluation measures.

3. The system and its model for implementation must be goal-oriented with an explicit statement of objectives or target behaviors whose achievement decision-makers consider important. These target behaviors (objectives) need to be discovered in the course of analysis.

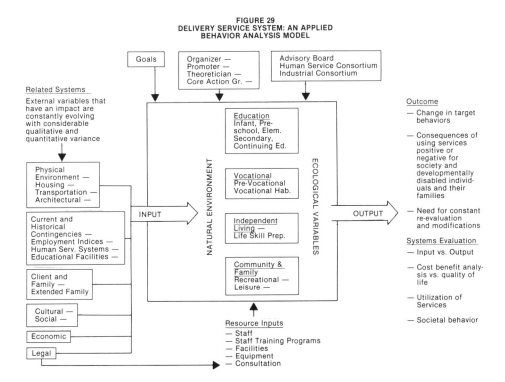

FIGURE 29
DELIVERY SERVICE SYSTEM: AN APPLIED
BEHAVIOR ANALYSIS MODEL

4. There should be alternate ways to reach desired goals, each of which require specific steps. Cost-benefit and effectiveness analysis is one technique used in this analysis. This can best be decided after the functional analysis stage as described in the next section.

5. Time lines should be established in incremental steps so as to shape behavior (barriers) toward the desired outcomes. A final plan of action is frequently used.

6. Finally, the systems analysis approach requires the assistance of a variety of individuals to help solve problems. Two groups of individuals comprise the "who" in the system: (a) staff and outside consultants: and (b) community leaders and groups (see next section) (Hyman, 1975).

Self-Modification Process. This system approach involves constant monitoring because of its evolutionary nature. It also requires the establishment of target behaviors to shape toward the desired outcomes. In order to accomplish all of these objectives, a problem-solving model that is capable of changing and monitoring itself is a prerequisite. In addition, the model must meet the criteria established earlier as well as address the seven major human service problems.

The self-modification model was selected because it meets these standards (Stark, 1976). Its "roots" can be traced back to learning theorists and applied behavior analysis. Also, its origins were based on the application to individuals and only more recently to organizational behavior. As Skinner (1953) notes, "Yet to a considerable extent an individual does appear to shape his own destiny. He is often able to do something about the variables affecting him. Some degree of 'self-determination' of conduct is usually recognized in the creative behavior of the artist and scientist, in the self-exploratory behavior of the writer, and in the self-discipline of the ascetic." He further states that an individual "chooses" between alternative courses of action, "thinks through" a problem while isolated from the relevant environment, and "guards" his health or position in society through the exercise of "self-control."

The techniques of self-control, self-monitoring, self-regulation, etc., can also be applied to an organization in order to regulate and gain control over its own future. The use of such a model allows for an organization to reduce the frequency of unacceptable target behaviors or barriers. To "choose" not to do so leaves an organization, in this case the community-based service system, too dependent upon the political, social, and economic contingencies of a given environment or government (Goldfried & Merboum, 1973).

Ecology and the Natural Environment. Perhaps part of the reasons for past failures of program development and the perennial problem of staff "burn-out" is due to the *system,* which frequently precludes success as a function of conflicting expectations, i.e., staff to client ratio and programming requirement (Shontz, 1970). The problem, however, may also be due to the situation that research has not provided the practitioner with answers regarding treatment approaches for use in a complex social or environmental setting. If a system and its model of implementation are to be successful, we must focus on the *place* in which barriers to services occur. Many of the solutions of the social and environmental dilemmas that the national, state, or regional organizations face may ultimately depend on an exact understanding of how client's or children's actions are affected by their everyday surroundings. Traditional methods of analysis, however, have been unable to fully explain behavior as it occurs in such ordinary places as classrooms, developmental centers, offices, clubs, and businesses.

Barker and Associates (1978) present a comprehensive overview of two special fields — ecological psychology and eco-behavioral science — which they developed to study behavior in real life contexts. These authors have demonstrated that human *actions* can be studied "naturally." In describing ecological-behavioral science, they demonstrate conclusively that the environmental settings in which behavior occurs can be identified and measured.

IMPLEMENTATION OF MODEL

The previous section explained the purpose, conceptual, and theoretical aspects of the model, and the major barriers that must be dealt with if the model is to be successful. Two questions remain to be answered. Who is going to implement the model and how long will it be done? No matter how good a model and its process for implementation are, the people who implement it will frequently determine its success. Perhaps the best way to select who should implement the model is to carefully analyze previously successful models in this area and the people involved.

Organization

The Eastern Nebraska Community Office of Retardation (ENCOR) has received international acclaim for its community-based model for providing services to its mentally retarded citizens (Menolascino, 1977). This program (model) is successful because of key individuals who are primarily responsible for its creation. Many versions have been offered regarding the reasons for this success. None seem to explain it as fully as an anology found in the insurance field. In a recently published book entitled, "Blue Cross Since 1929: Accountability and the Public Trust," the author, Anderson (1975), explains why this company and its product has been so successful. He explains that there is a latent division of labor which all social movements need — a theoretician, a promoter, an organizer, and a core action group of individuals.

When this example is applied to ENCOR, the key movers behind this social movement become clearer. The *theoretician* or idea person was the controversial psychologist, Wolf Wolfensberger, who has become one of the leading proponents of normalization and a national figure in the mental retardation area. The *promoter* or public relations specialist who got people excited was psychiatrist Frank J. Menolascino. The *organizer* was Robert Clark who administered the major program components in its early stages and has since become the director of a large community-based system similar to ENCOR. The *core action group of individuals* were committed idealists who enthusiastically took on the challenge of setting up a community system as a result of interactions with these leaders. Given time for these leaders to influence others, as was the case with Blue Cross, a self-determined group was formed. In ENCOR's case it was the Omaha Association for Retarded Citizen's parent group which provided the impetus for assisting in funding and legislation.

Anderson goes on to point out that a social movement is on its way if the concept is sound and the leadership adequate. If the concept is unsound and behind the time, or ahead of its time, any leadership will fail. However, if the concept expresses an idea whose "time has come" it will succeed even under barely adequate leadership but brilliantly under brilliant leadership. ENCOR was a concept of its time that has succeeded because of the key people behind it. As a result of over 50 town hall meetings across Nebraska, a State plan was formed, legislation enacted, and commuity-based programs were formed.

The same principles can be applied to other states and urban and rural programs in different countries. These key individuals should be identified at the village, county, state, and each regional or national level. The timing for a model utilizing a problem solving systems approach for the statewide alleviation of barriers to services appears to be excellent in view of legislation in the United States (Sections 503 and 504 of the 1973 Rehabilitation Act and the 1975 D.D. Act).

However, a network of key individuals influential in establishing such a system may not suffice in a state or county that is complex and heavily populated, particularly if deinstitutionalization and communal integration of our mentally retarded citizens is not a major goal.

In this system, indirect community influence is obtained by way of three groups, each constituted to reflect key sources of social control. The ability of these groups to shape and maintain positive community behaviors toward the developmentally disabled appears to be considerably enhanced if the group members have pre-existing socially reinforcing properties.

The first group is a "board of advisors" composed of individuals with the accessibility and ability to shape cooperative and attitudinal responses in the economic, social, political, transportation, and housing sectors. Effective representatives have been recruited from a variety of professional groups: industrial management, legal, educational, architectural/engineering, insurance, political, media, medical, public relations, mass transit industry, real estate, etc. The effectiveness of this board is contingent upon their responsibility for making the system work. Care must be taken to economically indenture such board members in order to avoid another "paper committee" while making it socially reinforcing for them to serve on such a board.

The second key group is a "habilitative cooperative association" of human services agencies, advocacy groups, and referral sources. The primary role of this group is the provision of guidance and cooperative monitoring for the state services in its efforts to meet the needs of clients. Critical benefits include improved communication and coordination among agencies and hopefully some avoidance of duplication of services. In most states in the United States, the major constituents joining the community-based system at the state, regional, or subregional level would include: Vocational Rehabilitation Service; Community Mental Health Centers; public and private schools (including child development centers, technical community colleges, and higher education); medical facilities; insurance companies; Office of Mental Retardation and Social Services; Association for Retarded Citizens; United Cerebral Palsy; Epilepsy Foundation of America Chapters; March of Dimes; and Easter Seal Society. Communities around the world have similar multiple agencies involved in the provision of services.

The third important group is an "industrial consortium" consisting of representatives from a cross-section of private industry and employment concerned agencies and organizations (Department of Labor, labor unions, Comprehensive Employment Training Agency, job services, National Alliance of Businessmen). The major role of this group includes the removal of employment barriers through the development of work stations, on-the-job training sites, and guaranteed job openings in cooperation with employers and labor unions. The function of this group is critical to the acceleration of access to job opportunities for our clients—a fact which can be illustrated by the following piece of data. A pilot project to train and place 45 moderately and severely physically handicapped individuals in the city of Los Angeles, obtained its placement in public service programs by way of direct arrangements with the Mayor (Vincent, 1977). This ability to go directly "to the top" with major employers is a substantial asset of the industrial consortium, and can obviously facilitate development of placement opportunities.

Of the three groups, the "habilitative cooperative association" plays the most critical role. The key to *successful habilitation of the mentally retarded will depend on inter-systemic coordination and cooperation.* This "human service consortium" should be the group of individuals who are willing to make the life-long commitment to being responsible to its constituents. Someone has to say to parents "regardless of programmatic fluxuations in the community we will be responsible for your son or daughter's care until they are completely independent of the system." The lack of this commitment by community-based programs is one of the major barriers to preventing institutionalization by parents. They are concerned about "what will happen to our son or daughter after we are gone." They often state that although they do not favor institutionalization, they at least know that their son or daughter will be taken care of by the state.

This "habilitation association" must carefully track all of its mentally retarded citizens to make sure that the appropriate agencies are providing the services they should and that no client falls between "the cracks." One of the major barriers to this coordination of client services has been the transition between public school special education programs and state vocational rehabilitation agencies. This problem will be exacerbated by the extension of age limits in which public school systems can provide educational services, e.g., 18–25. This process will have a dramatic impact on secondary special education programs in which decisions will need to be made regarding a shift from an educational institution to a vocational facility.

In addition, this "habilitation association" must build in an outside monitoring function for advocacy agencies to assure that the rights of our mentally retarded population are being met, as well as adding credibility and political power for the association in lobbying for legislative action.

Application

The process for accomplishing the goals and objectives (priorities of each regional planning committee) of a state/provincial agency could take various forms. For example, ENCOR uses a seven-step appproach in developing their five-year plan: (1) needs assessment survey; (2) defining the desired system; (3) problem identification; (4) goal statement development; (5) evaluation of alternatives; (6) recommend action; and (7) timelines for implementation. This particular approach is similar to the procedures used by many human service agencies (Weiss, 1972). The major difficulty with such an approach is the sometimes over-emphasis on what has traditionally been labeled "product evaluation." This involves an overemphasis on evaluating the end product — usually a report. Process evaluation allows for the constant feedback to the decisionmakers for program plan implementation (Stufflebeam, 1971).

What is needed then is a specific implementation process for a model, which would provide: (1) flexibility; (2) adaptation to local and regional needs; (3) constant feedback; and (4) equip the state and/or regional community-based service system with a monitoring model for its entire system operating in the natural environment with a complex matrix of contingencies. This system problem-solving approach utilizing a self-modification (S–M) process as conceptualized in the previous section involves three phases and eight steps.

Phase I—Problem Identification.   This phase involves three steps designed to identify target barriers and behaviors precluding accessibility to services, the ranking and selecting of specific barriers, and the frequency of occurrence of these barriers and behaviors.

Step 1—Identification of Barriers - This step calls for a listing of all of the possible or potential barriers that would diminish the goals and objectives of the organization.

Step 2—Selection of Barriers - Specify (define in behavioral terminology for measurement), select, and rank order the barriers that the community-based system wants to remove or modify. It has been demonstrated (Stark, 1973) that it is beneficial to identify both major and minor target behaviors to be modified. A major target behavior can be defined as a complex behavioral unit requiring extensive shaping and time to modify. An example of such a major target behavior (although it is not totally operationally defined here) would be to change "society's attitude" toward the mentally retarded.

This is obviously an important behavior to focus on, but it will require years if not decades to accomplish. A minor target behavior is less complex and thus requires less shaping. For example, the attitude of a small neighborhood toward group homes would involve less contingent variables for analysis and shaping. Minor target behaviors can also function as a percentage criteria of a major target behavior, i.e., the attitude of 20% of the community. Without the simultaneous focus on minor target barriers, behavior progress may not be as noticeable and "burn out" may occur as a function of not being reinforced by the system with some short-term progress.

The identification and selection of target barriers can be conducted at the local and regional level and on a statewide basis. Previous information to be considered would be the priorities identified by the state and regional planning committees. Considerable input should also be solicited from consumers, advocates, providers, advocacy boards, human service consortiums, industrial companies, agency staff, as well as the socio-economic and political sectors. Parent and client participation is critical to the ultimate success of the entire process. Quite often popular opinion polls will demonstrate the discrepancies between what parents and clients consider to be barriers and their order of importance and what is perceived to be barriers by society.

A positive side effect of this total involvement is the diminishing of resistance of some opponents; since they have been a part of the process, "the ideas" are consequently "their ideas."

Two demonstrably effective techniques for accomplishing steps one and two are the Nominal Group Technique (NGT) and the Delphi Technique. The Delphi Technique was created by Dalkey and his associates at the Rand Corporation in 1950. NGT was developed by Andre Delbecq and Andrew Van deVen in 1968. Both techniques have been widely employed in problem identification and program planning by human service organizations (Delbecq & Van deVen, 1971).

The Delphi Technique is a method for the systematic solicitation and collection of judgments on a particular topic through a set of carefully designed sequential questionnaires interspersed with summarized information and feedback of opinions derived from earlier responses (Turoff, 1970). NGT is a structured group meeting designed to systematically, independently, and then collectively make decisions via generation of information on problems and potential solutions (Gustafson, Shukla, Delbecq, & Walster, 1973).

Like other group techniques (e.g., force-field analysis and parliamentry procedure), NGT and the Delphi Technique are not a panacea for all group meetings. They are special-purpose techniques useful for situations where individual judgements must be tapped and combined to arrive at decisions which cannot be calculated by one person. They are problem-solving, creative decision-making, and idea-generating strategies (Delbecq, Van deVen, & Gustafson, 1975).

Step 3 — Measurement of Barriers – This step involves the collection of baseline data. The frequency of target barriers or behaviors is critical if the problem source is to be determined. Also, in counting target barriers, it is sometimes found that the behaviors are either less of or more of a problem than anticipated. The charting of these behaviors can be accomplished, although not easily, by a variety of staff including consumers utilizing observations in the natural environments, community surveys, etc., via the mass media.

Phase II — Problem Analysis. This phase involves two steps focusing on the functional analysis of the barriers and the environment in which they occur.

Step 4 — Ecological Description – By now it is apparent that each step in the S–M process is incremental. Thus far the identification, selection, and pinpointing of target behaviors has been accomplished. Baseline data is also being collected. However, in order to facilitate the next step involving a functional analysis process, a thorough description of the contextual natural environment is helpful. An awareness of the contingencies and ecology surrounding the target behaviors allows for a natural flow to the next step. Recent progress in ecological psychology and eco-behavioral science research now permits a scientific analysis of real-life situations in which mentally retarded individuals live, work, and play (Barker & Associates, 1978).

Step 5 — Functional Analysis – The functional analysis is the most crucial step to a successful self-modification plan. Behavior is embedded in a sequence: *antecedent-target behavior-consequence.* Once an organization is able to analyze the antecedent events that trigger its behavior and analyze the consequences that maintain it, its ability to problem solve increases dramatically.

As this skill develps, generalization is facilitated by its application to a variety of complex situations. An illustration of this is the common occurrence we are witnessing today across the country regarding the deinstitutionalization issue and class action suits against large institutions. The process of institutionalizing our mentally retarded citizens has a long reinforcement history for such behavior. Reinforcement was provided for parents (negative reinforcement — there were few other alternatives), for the institutional staff (positive reinforcement — social and financial), and for the state (positive reinforcement — economical and political). But large institutions are now facing legal action because of the lack of adequate facilities. Due to the reinforcement histories, some institutions are seeking funds to build cottages and meet federal standards. A functional analysis of this legal process reveals that the antecedent behavior of complaints brought by the plaintiffs results in exculpatory (target) behavior on the part of the institution (barrier to deinstitutionalization). This exculpatory behavior is maintained via the consequence of negative reinforcement (ending an aversial event — the court trial) and the avoidance of punishment (removal of history of reinforcement).

Many behavioral scientists focus mainly on the consequences of behavior, seeking to alter them and make them more contingent. However, in the S–M process, additional attention needs to be placed on the antecedent conditions. Awareness of the discriminitive stimuli that serve as cues in eliciting inappropriate societal behaviors can serve as a preventative function in seeking the removal of barriers.

Phase III — Problem Solving. This phase involves three steps focusing on the development and maintenance of a plan across settings.

Step 6 — Plan of Action – This step involves the development of a plan (state, regional, local) of action that details the type, frequency, place, and process of reinforcing the community or state's (and all the units thereof) behavior, so as to accomplish the desired goals and barrier removal of the organization. The consortia and board of directors groups can readily facilitate this process because of their accessibility and reinforcing "powers."

Step 7 — Monitor – This step involves a sophisticated monitoring system designed to measure the change in social variables and target behavior removal. The social policy indices to measure and monitor the barrier improvement may be community specific and will require careful analysis. For example, indices of mental health improvement have traditionally relied upon such indices as suicide, admissions to state hospitals, unemployment, crime rates, crisis calls, etc.

Step 8 — Generalization – This last step calls for the success reached with specific target behaviors to be generalized across categories and settings, e.g., employment, transportation, attitudes in urban and rural areas.

This self-modification model is not intended to serve as an eight-easy-steps-cookbook to social change. Rather, it is suggested that it functions as a framework for the provision of a problem-solving and functionally analytic process to barrier reduction.

BARRIER ANALYSIS

Many barriers may exist within an individual's environment. The handicapped must contend with barriers that are present in an internal and external framework. External barriers relate to the physical environment and to the attitudes of the general population. Conversely, internal barriers include the physical or mental (in)ability of an individual.

In this section, we review the seven major barrier categories, discuss the target behaviors and problems in each category and offer strategies for action in order to alleviate these barriers.

When analyzing the barriers related to the accessibility to services, it becomes apparent that of the thousands of specific barriers, many are interrelated. For example, in order to get a job, a handicapped individual must contend with attitudinal, transportation, architectural, employment, and financial problems. Any one of these barriers can preclude success even if the client has all of the social and vocational skills.

It is important therefore to analyze all of these barriers as they cluster into seven major categories: (1) Transportation; (2) Architectural; (3) Employment; (4) Housing; (5) Legislator Funding; (6) Services; (7) Social-Attitudinal.

Transportation

Lack of appropriate transportation constricts the life-space of any person, limits his/her capacity for self-maintenance, restricts activities with people, and may contribute to disengagement or alienation from society (Cantilli, Schmelzer, & Staff, 1971).

Target Barriers

A. Length in distance from one's home to the bus stops, particularly during the winter.
B. General lack of transportation in local neighborhoods.
C. Inaccessibility to available buses because of bus design.
D. Dependency, or the tendency for many disabled persons to rely on neighbors, relatives, or friends for transportation to work, recreation, medical care, etc.

E. High cost of other forms of transportation, i.e., taxis, specialized vans, redesigning care (Van Vechter, Pliss, & Barry, 1976).

Goals and Strategies to Bring About Change

A. Accelerate public education regarding the mobility needs of the handicapped via mass media, social, and political avenues.
B. Design a total public transportation system that will meet the needs of handicapped individuals with a variety of sensory, cognitive, and physical disabilities.

Architectural

The Architectural and Transportation Barriers Compliance Board has done a great deal to help improve accessibility to various buildings. Progress has been made in the last five years and it is essential to continue to remove architectural barriers that inhibit independence for handicapped individuals.

Target Barriers

A. Stairs and escalators
B. Restrictive toilets.
C. Narrow doors, revolving doors.
D. Water fountains, counter tops, elevator buttons, light switches too high.
E. Narrow aisles.
F. Elevators with buttons too high for reach and/or not marked with braille symbols.
G. Lack of enforcement of laws passed for architectural barrier elimination in all facilities receiving federal funds.

Goals and Strategies to Bring About Change

A. Undergraduate, graduate, and post-graduate training of engineers and architects concerning the needs of handicapped individuals.
B. Awareness in the construction industry that the cost for a barrier-free building is minimal, less than .5% over estimated construction costs (U.S. Department of Housing and Urban Development, 1975).
C. Architectural suggestions
    1. At least one building entrance at ground level.
    2. 32" wide doors that open easily.
    3. Sloping ramps instead of stairs.
    4. Convenient parking, accessible to building.
    5. Non-slip floors.
    6. Restrooms with wide stalls and grab-bars for wheelchair users.

7. Lower fountains and public telephones for wheelchair users.
8. Level walks with no curbs at crossways.

Employment

Mentally retarded individuals must contend with many barriers when seeking a job. They must be aware of unrealistic attitudes the public has toward them. They must consider architectural and transportational barriers, and finally they are faced with the dilemma "damned if I do work and damned if I don't" created through Social Security programs.

Target Barriers

A. Vocational rehabilitation programs which continue to train the mentally retarded for jobs that are non-existent.
B. Common stereotypes by employer (Perlman, 1975).
    1. Fear of higher insurance rates.
    2. Fear of higher than average absenteeism rates.
    3. Fear of higher accident rates.
    4. Fear of negative reactions from co-workers if a seizure should occur on the job.
    5. Fear of frequent and uncontrolled seizures.
    6. Need for extra supervision.
    7. Fear that the employee may harm him/herself as well as co-workers and damage equipment.
    8. Customers and other employees will react adversely to associating with obviously handicapped people.
C. Lack of educational and training facilities.
D. Societal stereotyping of jobs for the handicapped that are depressing, i.e., janitorial work, washing dishes.
E. Lack of self-confidence and poor self-image.
F. Impaired ability to read or review written work.

Goals and Strategies to Bring About Change

A. Public education and public relations campaigns through media coverage of successful handicapped workers in a variety of jobs.
B. Development of self-confidence through overtraining procedures and counseling support systems.
C. Electromechanical aids to help with communication difficulties.
D. Ongoing speech and language therapy.
E. Use of electronic technology such as OPTACON (Optical to Tactile Converter) for the visually impaired (Cook, Dahl, & Gale, 1977).

F. Alternatives in the work system such as apprenticeship training. New patterns are needed, such as the Australian plan of mixing handicapped and non-handicapped people in an entire industry. White collar and service occupations geared to handicapped people and sales programs providing meaningful income to disabled people are also needed (Park, 1975).

Housing

Target Behaviors

A. Barriers that affect the integration and utilization of community residential facilities.
 1. Neighbors
     a. desire to put mentally retarded individuals some place where they "won't get hurt."
     b. fear that the residential program in the neighborhood will devalue their property.
 2. Parents
     a. fear their child will fail in a facility with less restrictions.
     b. are concerned that it would appear as if they have failed as parents if their child is placed in a residential facility.
 3. Public Administrators
     a. issue rigid regulations.
     b. keep threatening the loss of funds.
     c. insist upon multiple agency inspections.
     d. don't plan for coordinated outcomes.
B. Geographic isolation, i.e., rural communities.
C. Lack of transportation.
D. Coordination among agencies.
 1. Need for State mental retardation agencies to support community programs over institutional programs.
 2. Need for more community facilities and services that can be supported by the funds available.
 3. Insufficient assistance by other federal, state, and local agencies.
E. Lack of knowledge about housing resources.
F. Lack of money to buy, rent, or repair housing.
G. Discrimination, lack of housing code enforcement.

Goals and Strategies to Bring About Change

A. There are four goals one should follow when developing housing for the mentally retarded:

1. Housing should be conventional in appearance, as undifferentiated as possible from surrounding living arrangements for non-handicapped persons.
2. Fit the type and scale of the neighborhood and "congregate" no more handicapped persons than can be absorbed into the neighborhood or community.
3. Offer a home environment in neighborhoods within the mainstream of community life.
4. Provide easy access to necessary supportive habilitative, rehabilitative programs based on a developmental model.

B. Match housing with service needs.
C. Assess the types of housing needs and demands.
D. Bring more technical knowledge and equipment into the homes to help with communication and employability.
E. There are four key components necessary for a national housing program for the handicapped.
   1. Staff with knowledge of the special design and management requirements of the living arrangements for a variety of the handicapped, as well as the array of services needed to sustain independent living in such an environment.
   2. A methodology for determining the handicapped housing market and the related need demand factors.
   3. Funds to provide essential services to sustain the handicapped in community-based housing.
   4. Funds for extra construction costs (Thompson, 1976).

Legislation — Funding

Target Barriers

A. The barrier to effective use of governmental funds for group homes and other community residential programs.
   1. Many programs are under-funded to the point where they are rendered incompetent but too dependent to turn down funds.
   2. Politicians do not have a long-standing commitment to the mentally retarded and are reluctant to become involved in something they understand poorly, if at all.
   3. There are gaps in funding in that construction funds and start-up support are much harder to come by than operational funds.
   4. Various governmental programs must be pieced together into a cohesive funding package — a formidable undertaking, given differing program managers, operating procedures, and eligibility standards.

B. Problems with Social Security program.
  1. Social Security payments meet room and board costs, but are often inadequate to meet actual costs and therefore individuals must be financially supported by the State or through some other source. A number of local governments supplement the federal payments on a marginal basis, some not at all.
  2. Eligibility is limited to those persons with mental retardation who are unable to earn substantial wages or engage in "gainful activity."
C. Disability insurance programs.
  1. Coverage is limited to persons whose parents are themselves retired, deceased, or disabled and covered under Social Security program.
  2. Disability coverage is limited to individuals over 18 and whose disability originated in childhood.
D. Problems with Section 8 H.U.D. regulations, Housing Assistance Payments.
  1. H.U.D.'s lack of familiarity with or commitment to small group homes for mentally retarded persons has created serious attitudinal barriers to using Section 8 funds.
  2. The minimum property standards are not appropriate to normalized living.
  3. Requirements that Section 8 be consistent with the local community's Housing Assistance Plan means that sponsors must convince their communities to include small group housing for mentally retarded persons in their housing plans.
E. Section 202, H.U.D. regulations, Projects for Elderly and the Handicapped.
  1. H.U.D.'s requirement that Section 202 sponsors also obtain Section 8 operating subsidies, which sometimes present conflicting regulations for housing handicapped individuals.
  2. H.U.D.'s criteria for evaluation of Section 202 applications stress past experience in operating housing programs and long-term financial stability that eliminates many applications for small group housing for developmentally disabled persons.
  3. H.U.D. is reluctant to fund small scale applications with the result that those few projects funded for developmentally disabled persons to date have tended to be clusters of community residences in one neighborhood or large facilities in the community.
  4. Also, competition is intense for funds.
F. Title XX problems.
  1. A financial ceiling on Federal social service expenditures has created intense competition for Title XX funds. Funds for new programs can come only if old programs are cut back or eliminated.

2. Decisions on what activities to fund rest with the state.
G. Medicaid Title XIX of the Social Security Act.
   1. H.E.W.'s ICF/MR regulations are not generally appropriate to the service delivery style of the typical group home. Also, many states won't release funds for residential facilities receiving the funds for institutions.
H. Problems with Developmental Disabilities services and facilities.
   1. Very limited funding level of the D.D. program, coupled with intense competition for D.D. support, creates obvious limitations on the role of the D.D. program in supporting group homes (Manes, 1976).
I. There are too many agencies responsible for providing services/funds to the mentally retarded (Hitzing, Hoffman, Killenbeck, Loop, Neil, & Wood, 1977).

Goals and Strategies to Bring About Change

A. H.U.D. Programs
   1. Community Development Block Grants help to remove architectural barriers, restrictions to mobility, provide services, i.e., counseling, vocational rehabilitation, job training, day care, etc.
   2. Comprehensive Planning Grants (Section 701 Program) funds for planning public services, natural resources and land uses, financing, etc.
   3. Direct Loans (Section 202 of Housing Act, 1959) to finance the construction or substantial rehabilitation of housing projects.
   4. Congregate Housing (Section 7, Title II), living quarters with meals and at least minimal kitchens in each living unit.
   5. Lower Income Housing Assistance (Title II of the Housing and Community Development Act of 1974) to provide for payments on behalf of eligible families occupying newly constructed, substantially rehabilitated, or existing rental housing.
   6. Low Rent Public Housing enables PHA's to provide safe and sanitary housing for low income families.
   7. Start-up Loans/Short-term Loans to cover early costs of building or rehabilitating buildings for use by the handicapped.
   8. Mortgage Insurance to assist in providing new rehabilitated rental housing.
   9. Home improvements. Insured loans for improvements to increase the utility or liability of property (H.U.D. 467-H(2), 1978).
B. Raise ceiling on Title XX. Many states have reached funding ceiling which has cut back community programs (Hitzing, et al., 1977).
C. Title XIX funds should be used to provide for the establishment of small group homes of eight to ten clients with a full range of services needed by

the people they serve (Kral, Crowther, Edwards, Howie, Morrill, Stacey, Svoboda, Wood, & Girardeau, 1978).
D. Possible shifting of Title XIX funds to Title XX, out of the Medicaid/ Medicare model with a re-focus on strong definition of rehabilitation as training, including residential and life skills development (Hitzing, et al., 1977).
E. Title XX redirection should possibly be contingent on Title XIX re-focus.

Service — Education and Training

Target Barriers

A. H.E.W. and State Vocational Rehabilitation Agencies need to (U.S. Department of Health, Education, and Welfare, 1977):
   1. Define an appropriate role for the vocational rehabilitation program for assisting in deinstitutionalization.
   2. Provide more assistance and guidance to States and monitor and evaluate their efforts relating to this goal.
   3. Clarify the definition of severe disability for the developmentally disabled and make sure that decisions to deny vocational rehabilitation services are made in accordance with its regulations.
B. More counselors are necessary for homebound clients because they have to travel to the home and cannot work directly from their desks.
C. Counselors are called upon for knowledge in many areas, i.e., accounting, marketing, business design; often, these counselors don't have the knowledge.
D. "Fewer than five percent of the homebound have access to any rehabilitation service" (Walker, 1973).

Goals and Strategies to Bring About Change

A. Child-find services. Identification of individuals in need of services and direction to these services (Nebraska Department of Education, 1977).
B. Neighborhood facilities for training to utilize a more realistic environment to reinforce the acquisition of independent living skills.
C. Bring in specialists in various fields to help the clients with their special problems.
D. Improve accessibility to school facilities (U.S. Department of Health, Education, and Welfare, 1975a):
   1. Integration through mainstreaming and curriculum development.
   2. Extending research and vocational education for post secondary youth through career education, vocational guidance, job design and placement, and vocational assessment and evaluation.

3. Supply teaching and paraprofessional personnel for special education through new approaches to evaluation, teaching, training programs, and technological systems to aid performance.
4. Increase knowledge through alternative methods of curriculum design, utilization of technology, and diagnostic techniques.

E. Title XX funding should allow for access of mentally retarded persons to all service options, not just those specifically designated for special handicapped populations, with incentives and dollar increases in those categories, i.e., foster care, day care, homemaker/HHA, and counseling services (Hitzing, et al., 1977).

Social – Attitudinal

A. Achievement by the handicapped is almost always measured through jobs or working. This attitude is widespread in the United States, which makes it "virtually impossible for the handicapped individual to achieve any measure of satisfaction or success in activities that do not produce financial rewards" (Park, 1975).
B. Frequently, there is denial of remedial, corrective, medical, and dental services because of the belief that mentally retarded persons do not benefit from such services (U.S. Department of Health, Education, and Welfare, 1975b).
C. Beneath the acceptance of the harmless child is still the concern of a threatening adult whose difference from us is viewed with exaggerated alarm and whose presence in the community makes us uncomfortable, especially if we see the handicapped adult as a threat to the wage structure, or to property values (Packard & Laveck, 1976).
D. Lack of information, fear, misconception, or childhood experiences are often stated as the reason behind the negative attitude our society holds toward the disabled. Certain types of disabilities elicit various negative responses from the non-disabled (Reeder, 1975).

Goals and Strategies to Bring About Change

To achieve a firm and deep acceptance of developmentally disabled persons as members of the social community and as citizens in their own right. The goals and strategies are:

A. "Advancement of those values which emphasize the worth of every human being without regard to his material possessions, his job status, his productivity, his I.Q., or his beauty, and which recognize the importance of diversity and the right to be different" (Packard & Laveck, 1976).
1. Appropriate attention must be given to the areas of human values, of working with minority cultures, in-service training, and the development of curriculum in these areas for all present teachers.

2. An exposure of all students during the elementary and secondary years of various aspects of handicapping conditions and a sensitivity to developmentally disabled individuals.
3. H.E.W. must continue to move forward under the authority of Part D (94–142) of the Education of the Handicapped Act, which provides not only for the training of special education personnel but also for the training of regular teachers in developing a sensitivity to the needs of the developmentally disabled.
4. The states should continue to mandate exposure to handicapping conditions as a requirement in the certification of all teachers.
5. Department of Education should develop specific curricula units on teaching the handicapped as part of the curriculum for all students.
6. Courses on developmental disabilities should be included in the curricula of all students of medicine, dentistry, nursing, law and law enforcement, education, religion, psychology, social work, and any other field in which professional practice involves contact with mentally retarded persons.
7. The continuation and expansion of the "education for parenthood" program is essential, with inclusion of material on mental retardation.
8. Civic organizations in each community should search for creative ways to enhance community regard for the teachers, social workers, recreation leaders, employment counselors, residential aides, and all others who provide supportive services to retarded persons.

B. ACTION, The National Center for Voluntary Action, and corresponding groups in every community should intensify the enrollment of volunteers in activities involving direct contact with mentally retarded persons.
C. Continuation of public education programs and use of the mass media to promote: (1) a greater understanding and appreciation for handicapped persons as neighbors and fellow citizens, and (2) understanding of the means of reducing the occurrence of mental retardation.
D. The mentally retarded individual must serve as a model in changing attitudes in order for each succeeding generation to progress.
E. Mainstreaming handicapped children in public and private school systems as well as shaping public policy to mainstream mentally retarded individuals throughout the community.

SUMMARY

Writing this chapter was an ambitious and difficult process. The reason for this was not the typical problem of a lack of information. Rather, it was the result of analyzing over 1500 reports, studies, etc., and reviewing the 142 computer citations. It is obvious that this review was ambitious when one also considers that there are over 140 national and international organizations that publish 93 journals associated with a multi-billion dollar industry and mediated through 91 federal programs in the United States.

The strengths and weaknesses of these research studies were investigated along with the six most significant studies on barriers to services for the mentally retarded. The major conceptual and theoretical components of the model were studied in order to provide a rationale and scientific basis for its use.

The implementation of the model centered on two aspects: the organization (who) and the application (what and how). Successful models and programs were critiqued in order to identify the key change agents who are responsible for a model's success. Suggestions were also given on ways to effectively utilize influential groups and consortias in the community. The model application involved three self-modification phases with eight discrete steps.

The barrier analysis section presented seven major barrier components with specific target behaviors and goals identified. These barriers are not meant to be all-inclusive, but representative of the more critical barriers requiring our immediate attention. In sum, the purpose of this chapter was to demonstrate that of all the complexities inherent in this field, significant progress can be accomplished if comprehensive models and methodology are applied. Finally, the ultimate question is not an idealistic one of whether we can afford to eliminate these barriers, but rather can we afford not to in lieu of legislative mandates, spiraling costs, and ethical and human concerns.

8 The Delivery of Services in Rural Settings

INTRODUCTION

The purpose of this chapter is to describe the process in which generic professional services can be delivered vis-a-vis the role of the community-based program in rural settings. The major criticism leveled against deinstitutionalization and mainstreaming into rural areas is the lack of resources, i.e., specialized staff and comprehensive programs. We frequently hear arguments that rural programs don't have the money, staff, knowledge, or support to implement the federally mandated programs.

In this chapter we attempt to demonstrate that these concerns need not be a barrier to serving mentally retarded individuals and their families in rural settings. In our attempt to dispel some of the myths surrounding this controversial issue, we have divided the chapter into four sections.

RURAL SETTINGS

A major perspective on the problems in expending generic rural services is to examine the unique features of the rural setting. First we examine the issues that are generally held to be problematical in regard to delivery of services in a rural area:

1. Those who deliver primary health care are both proportionately fewer and further away.
2. Social service providers and teachers are often less up-to-date regarding mental retardation.

3. Secondary and tertiary health care facilities are remote.
4. Problems do not cluster often enough to allow development of specialized expertise.
5. Families in such areas are generally less affluent.

In other words, the basic problems concerned with providing rural services are distance, transportation, shortages of service providers, and inadequate training for service providers. Radford (1978) describes a number of common factors that contribute to health problems in less developed countries. These include lack of knowledge, poverty, isolation, lack of resources, and holding to traditional concepts of agricultural practice and health-related behavior.

Vail (1973) contends that the rural versus urban distinction is not as important as the distinction between socioeconomic levels. He emphasizes that it is the socioeconomic level of an area that is crucial to the occurrence and prevalence of mental retardation. Moreover, he claims that indeed the financial or economic issue is the key to overcoming problems of distance and the other effects of sparse population. In terms of the transportation issue, Vail contends that anything beyond an hour drive causes a marked decrease in the use of a primary care facility. In discussing manpower issues, Vail notes that professional establishments tend to have a somewhat counterproductive effect. That is, while the professionals will make noble statements about expanding manpower utilization, nevertheless, they still look first to the continuation and maintenance of the power of their own professional establishment. Unfortunately, universities and major agencies in general have perhaps unknowingly contributed to this problem by emphasizing the training of professionals as opposed to paraprofessionals and parents.

Another issue is that of cultural attitudes. The stereotyped view is that rural citizens have strikingly different cultural attitudes than urban citizens. Although this is a commonly held view, there seems to be evidence disputing this. Hassinger (1976), in reviewing the evidence on differing values and norms, concludes that it is very easy to overstate rather than understate this difference between urban and rural beliefs and values. The stereotype of rural people being more conservative, religious, puritanical, work-oriented, ascetic, isolationistic, etc., was only thinly supported. Moreover, such research has always failed to obtain consistency and consensus on values among rural respondents.

One different factor that has emerged is more a function of social organization than values. For instance, Hassinger notes that there is a tendency among rural individuals to be more person-oriented in terms of important interactions. Urban dwellers on the other hand may be more object or materially oriented.

In short, there are a number of supposed problems affecting the delivery of rural services. These include distance, transportation, communication, manpower shortages, and differences in values and beliefs. It appears that these may indeed represent more of the surface than the deep aspects of the problem. A problem-solving focus must look beyond this common view of rural issues, towards some of the real underlying issues. For example, should transportation really be an issue? People in rural areas take care of all their other transportation problems in terms of getting supplies, agricultural equipment, and moving merchandise to market. All of these activities are completely taken care of their own initiative. So transportation doesn't seem to be a problem in and of itself. Perhaps more focus should be directed to social matrix. The use of transportation may follow when rural individuals are educated on the needs of services. Thus, the real issue is on education.

Hassinger suggests a sociological approach to the process of spreading ideas in rural areas. He suggests a two-phase process. First of all, there is a communication phase within which mass media may present new ideas on health practices. He notes that it is most important that such information goes to certain people in a rural area. He describes these individuals as the cosmopolites. These individuals are looked up to by others and are the natural change agents to be spreading information. Given the completion of the communication phase, comes an adoption phase with a number of steps including awareness or the getting of the information, a cultivation of interests during which more information is obtained, evaluation of the information, trial of the information, and finally adoption. Hassinger submits that efforts to change patterns of health care (and we might add patterns of care for the mentally retarded) are based on dissemination of information. Dissemination of information in turn must be based upon a sensitive appraisal of the mechanisms for this within rural areas.

Similarly, a sociological perspective should be taken on the behavior of interests. For instance, one behavior of interest is the seeking of services; another, as mentioned earlier, is the adoption of a new health or care behavior. Another set of behaviors is that of caring for a handicapped individual within a family constellation.

Recasting the issues in a more sociological light suggests that the real problems in terms of rural services are concerned with *education* and the provision of basic *technology* to rural individuals and the careful study of the *processes* whereby such new ideas and practices are *learned, adopted,* and *used.*

CONCEPTUAL ISSUES

A second perspective on problems and issues in rural services concerns a number of philosophical conceptual issues surrounding the provision of rural services themselves, and particularly, the role of community agencies in providing such services.

Programs Versus Services

Vail (1973) emphasizes that there is a crucial difference between the terms "services" and "programs." The concept of services emphasizes an input model. It focuses on both the professional and material inputs. The entire issue of providing services becomes something that is carried on in and of itself. Such a service orientation frequently does not focus on the impact and effectiveness of the services. Vail instead poses a programmatic approach that takes into consideration the *who, what, how,* and *why* of providing services. He suggests that any program should be built upon *five* criteria. These include:

1. A rational ordering of a wide range of personal social problems.
2. A clear differentiation between public programs and non-public programs.
3. A mandated local public agency to implement any public program.
4. A local agency to plan for the coordinated implementation of both public and nonpublic programs.
5. A state or governmental body that must concern itself with the entire range of programs.

While the second through fifth points made by Vail applied to the structural aspects of a program, the first point is of particular importance. This point insists that there be a careful ordering of the wide range of personal and social problems. In other words, these problems must be identified and placed in some kind of a priority order. Perhaps a point here is that only those issues that individuals in rural areas perceive as meaningful or that effect their life are going to be ones in which they are willing to make an effort to create change.

Certainly Vail's point is well taken and perhaps the emphasis should be more programmatic and thereby impact-oriented rather than merely service-oriented.

Appropriate Technology

Another issue that is particularly important for a community-based program's concern is making program technology as approriate as possible to the environment. Perhaps the most comprehensive and penetrating analysis of the issues involved in appropriate technology are raised by E. F. Schumacher in his book, *Small is Beautiful* (1973). He emphasizes that the key point in the application of technology is to focus on the human resources. For anything to be carried out, the people must maintain a strong morale. They must be self-determining and have a role in decision making. The focus of technology should be to improve self-reliance and self-help. Given this perspective that human resources are the most valuable, the crucial facet becomes the education that accompanies the technology.

Schumacher insists that education must be combined with values. It is the values that indicate the use and meaning of the technology. It would seem that such considerations are particularly crucial in the area of providing services. Can people provide help for others without some convictions in terms of values of providing such help?

Development in Schumacher's mind does not start with material goals. It starts with people, their education, organization, and discipline, the foundation of development. Poverty is ultimately a deficiency in education, organization, and discipline. In Schumacher's mind the possible pernicious effects of lower socioeconomic status are not limited to less wealth, but include less education, organization and, discipline. Thus, for technology to be appropriate it must facilitate education, self-reliance, and self-help.

Other issues in making technology appropriate should include an attempt to meet a given end with minimum means. This suggests that the use of local resources to meet local needs is a crucial consideration.

Consumer Involvement

Another conceptual issue related to appropriate technology and programmatic development is that of consumer involvement. Appropriate technology stimulates consumer involvement, and programs are built on consumer identification and prioritization of need.

Consumer involvement means starting with the rural people. It means allocating scarce resources to a community's perception of need. It means drawing on the interests of the community to begin a process of search and discovery and innovation. An informed consumer is a wise consumer. Information on choices should be made available to the consumer. Professional care workers should attempt to join with community members to raise their consciousness and to enable them to make the best use of available resources.

Hatch and Erpp (1976), in describing the Tufts-Delta health project, present a good example of consumer involvement. Rural citizens identified hunger and malnutrition as their number one problem and expressed interest in ideas and technology to help them overcome this problem. After working readily with the Tufts University staff to solve these problems, a sense of "consumer involvement" had developed and the Tufts professionals and rural citizenry were able to identify additional problems.

There are a number of other factors related to consumer involvement. Hatch and Erpp (1976) suggest a successful integration of consumer involvement with outside professional expertise, organizational know-how, and resources. Perhaps there is a continuum of community participation and professional participation. Obviously the right balance has to be achieved in order to create innovation, based on profesional expertise, and appropriateness and long-term community commitment to participation.

Philosophy

Technology without a guiding philosophy seems to be empty and problematical and destined for either failure or non-utilization. On the other hand, health and service technology that is guided by a powerful philosophy can have tremendous impact. For instance, in Nebraska, the Eastern Nebraska Community Office of Retardation (ENCOR) program for providing community residential services for the mentally retarded was guided by the philosophical belief in normalization – the idea that retarded individuals should have an opportunity to have as normal a life as possible. Such normal life patterns are seen as a great help for the optimal development of the retarded individual and for all of society. This principle, combined with the active idea of deinstitutionalization, has had a tremendous influence in mobilizing families, aides, social workers, school personnel, and general citizenry in providing community services for mentally retarded individuals. Too often our educational facilities have emphasized technology without considering the values involved in the application of such technology.

The major values of rural programming are that of self-reliance and self-determination, values that underlie Schumacher's view of appropriate technology. Another example of a guiding philosophy concerns the barefoot doctors in China who hold as a paramount value serving their fellow man. Here is a notion of service, of providing service that is held to have particular value. All too frequently community-based programs have not been a benefit in providing a vital guiding philosophy. It will be crucial in the future for the community-based programs to address this deficit.

SUMMARY OF PROBLEMS

The problems effecting the delivery of generic services for rural mentally retarded citizens are many. A cursory overview of these problems suggests that additional work may be needed to identify actual problems. Traditionally, the focus has been on the obvious issues of spatial isolation, transportation, communication, manpower shortages, and slow information flow. Nevertheless, many sources are suggesting that these named problems provide only a superficial view and that perhaps the real problems have much more to do with socioeconomic status. Another perspective holds that the socioeconomic level is in turn merely a reflection of the awareness and/or educational level not necessarily in a formal sense but in a sense relevant to the problem of providing services. Another perspective suggests scrutiny not of broad areas so much but of the processes involved, i.e., what factors contribute to and inhibit the flow of ideas and the delivery of services within a rural area.

Above and beyond these considerations are a number of basic conceptual issues concerning the program versus service dichotomy, the issue of philosophy and values in providing services, the issue of appropriate technology, and the issue of consumer involvement. And, of course, the dynamics of the structure of the community system along with planning and policy trends within the communities must be kept in mind. Obviously, the community personnel must be cognizant and sensitive to this full range of problems and issues in formulating future programs.

CURRENT MODELS

The purpose of this section is to review the six major types of models currently being used in the delivery of human services in rural settings. We also examine alternative international models that have intriguing implications for the continental United States. This review of what models are currently being used naturally leads us to the next section on what a new model or system could be like.

Continuing Education Model

As mentioned in the previous section, the essential issue is to bring those skills, those new treatment tactics, and the programming strategies developed within the urban community-based system out to service providers and to mentally retarded citizens in the rural area. In contrasting the effects of rural-urban and urban vocational rehabilitation, Goodyear, Bitter, and Micek (1973) noted that there are several important differences in rural rehabilitation. They suggested that the habilitation professional for rural clients needs to be more of a generalist and in particular, drawing upon the suggestions of Daniels (1967), the counselor needs to provide resource engineering, consultation education, and community organization. In other words, the role of the service provider in a rural setting is much more likely to involve service coordination as opposed to service provision. The different phases of service coordination indicated above have several advantages in that an attempt to utilize existing resources that try to provide for people where they are and attempt to stimulate community participation and can be efficiently integrated if approached correctly. Essentially this model suggests that a unique set of skills is needed by the service provider in the rural area. An important role of the community-based program is to provide training sequences that facilitate the acquisition of these unique skills. It is also to provide continuing education in terms of the development of these coordinating skills. The problem with this model is that essentially it has never been implemented in a massive or consistent fashion.

In most counties there are a number of service providers, including social workers, rehabilitation counselors, and psychologists who for the most part do not receive specialized training in these areas. In most cases these professionals were not identified as potential rural service providers during their training. This means that while graduate training emphases on rural service provisions are important, probably more important is the aspect of continuing education in the provision of rural services. In particular, this means that continued research on the refinement of those skills required are crucial. Another problem that would be part of this model is the content of the material presented in training. All too often training tends to emphasize the need for *recreating* those programs carried on in the educational setting. Those programs are frequently characterized by high levels of technologies, manpower support, and financial support. The total technological level may frequently not be appropriate for rural areas.

Transportation Models

Transportation models are composed of basically two approaches. The first is to decrease the distance between the primary care services and the individuals requiring those services. Perry (1976), in discussing rural medical health care, notes that several communities have set up patient systems utilizing mini-buses that make regularly scheduled trips to medical centers. Other possibilities include using school buses and other vehicles for transporting those requiring services to the service agency. However, he notes the considerably high cost of such transportation systems, which many rural areas cannot afford.

A second approach is the use of mobile facilities to bring primary care to rural areas. Mobile health units were originally developed to deal with the epidemics and sickness in Africa between 1915–1940 and they are now used fairly frequently throughout the world. With mobile units there is a trade off between the amount of equipment that can be transported and the mobility of the unit. In other words, the larger and the more inclusive and equipment laden the unit becomes the less mobile it is. Mobile vans have been used for screening and evaluation of the mentally retarded.

Again, the problem with this approach is the expense. Another problem of this model in that the burden for providing services is placed on urban areas and we simply need to make these services available to the rural population. In some instances these services as they are presented and used in urban areas may be appropriate. On the other hand, it is often the case that these particular services are not tailored to the needs of rural citizens. A third problem is that these forms of service do not necessarily involve the people for whom the services are being provided. In other words, *it is an outside technology that is either brought in to the people or the people are brought to the outside technology*. Such an approach can create a dependency on outside technology rather than stimulating initiative and self-reliance on the part of rural communities in dealing with these problems.

Cooperative Extension Services

Through the cooperative extension services of land grant colleges, educational teams have been established in almost every one of the 3,000 counties of the United States. These teams traditionally consisted of a county agricultural agent, home economist, and a home youth worker. One possibility is to add staff members who would provide educational resources in service to the mentally retarded. It is somewhat difficult to envision just exactly what this person's total job would be. It might be broadly defined in the field of health education and the development of services for the handicapped.

The possible problems with this approach are a shortage of trained manpower and an insufficient research base to support health education programs. In response to these criticisms it must be stated that a great deal of research has been conducted in the care of the handicapped. Possible advantages of this system are that the cooperative extension has an already operative and known educational delivery mechanism functioning at the local level. In terms of responding to the issue of qualified manpower, it may be necessary to train a new kind of professional/parent professional as health educators. This training would emphasize the provision of information on how to deal with the most frequent issues that bring people into primary care. The emphasis here is going to have to be not so much in providing health education in the field and the most technical aspects of care for the mentally retarded, but for providing resources and education in dealing with the most common problem that the people in the rural areas are affected with. The treatment modalities and the training techniques again must emphasize the technology that is appropriate to the rural area.

Telecommunications

One way of overcoming the distance problems of the rural service model is to take full advantage of modern telecommunications, which can cover distances with relative ease. Urban-based programs can, as part of their activities, train individuals for work in rural settings. Nevertheless, limitations of resources do not allow them to fully meet this need for trained personnel in rural areas. In many cases the further one travels from the urban-based program, the less they are influenced by that facility. For example, one grant project by the Alternate Media Center of New York investigated the possibility of using telecommunications in the developmentally disabled field and noted the following: "Telecommunications may help those serving DD persons in rural areas to be more informed about seeking assistance. They may help in providing the access to training programs, consultation services, and information on demand. And they could have a part to play in facilitating collaboration in treatment planning or feedback following referral" (page 19, volume 2). In this light the role of telecommunications is to assist rural service providers with up-to-date information on treatment and available services, including training programs, consultation, and related information services. Another use suggested here is that when a referral is made to a community-based program, the information on the results of the evaluation for training could be transmitted via telecommunications to individuals involved in the primary care of each client.

Additionally, the telecommunications process could assist in increasing public awareness and providing education on the nature of mental retardation. Information could also be presented on possible resources in appropriate responses to the mentally retarded individual. In this case a solid relationship with the commercial and cable TV networks would be of considerable value.

The Alternate Media Center concept proposes in addition a number of other specific applications of telecommunications technology in providing services for this population. For example, in assessing children's response to training methods, it is often more enlightening to monitor them in their natural home or school environment than to do so through observation of behavior in the urban clinic. Setting up a video link would facilitate a very systematic observation. Another possibility is to provide the support of information for parents of needy children in isolated areas. A conferencing link network could be provided for needed interaction among indiviuals or groups of parents and professionals on a regular basis. This may be accompanied by a series of programs on certain issues, such as audio cassettes that individuals could either call up for or purchase. Another specific suggestion is to provide telecommunication links with the urban community center to group homes and foster care programs. These ongoing links could provide information as well as consultation.

Another potential area of emphasis is for community-sponsored training seminars. Currently, such seminars are usually held at a large urban program and require rural staff to travel to the program. Telecommunications at that selected site might allow better access to training seminars. There are other specific areas for linking up with service providers in rural areas, including primary care individuals who may not have a great deal of experience with mentally retarded clients. Also school systems, now under the mandate of mainstreaming, will be having increased contact with mentally retarded clients. Both of these groups could, through audio conferencing or televised presentation, be given up-to-date information. One concept that has been utilized in providing rural health care is that of the rural clinic accompanied with satellite centers. Telecommunications links can improve the coordination between home clients and the satellite centers. Essentially such a telecommunication link between the urban center and the satellite would reduce the travel needed to provide technical consultation but maintain close relationships and would provide back-up in emergency settings.

There are, however, a number of problems associated with telecommunications. For one, telecommunications equipment, generally speaking, is expensive. Initial expense is compounded by continued maintenance cost, which in turn requires trained personnel who can both operate and maintain the equipment. Another aspect of telecommunications that can limit its ability deals with the manner in which it blends in with currently existing modes of communication. At times the establishment of a telecommunications outlet can be viewed as intrusive. At other times it can clash with current systems such that the use of the equipment involves extra effort. From a learning perspective such extra effort to utilize the equipment is similar to a response cost contingency and thus may act to reduce the frequency of use of such equipment. But even more important is that in some manner the equipment must interface with the ongoing social organization system. This returns us to some degree to the issue of appropriate technology. In some cases the application of telecommunications as a technology may not be appropriate and useful for the actual service needs of the people it is trying to help. Applications of video channels in industry have not been very successful.

In summary, while there are a great number of theoretically attractive applications of telecommunications for improving the provision of services to rural mentally retarded individuals, the possible advantages include certainly the increased rate of dissemination of information, the ability to keep rural service providers up-to-date on the latest findings, the potential for decreasing the sense of isolation of rural service providers as well as providing tools for improving direct service via telecommunications based consultation, and the facilitation of training. Nevertheless, the disadvantages in terms of costs in the initial expense and maintenance coupled with a crucial issue of compatability, suitability, and appropriateness would suggest that the area of telecommunications applications is one in which carefully planned programs should be initiated. Moreover, such programs should be cautiously evaluated as to their effectiveness.

The Consultative Model

Another model whereby urban community-based programs can provide support for rural mentally retarded services is by providing consultants. This, of course, has come to be known as the consultation model. Via this model, rural service agencies, when confronted with difficult assessment/ diagnostic or when confronted with a problem in treatment and program development for the mentally retarded individual, could call on a program for a consultation to help resolve some of these issues. Someone would then visit the rural area, evaluate the situation, and come up with recommendations and/or provide actual intervention or follow-up services. There are several advantages to the consultative model in that bringing in an outside consultant is equivalent to bringing an objective or fair opinion into a situation that not unfrequently is quite polarized. The consultant in this role may be able to provide fresh ideas or confirm the estimates of a rural service provider.

However, there are a number of potential disadvantages with the consultant model. First of all, the burden of initiating this consultation lies completely on the rural providers. Not only does this mean that the rural service provider has to have some kind of a crisis to develop a request or initiate action but that he or she knows the correct access route to the consultant. In many circumstances this may not be an easy task with the least experienced rural service provider and their familiarity with the personnel at the urban center. Another problem involves the time lag. Frequently individuals associated with the urban center have a number of other time obligations and there may be a considerable lapse of time between when the request for the consultation is originated and when the consultant actually appears on the scene. Frequently, this time lapse can be detrimental in terms of service provision. A further disadvantage exists in the consultant's potential ignorance of the political, economic, and social realities of the rural setting. Lack of knowledge of these factors may lead the consultant to make recommendations that, from a theoretical ground, may be solid but nevertheless inappropriate to the given setting. Moreover, he/she may make recommendations that individuals who are providing services may not have the skills to carry out consistently or thoroughly.

In summary, the consultation model has a number of possible advantages, and a number of disadvantages that hinder its effectiveness. Of course, one of these is again the issue of expense. Just who is going to pay the transportation and the wages of the consultants remains a major barrier.

Alternative Models for Spreading Technology to Undeveloped Areas

As mentioned earlier, the issue of spreading rehabilitative care technology from areas of high concentration such as urban community clinics has been one of worldwide concern. In this section we examine some of the attempts that have been made all over the world to deal with these problems. We review some of the models that have been developed particularly in the area of more general medical care and see if there are important aspects of these models that would make them useful in terms of programs for mental retardation services.

The People's School in the Phillipines.   The Peoples School was established by the government in the Phillipines to raise the economic and social standards of rural people via self-help approaches (Flavier, 1978). It was designed to make appropriate science and technology available to an increasing segment of the rural population at an affordable cost. Previous experience in the Phillipines was derived from a farmer-scholar program in which selected farmers (individuals chosen by the fellow villagers) attended a government course in some area of agricultural production. Participants then returned to their villages to share their knowledge with fellow villagers. This project resulted in increased income on the part of the farmers who participated.

Other studies indicated the importance of identifying the true leaders in the villages as opposed to those who held legal/judicial posts. It was found that leaders who had real social power were much more effective in initiating change based on the technology. The People's School was designed to provide assistance in the area of economics, health, education, culture, and self-government. The actual title was "Paaralan Ng Anak Pawis." This title literally translated means "school of the children of sweat" or paraphrased "people's school." In implementing this program, the first step was inviting the village leaders to a conference where a school proposal was presented. These leaders then were responsible for forming within the village a committee which selected school participants and implemented a program at the village level. Moreover, all members of the village committees were invited to a conference to further describe the purposes of "The People's School." Then the committees selected scholars based on the criteria of a minimal level of literacy, permanent residence in the village, social characteristics acceptable to the villagers, and a willingness to share their newly gained knowledge with others. The village committees agreed to provide transportation and food for the trainees while the government school charged neither tuition nor lodging fees, and provided materials. The organizational system is of particular interest here in that the scholar not only has social status by being selected but also a certain sense of obligation to the entire village, since village funds are paying for food and transport.

In addition to the training course itself, which was designed to present appropriate technology to the villager, a number of procedures were designed to facilitate maintenance and generalization of the skills required. The follow-up system included continuing education support, supervision, evaluation, motivation maintenance, and morale for both the scholar and the village committee. In terms of health care the scholars have become partners in the total rural health program. Many of the scholars developed medical supply systems in their villages, providing treatment and preventive care, and facilitating referrals for problems that they couldn't handle through government health centers. The latter process and the ensuing consultation provided a matrix for continuing education of the rural health scholars.

In evaluating problems that emerged through the "People's School" project, several points become apparent. The greatest issue is the selection of the scholars themselves. The issue of follow-up for the scholar and the village committee is also particularly important in the more technical areas.

Another issue was the difficulty experienced by some villages in raising funds to support their scholars. Yet another issue was the selection of the instructors at "The People's School." In terms of their qualifications, the most effective instructors appear to be health specialists who have considerable years of living and working in rural settings. There is some suggestion that current rural scholars may make future instructors.

There are several points that need further clarification in understanding this program. First of all, a great deal of planning went into designing this transmission of technology to be maximally sensitive to the economic and social realities of the rural areas. It was the result of interaction among the government staff and the village leaders and village counsels. The training courses always focused on an integrated approach, one linked to a total picture of self-help and rural reconstruction. Also, the emphasis was not only self-help by individuals but mutual help in terms of community cooperation; instructors were strong in practical experience. This was also an important factor and a team spirit approach was emphasized throughout. It is somewhat of interest to examine the credo of the government agency in its efforts for creating economic and social improvement. This is in the form of a poem.

> Go to the people.
> Live among the people.
> Learn from the people.
> Plan with the people.
> Work with the people.
> Start with what the people know
> and build with what the people have.
> Teach by showing.
> Learn by doing.
> Not a showcase, but a pattern.
> Not odds and ends, but a system.
> Not piecemeal, but with an integrated approach.
> Not confirming, but transforming.
> Not relief, but release.

Health Care in North Viet Nam.   North Viet Nam presents a system that is designed at once to simultaneously provide centralized and well-organized health care delivery and communal human services based on mass community involvement (Djukanovic, 1978). The bottom level of this system is the family health worker. In each family one member is designated as a member of the Red Cross and he or she receives training by a local health specialist to carry out basic health tasks. These include ensuring proper maintenance of septic tanks and bathroom facilities, providing first aid and, in the event of more serious problems, appropriate referrals. This member also provides care for the sick and is responsible for maintaining the family medicine supply. The next level is that of cooperative health services. Each village is organized into a cooperative. The members of the co-op are elected by the general assembly of the members. Each co-op has a health worker and a hygienist who is paid by the cooperative. The co-op selects individuals to be trained as nurses. Trained at district and communal health centers, these nurses provide health education information on sanitation, first aid, and treatment of minor and common diseases. Moreover, the cooperatives are also concerned with production and labor management and maintaining the living standards of the workers. Thus, considerable coordination can be exercised between health care and overall community activities. For example, the cooperatives participated in the creation of kindergartens and various day nurseries and provided food and resources for the children.

The next level of care is a communal health center built and managed by each community. This center is designed to provide basic curative and preventative health care.

Proceeding to the next level, a district health center composed of dispensaries, a poly clinic, laboratory, and a hospital provides educational facilities, preventive efforts, diagnostic, and treatment capacities. These centers have very close links with the communal health centers. At the provincial level there are health care centers which consist of a variety of generalized and specialized activities. These centers are responsible for coordinating technical and administrative support in supervising all the district institutions in their specialized programs. Finally, there comes the central level which constitutes a highly specialized structural level of the service delivery system. This level is tied directly into the Ministry of Health and maintains research institutes, central general hospitals, specialized clinics, medical schools, and other postgraduate training schools, pharmaceutical factories, etc. This constitutes the highest level of a nationwide referral system. In addition to this hierarchical organization they have several lateral tie-ins in the form of voluntary organizations such as the Red Cross, which may focus on particular health issues such as maternal care or vaccination. Also, special committees may be set up with the cooperative level. An example of this is a Tuberculosis Control Committee, which focuses particularly on the curative and preventive care of this problem.

Of considerable interest in the Vietnamese system, is that it is highly centralized and yet structured to include input in both decision making and in the administration of health services. As emphasized by Djukanovic (1978),

North Viet Nam attempted to implement this program under the strained conditions of conducting 30 years of war. Their success in spreading health care and services to the mentally retarded indicates in Djukanovic's words that the "developing countries' dream of providing basic health required for all populations is not the utopian but entirely possible to be realized."

China: The Barefoot Doctors.   Post-war medical care for rural China was characterized by a physician-dominated medical delivery system. Moreover, the services of these physicians were expensive to the degree that those who are called middle, lower, and low peasantry were simply not able to afford medical care and medicine. Efforts to eliminate this problem in the immediate post-year wars were not successful. In addition to the low availability of the medical services, the rural areas were characterized by a number of unhygenic practices and unsanitations in personal hygiene. One of the focal points of the cultural revolution was on the improvement of rural health. One part of this program was the training and subsequent work of what has become to be known as the "barefoot doctors": those "who have blisters on their palms, mud on their legs, medical kits over their shoulders, and a close concern in their hearts for the poor and lower middle peasants."

The training of these barefoot doctors has a certain degree of flexibility. Nevertheless, there are several consistent principles. (1) The barefoot doctors in terms of a class perspective come from the rural peasantry. They continue with their role as agricultural workers. The foundation of the actual training is philosophical; the concept being that without the right orientation, knowledge is aimless and is of no use at all: Technical training must follow a philosophical education. This philosophical education is not abstract or speculative metaphysics, but is social-philosophical in nature, encouraging the barefoot doctors to work with the people wholeheartedly and consistently. It should be noted that even though within the Chinese setting, a good deal of the philosophical training is couched in Marxist-Leninist terminology, emphasizing a system of agricultural collective, productive labor, and the collective distribution (collective, productive labor and the collective distribution) system, as well as developing a notion of casting out bourgeois ideas and influences. Nevertheless, above and beyond these political perspectives is a strong emphasis on direct service to the people. In other words, there is a tremendous emphasis on the importance of the primary care activities.

A third basic feature of the training program regards the teaching methods and contents, with an emphasis on practice that parallels Chairman Mao Tse Tung's emphasis to learn warfare. In terms of presenting medical information, courses in basic theory and clinical knowledge are closely combined. In addition, right from the beginning, the barefoot doctor in training spends time working with patients in hospital settings. These trainees spend some time each week visiting and working in the commune hospital and in an exchange program that permits the barefoot doctor to work for a period of time in the hospital specifically with the mentally retarded. A fourth feature is the persistent attempts to integrate training and practice. Now this involves employing both traditional Chinese medicine and modern Western medicine in terms of medical practice, nursing, and pharmaceutical work, at all times with an eye toward the actual conditions in rural areas. The Chinese people are well aware of the importance of preventing mental retardation via their health care program.

Preventive efforts have placed the barefoot doctors at the forefront of nationally publicized health campaigns centered on wiping out major hygienic and sanitation problems. Simultaneously the barefoot doctors have lead the effort to create a new approach to spread health knowledge thereby creating a new consciousness of preventive care as it applies to mental retardation. In addition to the emphasis on preventive measures, the barefoot doctors symbolize a spirit of self-reliance in terms of health care and community services. Whereas in the past, rural individuals sought medicinal products from private clinics at high costs, now almost every rural area has set aside some land for the cultivation of medicinal herbs used to deal with many of the common health problems.

SUMMARY OF INNOVATIVE APPROACHES TO RURAL HEALTH CARE AND DELIVERY OF HUMAN SERVICES

The three systems reviewed here have shared many points in common and yet have had unique emphases. Perhaps these shared points are most thoroughly assembled in a listing of the 18 axioms of medical care that were developed at the Makerere Conference in Uganda (King, 1966). These are listed below.

Major Axioms

1. The medical care of the common man is immensely worthwhile.
2. Medical care must be approached with an objective attitude of mind; free as far as possible from preconceived notions exported from industrial countries.
3. The maximum return in human welfare must be obtained from the limited money and skill available:
   a. In estimating this return, means must not be confused with ends.
   b. Medical care must be adapted to the needs of an intermediate technology.

Pattern of a Medical Service

4. Medical service must be organized to provide for a steady growth in both the quantity and quality of care.
5. Clients, including the mentally retarded, should be treated as close to their homes as possible in the smallest, cheapest, most humbly staffed, and most simply equipped unit that is capable of looking after them adequately.
6. Some form of medical care should be supplied to all the people all the time.
7. With respect to most of the common conditions there is little relationship between the cost and size of a medical unit and its therapeutic efficiency.
8. Medical care can be effective without being comprehensive.
9. Meeting the health needs of a community must be based upon its perceived priorities.

Roles of the Health Workers

10. The role played by auxiliaries is both different and more important in less developed countries than in more developed ones.
11. Health workers should be trained to a level approaching, but not exceeding, the threshold that enables them to leave the environment in which their services are wanted (King, 1966).
12. Health workers should undertake any tasks that they can be readily taught to perform with an acceptable degree of competence and in a cost-effective manner (Radford, 1978).
13. Every health worker deserves regular supportive (as distinct from inspectorial) supervision and continuing education. Generally speaking, their effectiveness is related to the amount of each which they receive (Radford, 1978).
14. The role a doctor has to play in a developing country differs in many important respects from that which he plays in a developed one.
15. All medical workers have an educational role that is closely linked to their therapeutic one.
    a. Skilled staff members have a duty to teach the less skilled ones.
    b. All medical staff have a teaching vocation in the community they serve.

Adaptation of Medical Care to Local Conditions

16. In developing countries, medical care requires the adaptation and development of its own particular methodology.

17. Medical care and the local culture are closely linked.
    a. Medical care must be carefully adapted to the opportunities and limitations of the local culture.
    b. Where possible, medical services should do what they can to improve the non-medical aspects of a culture in the promotion of a "better life" for the people.

Another might well be added:

18. Community participation in the establishment, conduct, and maintenance of health services increases with the understanding of their relevance and the visible outcomes of the effectiveness of such services. This, in turn, increases the community's utilization of the services.

Perhaps what is of interest in comparing the three models is the ways that they have found to implement these different axioms. For instance, the first major axiom within the Chinese setting is emphasized through a total social-political philosophy. In terms of the fourth axiom, perhaps the Vietnamese have put the most work into the total organization that is aimed at continual growth in quantity and quality of medical and educational care. The Peoples School in the Phillipines of course emphasized the selection and community organization aspects as well as the follow-up aspects of training effective rural health and service workers. Thus, the emphasis can vary from situation to situation. Nevertheless, these axioms seem to provide a very comprehensive foundation for providing effective rural services to the mentally retarded and developmentally disabled.

Role

Our opinion is that the primary focus of a community-based system should be on the development of human resources; on training individuals and agencies to take care of as many of their own problems and issues as possible. This educational and training dissemination effort obviously should focus on professionals, paraprofessionals, and other influential individuals within the rural setting.

Prior to the implementation of any training efforts, there should be a clear understanding of the *role* of the community-based system in expanding generic services. The evidence and discussion found in the literature suggest that several cardinal principles should be included in the community-based program. These parallel to some degree the major axioms listed previously, but they are modified to cover the somewhat unique role of the community-based system. These principles are:

1. The habilitation of the developmentally disabled person needs to be in the least restrictive setting. This is not only the best way to provide services, but it should also be mandated by law in many countries.

2. Services for the mentally retarded individual must be approached with an objective attitude as free as possible from preconceived notions of services that pertain to other populations and particularly from notions about services in urban areas.

3. The Maximum return in human welfare must be obtained from limited money and skills available in rural areas: (a) In estimating this return, means are not to be confused with ends; (b) service delivery must be adapted to the needs of an intermediate technology.

4. Generic services must be organized in a way to provide steady growth in both the quantity and quality of these services and programs.

5. Individuals should be served as close to their homes as possible in the smallest, cheapest, most humbly staffed and most simply equipped unit that is capable of adequate habilitation. Habilitation programming should be supplied to all mentally retarded people all the time. The total implementation of the concept of a "continuum of care" is seldom found in rural programs.

6. Frequently there is little relationship between the cost of a unit and its habilitative efficiency. Habilitation services can be quite effective without being comprehensive.

7. The habilitation support to a community must be related to their "needs and wants." Health workers in rural areas should be trained to a level approaching but not exceeding the threshold that enables them to leave the environment in which their services are vital.

8. Habilitation workers should undertake any task that they can be readily taught to perform with an acceptable degree of competence and in a cost-effective manner. These tasks should not be prescribed and/or limited by any professional boundaries.

9. Provisions should be made for regular supportive supervision and continuing education.

10. The role of habilitation professionals may be expected to be entirely different in rural areas than in urban areas.

11. All habilitation workers have an educational role and teaching vocation closely linked to their therapeutic role in the community. Skilled staff have a duty to teach less skilled ones.

12. Habilitative services must be carefully adapted to the opportunities and limitations of the local culture. Where possible habilitative services should do what they can to improve all aspects of a local culture with an eye toward promoting a better lifestyle for its constituents.

13. Participation of the community in the establishment, conduct, and maintenance of habilitation services and programs is to be sought. This in-

creases the understanding of the relevance of such programs and the visible outcomes and effectiveness of such services. This in turn increases the community's perception of the need for and utilization of these services.

These guidelines establish a framework that can be used to adapt community-based programs to rural areas. These guidelines, in fact, mandate particular flexibility and adaptability on the part of the community-based system in terms of the rural areas that they serve. The precise form of this service and the community-based system's function in it may well vary from setting to setting, but developing technology is helping to apply this basic framework. This technology can be shared by many community-based systems and the overall ability to expand generic services in rural areas can be improved. Several possible approaches that community-based systems might take in employing these perspectives are described in the following.

Needs Identification

As described previously, many of the successful rural medical programs were based on an accurate knowledge of the real common problems of rural people. This information was gained through several processes. One source was epidemiological research. For example, in applying health services to rural areas in New Guinea, researchers were able to identify the most common medical needs. This provided them with the goals for the technology to be taught to the rural citizens. An example of this is the barefoot doctors of China who are trained to deal with those problems that are most common. In this area, the problems are infectious disease, respiratory ailments, and malnutrition (all of which are contributory to mental retardation in the country).

In many cases epidemiological research can be conducted on the basis of documents and diagnostic survey material obtained within the rural area. Occasionally, however, such data may need to be intensively collected for random sample areas.

In collecting needs information on the mentally retarded, as opposed to general medical needs, there are some important differences. Medical needs tend to cluster around basic problems for the general population. However, with the mentally retarded the needs range is much greater. Thus, epidemiological research may well find very few diagnostic clusters for this group. It is suggested then that such survey research conducted by community-based systems be directed not so much at the diagnostic clusters but focus on the functional problems created by these clusters. In our opinion, by understanding and using this approach, a fairly cohesive set of needs could be identified.

Another approach to needs identification involves not so much the epidemiological survey approach but an actual exploration of exemplary cases in the rural area. This would involve interviewing and systematically questioning all rural families and mentally retarded individuals as to their needs. Given a precise needs identification, the community-based system can then move on to developing the required technology.

Developing Appropriate Technology

Once the general needs have been established, the next major effort is to train rural individuals to maintain self-reliance. They should learn the skills to deal with most problems, yet have ready access to a referral network to deal with the occasional difficult and exceptional problems. Subsequent to the needs identification, community-based systems should begin to match remedial therapeutic and educational technology to resolve these problems. In many cases such technology may currently exist in highly served urban areas. In other cases, specific technology may need to be developed to deal with certain problems. The really crucial problem or issue for the community-based system personnel is to adapt this technology so that it becomes appropriate and practical for rural areas. This means that it needs to become usable, applicable, and practical for families, school personnel, parent groups, and other potential local service providers. More than likely, this process of developing appropriate technology will need to be a heuristic process that is empirically verified. By this we mean that trial and error attempts must be made based on the interaction between proposed appropriate technologies, which are investigated out in the field and from which feedback is obtained from the rural constituents. This process of feedback and refinement should continue until an appropriate technology is developed. Simultaneously, such a technology must receive empirical verification in terms of its impact or output.

Trainee Selection

The next step in the model delivery service process is to identify individuals to receive training in the use of appropriate technology. Perhaps one of the most successful of the rural medical care models has been to have the actual groups concerned select personnel to receive the training. In rural areas it would be important to tap into already on-going social structures from whom individuals could be chosen. This might include fraternal organizations, parent groups, school systems, and churches. As was done in the Phillipines, it may be important to establish guidelines and criteria for this selection of trainees. It is extremely important that the trainees be individuals who are respected and considered competent by the germane social group. Also, the trainees should be individuals who most likely will remain in the rural area. And finally, the trainees should be individuals who can function well in the role of an educator and competently spread those skills that they might obtain.

Training Procedures

Again, lessons might be learned from the training experiences of rural medical care models. It was emphasized that in these models there is considerable need for a "practical" based training. This training, however, should not separate academic and theoretical material from actual clinical or applied material. In this regard it may be necessary for the appropriate community-based system or its satellite to be located within or near rural areas. Also the trainers should, to some extent, be individuals who are involved in and familiar with rural services. In short, individuals with long experience in working in a rural setting should be instructors for the program. Also, the content of the training programs should have some flexibility in that it is sensitive to these unique needs of the trainees.

Follow-Up Services

An important aspect to include in model rural delivery system models described above is to build in options for continuing education and training. These could include on-site seminars for trainees within a given area, and periodic visits back to the community-based system for specialized training. This also could be an opportunity for using appropriate telecommunications for in-service sessions and continued training. The community-based system could play a very important role in providing such needed follow-up services.

Referral System

An important aspect for having "the people" carry on the work of habilitation is that they also have access to more comprehensive services when need for such services should arise. The community-based system training can facilitate the establishment of such a referral system. An additional effect of this is that the trainees will have knowledge of the workings of the community-based system, the services that it can provide, etc. In addition, the trainees will have some personal contact with individuals from the community-based system. It should be possible for the system to assign specific staff as a referral coordinator for a given rural area. Again, selective use of telecommunications may facilitate and improve the quality of a referral system. Telecommunications may be used in the exchange of information and/or live broadcast of individuals who need additional services. In some cases it may be possible to give suggestions on programming and services from a distance. On the other hand, there may be a referral to more comprehensive services that are either provided by the community-based system or by other service providers within a more densely settled area.

Consultation

Another function that a community-based system may serve is to provide consultation within this rural habilitator model, such that difficult problems are brought to the attention of a community-based system consultant. This consultant then would serve a dual role. First, he/she could consult on a specific problem. Simultaneously, he/she would be educating the rural habilitator in terms of the services and necessary technology of treatment, education, and/or habilitation. As with the referral system and follow-up, there are also tremendous potentials for the selective use of telecommunications to facilitate this consultation process and overcome the problems of distance.

Feedback Loops

Since this whole system of the rural habilitator is based on needs identification, there should be an on-going assessment of needs. Rural habilitators could play a key role by collecting data on the types of cases they deal with, and on the needs, problems, and difficult issues that they face. This information then could be fed back into the selection, training, and other parts of the process.

Financial Assets

Obviously one of the most important issues is that of financing a rural habilitator system. Obviously some of the burden to provide training falls on the community-based system. Some funding could come from federal sources for setting up training staff. Nevertheless, it is to be expected that there be a mutual responsibility from the beginning and that local groups and social organizations be requested to finance part of the actual training process. Again, in line with the philosophy and perspective laid out in the beginning of this section, it will be crucial to work within the financial limits of the real situation. Likewise it is suggested that there be a sufficient number of trained rural habilitators who do their work not as a full-time professional career, but in addition to their other life work. Telecommunication links used in follow-up referral and consultation services may be expensive. That is why they must be used selectively and impose as little expense in terms of operation and maintenance as possible.

Training of Rural Professionals

Obviously there has not been a great deal to differentiate the training of those social workers, psychologists, and/or rehabilitation counselors who work in rural areas from those who work in the urban areas. It is suggested that community-based systems might establish modules for professionals that would prepare them to deal more successfully with rural issues and with rural programs. It has been pointed out earlier in this chapter that a key issue for rural mental retardation services is community development skills. These comprise an important part of the training of skills that a rural professional should possess. In addition, the training for the rural professional should include a section on working with and training paraprofessional rural habilitators. Another aspect of such training would be the effective use of telecommunications equipment for facilitating rural community-based system program links.

Moreover, the training should tend to focus more on the process involved in the development of human resources in rural areas. This will include sociological aspects of how people change behaviors and how people incorporate new ideas. Also, the rural professional should be trained in the development of appropriate technology. Not only in techniques developed but in the whole philosophy of appropriate technology.

SUMMARY

These suggestions delineate the role that the community-based system might play in creating a number of rural habilitators who would act to carry out habilitation and training services. These rural habilitators will be part of a new model, a model that gets away from the *expert model* that is currently being dictated to rural individuals. This model would attempt to use local people to deal with perceived local problems. It would emphasize a philosophy of normalization and of provision of service to one's neighbors. Obviously, the model of the rural habilitator and of the rural professional represents a number of dramatic shifts in our thinking. At present we are caught up in the respectful worship of high technology, of the role of the professional and the expert. Our view of rural health problems, of rural services to the mentally retarded person has been essentially materialistic. The commonly held view is that by dumping resources, masses of professionals, and masses of sophisticated equipment, and complex services into the rural areas, we can overcome the difficulties in providing services within these areas.

We suggest that our perspective on all of these counts must change. The focus for service provision must move away from the professional and expert and must focus instead on the people who really live there, work there, and know life in the rural area. Rather than fostering a sense of dependency on experts, high technology, and highly trained professionals, community-based systems must focus on cultivating within the rural populations a sense of self-reliance and an attitude of handling their own problems as well as possible. In addition this emphasis must lead to the continued development, refinement, and elaboration of material resources and must focus on the development of human resources.

Rural services for mentally retarded individuals and their families can be improved most directly, most effectively, and most permanently through the development of human resources. Similarly, the training of rural professionals must focus on those who can best facilitate this process in a practical sense. Rural professionals should not be set up as local experts but more as facilitators; people with the skills to help people help themselves. Such training obviously will include a number of topic areas that are particularly crucial for this facilitative role.

As our nation increasingly gets caught in the crunch of the cost-benefit analysis, as the imbalance between unlimited needs and limited resources is driven home again and again to our citizenry, it is going to become increasingly important to focus our efforts towards improvement of the development of human resources. We are beginning to realize that there is a limit to material resources. But human resources are virtually untapped. It is the role of the community-based system to provide quantitatively and qualitatively improved services for the rural mentally retarded citizen. This role can only be fulfilled if the community-based personnel are able to find, refine, and apply those techniques that will help to develop the human resources of rural America and any other country with rural programs.

However, this programmatic thrust must be built on a firm philosophical understanding of the what, why, how, and who of such an effort. In other words, this development of human resources cannot be a purely technical thing but must include basic philosophical considerations. It has been suggested that such a philosophical underpinning include the principle of normalization and the principle of an altruistic service.

FUTURE CONCERNS AND CONSIDERATIONS

There are many external and global variables and trends outside of the delivery of services in rural settings that will greatly affect rural programs in the future. Five major areas will have direct and indirect effects on future programs.

1. Factors that influence population changes (fertility, morbidity, mortality, migration, and inflation) have a direct causal relationship on the habits, beliefs, attitudes, and practices of clients and their subsequent care in rural settings. Twentieth century demographic trends in the United States point to several population changes which have been or soon will be major determinants for the nation's emotional, mental, and physical well being. They are:

a. Life expectancy rates in the United States have increased significantly
    from 47.3 years in 1900 to 72.8 years in 1976 and will climb to 81 by the
    end of the century.
b. The rate of U.S. population growth has slowed substantially with 4.3
    million to 2.8 million births from 1950 and 1980 respectively.
c. By the year 2000 the number of people over the age of 65 is project-
    ed to increase by approximately 9 million or from 10.7% to 12.2% of
    the total population. This trend increases demand on facilities as the
    elderly are generally in need of greater and more comprehensive service
    care. These demographic data reveal a tremendously changing client
    population whose needs require more comprehensive and extended
    services particularly in the rural areas if our goals and objectives are to
    be achieved (U.S. Department of Health, Education, and Welfare,
    1978).

2. Spiraling inflation and the continued shortage of natural resources and
the subsequent cost for energy will force dramatic changes on the lifestyle of
typical agricultural rural communities, requiring the expenditure of more
monies on natural resources, which could result in a shifting of funding away
from human resources. Transportation will be a major concern in view of
these constraints. However, limitations in this area should be offset within
the next two decades by advanced technological improvement via
telecommunications systems, video discs, and exchange of training information devices.
3. Deinstitutionalization and mainstreaming efforts will impact even
more directly on rural settings. With the increased legislative demands on
mainstreaming handicapped individuals in the public school system and services from 0–21 years of age (and above in some states), schools will be required to provide extensive services in a local community regardless of their
ability to meet manpower requirements, funding, space facilities, etc. Philo-
sophically and functionally our society over the years has shown that when
persons can be taken care of within their family it is better to do so than to
provide other environments that may be of a more restrictive nature. In addition, increasing emphasis will be placed on returning currently institutionalized individuals over age 21 to their local communities. There are
considerable legal and moral imperatives, as well as research evidence, which
demonstrate the necessity to further our efforts in this area. The solution to
meeting these concerns and problems will result in a continued network of
services throughout each state as well as a combination and collaboration of
various agencies, which will take the form of a local consortium of human
services.
4. University structures and their ability to respond is a complex issue. A
recent survey of interdisciplinary centers around the country has revealed

that academic departments, having lost some of their appeal as recipients of federal funding, continue to exercise leverage in university politics, enough to frustrate the efforts of centers in their attempts to gain funding at a time when academic financing is tight and tenure no longer guarantees job security (*Behavior Today,* 1979).

University administrators continue to show an impatience and distrust for the kinds of programs that "reach out into" local communities and that are service-oriented as well as research-oriented. This is despite the fact that federal funding is increasingly directed towards service providers of researchers and also despite the fact that national associations in the social and behavioral sciences all agree that applied work is the major thrust at this particular time. Universities rarely understand what is meant by interdisciplinary programs and in cases where they do there seems to be direct efforts to sabotage cooperation among such programs. The additional indirect costs of between 50 and 150% with some universities is increasingly taking its toll as money becomes tighter. As a result, money is being directed to state agencies in specialized centers for the delivery of services.

5. New federal guidelines and the expanded definition of developmental disabilities will put an increased burden on the already strained system for the care of our mentally retarded citizens. Additional funding will simply be needed if we are to meet our demands and this is not likely to happen from a federal support process. The new "federalism," however, is encouraging a decentralization process in which monies are being sent to states in a "block grant" process for the state and local bodies to make decisions as to the reduced allocations and support of human services. In addition to this, the realignment of the Health, Education, and Welfare Programs will have a significant impact at least until the late 80's as hundreds of thousands of employees in these departments try to adjust to the new legislation splitting up this conglomerate. By creating a Department of Education, programs have been split out in that special education, education, and rehabilitation service programs will be under this new department. Another major trend will be in the development of alternative residential service systems and it appears that we now have the technologic know-how to develop these residential services as stipulated in other chapters in this book. Our task and challenge now is simply to find dedicated people who are willing to spend the next ten years carrying out these challenges.

III SPECIAL POPULATIONS AND ISSUES

9 Serving Mentally Retarded-
Medically Fragile Persons

INTRODUCTION

We have demonstrated that in ENCOR the most severely mentally retarded persons are capable of being served in dispersed, comprehensive, community-based service systems. Biklen (1979) in his review of community-based programs in the United States pointed out several others besides ENCOR which are also serving the severely mentally retarded. Likewise, many nations are starting to develop programs and service in the mainstream of community life (Servicio Internacional del Informacion Sobre Subnormales, 1975; Mitler, 1980; Smith, 1981). Severely mentally retarded individuals with allied medical needs represent the last frontier in the application of state of the art ideological and programmatic breakthroughs. They comprise the ultimate test and challenge in fully actualizing the principle of normalization and the developmental model.

In this chapter we define and examine the basic issues inherent in serving severely mentally retarded individuals with allied medical needs in community-based programs. The primary issues are: (1) the necessary developmental approach that caregivers must take in serving severely mentally retarded, medically fragile children and adults; (2) the types of programs and services that must be developed and ensured in order to serve this population; (3) cost-benefit approaches to serving this population; and (4) manpower development for caregivers involved with this population.

This population presents a special ideological and programmatic challenge to parents and professionals (Menolascino & McGee, 1981). They fall under a large umbrella of allied disabilities such as organic brain syndrome, Lesch

Nyhan Syndrome, celebral palsy, children with poorly controlled seizures, etc. (Menolascino & Egger, 1978). Each of these symptoms adds up to the potential for custodial care and segregation if adequate and individualized services are not mobilized. The severity and multiplicity of the basic human needs of these children and adults often leaves them the last to be served, the least likely to be served, and unfortunately, the most subject to abuse (McGee, 1979). Persons with these complex needs represent a small percentage of the mentally retarded population who seek help, yet they present a high level of challenge to their caregivers and advocates both ideologically and programmatically. Although not a large population, mentally retarded-medically fragile persons are characterized by a multitude of medical needs that make both developmental intervention and community support a complex proposition. Figure 30 gives an overview of the types of common acute and chronic medical involvement presented by this population.

In the ENCOR program, with a population base of approximately 500,000 inhabitants, at any given time over 1,000 clients are receiving direct services. Of these 1,000 persons approximately 20 are mentally retarded persons who have acute medical needs requiring special medical supports. Thus, a small percentage of the community-based population will likely require the special ideological and programmatic supports due to medical needs—which we discuss in this chapter. At any given time, according to the ENCOR experience, there are another 100 persons in the community system with stabilized, yet sub-acute chronic medical needs. These persons also require specialized back-up supports.

Community-based services to the mentally retarded-medically fragile follow the same general structure as those provided to other retarded persons, although requiring (1) more intensive developmental interventions (e.g.,

FIGURE 30
CLUSTER OF ACUTE AND SUB-ACUTE CHRONIC MEDICAL NEEDS

Symptom Cluster	Etiology
1. Poorly controlled seizures	Infantile spasms
2. Cardiac and respiratory diseases	Multiple congenital defects
3. Extensive motor involvement	Cerebral palsy, massive hypotonia, persistent and primitive reflexes
4. Marked, multiple sensory impairments	Rubella, cytomegalic viral diseases
5. Failure to thrive (feeding and positioning problems)	Microcephaly, hydrocephaly
6. Frequent and recurrent infections, gastrointestinal and respiratory disorders	Cornelia de Lange Syndrome, etc.

physical therapy, speech therapy, and on-going medical consultation); (2) the availability of necesary prosthesis (e.g., positioning chairs and communication systems); and (3) the availability of generic back-up, medical support when necessary. Once out of need for acute medical care, these children and adults can return to their natural families, alternate families (in-home teachers), or small group homes. The key issue in serving this population is the provision of adequate and necessary services based on the person's needs in the most integrated setting possible. As communities develop programs for the mentally retarded, the question of serving medically fragile children inevitably arises. Two factors should be kept in mind: (1) Only a small percentage will have such needs; and (2) these needs can generally be met in ordinary community alternatives (homes, schools, and training centers), given appropriate supports. Parents and professionals need to focus on the care of persons with these needs in the mainstream of community life. Initially many parents and professionals may feel that all retarded persons are "sick." This, of course, is not so. Mental retardation is a disability which relates to learning and the ability to adapt to community life. Others may over-react to allied medical conditions such as epilepsy.

A MODEL FOR SERVING THE MEDICALLY FRAGILE

For those who do have allied medical needs such as those depicted in Figure 30, parents and professionals need to ensure that those needs be met. In the early stages of its development, ENCOR was confronted with this challenge. In 1972 a residential service was started and originally was considered as a maintenance of life program; but it soon evolved into the Developmental Maximation Unit (DMU) when it was seen that even the most profoundly retarded children with major medical needs were capable of development. Originally parents and professionals were hard-pressed to apply the principle of normalization and the developmental model to persons with these complex needs. For example, with the medically fragile, it was originally felt that some retarded individuals were so impaired that they would require basic services necessary to merely sustain life. The profession most suited to offer this service was deemed to be the medical profession and its related disciplines. The DMU service was administered by medical personnel, and operated on a hospital model. Further, it was felt that such units should be subdivided, according to age, and care should be taken that individuals were not placed in these facilities merely because they were multiply handicapped, but because they did in fact, require medical care more than any other single service. In ENCOR's initial development and residential services for the medically fragile population several issues had to be confronted:

1. Overcoming negative public and professional attitudes such as: "What can you do with these 'vegetables'?"; "If my child is at least getting something at the institution, why upset him by moving him elsewhere?"; "Aren't you just exchanging a small ward for the hopeless for the much bigger ward they are now in at the institution?"; "Why spend any money on these kids beyond three meals and a bed to sleep in, especially when you can't prove that a better alternative exists?"

2. Concerns of potential professional staff (i.e., "I've been able to help many retarded children, but these children have too many handicaps"; "These children seem too medically fragile — will they stay well long enough for periods of time for us to get a chance to teach them anything?"; "Will they ever be able to leave the DMU? It seems that they will be here until they die.") The expressions of deeply felt concerns on the part of parents who had had to fight for any services (without available alternatives), and low professional horizons of expectations for the severely retarded persisted then, and, unfortunately, continue at this time. Program personnel in DMU who had been accustomed to working with less disabled children who would make rather rapid developmental gains (and hence progress to new programs in special education classes in the community), were understandably perplexed by children who displayed so many signs and symptoms of misled developmental delay.

3. The relative paucity of information concerning programs for the severely retarded multiply handicapped as to curriculum components, equipment, and developmental expectations. This information is still scattered in the professional literature, despite attempts to disperse it (National Association for Retarded Citizens, 1973).

PLANNING CHALLENGES

The initial plan was to provide a 16-bed unit within a non-hospital model. When ENCOR was not able to locate such a facility, it was decided to initiate the program in an unused ward at a local hospital. This setting presented various problems: (1) This hospital's operating policies stated that visitors to a childrens' unit had to be restricted in number, had to wear surgical botties over thier shoes, masks on their faces, and children visitors were not permitted; (2) the kitchen facility in the unit was not considered sterile enough — yet a sterile kitchen would not meet the requirements for a home-like setting; and (3) hospital dress was a tradition. A major challenge involved training paraprofessional staff under such difficult conditions. A corollary challenge was the preparation of staff members — especially the education personnel — for the death of some of their children.

From the beginning, it was decided to have only medical and other consultants rather than full-time or part-time medical personnel. Accordingly, the medical service inputs were viewed as secondary to the full-time educational developmental thrust of the unit. Personnel selection focused on hiring a core staff of experienced persons and/or young and assertive individuals who had a positive attitude toward the children and the teaching skills so necessary to work with these children.

The children who resided at the DMU were similar to the youngsters who were typically found in infirmaries in institutions for the mentally retarded. Yet, these youngsters once placed in the DMU, were immediately involved in the routines of daily living experienced by non-handicapped peers in the community, (i.e. out of bed, dressed, involved in educational activities, etc.). The unit staff was composed of a combination of nursing and educational personnel. All staff were dressed in street clothes to de-emphasize the traditional "medical approach" to serving the severely multi-handicapped-medically fragile.

THE PROGRAM

The on-going goal of the DMU has been to prepare children to move into less structured residential and educational programs in the community. The focus of the unit's activities has been to remove obstacles to developmental growth and to discover ways to support the child when necessary. Children who are admitted to the unit are first given an intensive medical work-up by the facility's consulting pediatrician as well as other medical consultants when appropriate.

The fallacy in the original concept of a "maintenance of life" type of service was that the focus was on the mechanics of keeping a human being alive. ENCOR's initial experiences with even the most medically tenuous infants has shown that these individuals either will not be maintained at all or they will improve. Thus, life maintenance became a very transient issue and the focus shifted towards preparing to deal with the developmental growth needs of children. The new name of the service (Developmental Maximation Unit) focused on seeking the maximum developmental attainments in any youngster, despite the nature or extent of his handicaps!

A crucial first step in the DMU is a comprehensive medical screening, performed for two reasons: (1) Many children coming from the institution have precious little or no reliable medical data provided; (2) in order to establish significant learning objectives, the initial medical evaluation must focus on interventions capable of removing or managing medical deterrants to growth and development. For example, a child who is frequently seizuring has very little energy or time left for educational or social activities. A child with a complete hip dislocation cannot be comfortably placed in an upright position so he/she may interact with the environment. A child with frequent upper respiratory infections must spend a major portion of the time in a croupette or isolation. These initial (and periodical) diagnostic services are provided to every child *regardless* of the degree of handicap or the prognosis from previous medical opinions derived elsewhere.

The nursing staff is responsible for the administration of medications and treatments ordered by the unit's consultants, providing direct nursing care to critically ill children, and assisting both the unit's medical and other consultants in providing services to the residents.

A significant proportion of medical procedures are performed by the unit's educational staff. The rationale for this approach is that many procedures traditionally assumed to be medical maintenance activities can be seen instead as having direct implications to the child's overall learning process and can be incorporated as part of the educational day. For example, passive and active range of motion, postural drainage, and therapeutic bracing activities are provided by the teaching staff. The educational curriculum focuses on the areas of gross and fine motor development, self-help skills, pre-language development, and socialization. These curricular objectives are often very basic. For example, self-care objectives may signify such learning as sucking and chewing. Language stimulation may signify visual teaching, gestures indicating "yes" and "no." It is necessary to define education in very basic terms. Program staff continuously monitor growth, in both educational and medical maintenance activities through the use of precision teaching techniques (Koenig, 1972; Lindsley, 1964).

Because of the need to provide culturally appropriate routines and rhythms, the children's daily schedule of activities approximate as closely as possible to those routines experienced by normal children in the community, i.e., more informal activities on weekends and holidays. Children are taken out into the community in small groups to restaurants, shopping centers, movies, the zoo, etc., using the community as a classroom. Through the use of a staff advocate system, the children are taken out "individually" into the community at a high frequency. Also, parents are encouraged to take their children out in the evenings and on weekends. If the child cannot go out, parents and siblings are allowed to visit at any time. Many parents take their child home for weekends and holidays.

As soon as a child demonstrates reasonable medical stability (i.e., tolerates supported sitting position, infection free, seizures fairly well controlled) he/she moves to an alternative day program in the community as a first step toward "graduating" from the program.

Since its inception in 1972 the DMU has "graduated" over 150 medically fragile children into their families or surrogate families in the community.

Once medical needs are stabilized the children invariably move into family settings with the support required for each child.

Jenny is a typical example of a child who has received the services of the DMU. Jenny was admitted to the DMU in 1972 at age three. She had been in a state institution since three months of age after surgery for spina bifida and hydrocephaly. Her parents had been told that she would never to able to learn, care for herself, or even respond to the world around her. When she entered the DMU at age three she had a chronic urinary infection that was threatening her life. This condition was corrected through surgery and her subsequent physical improvement was dramatic. Within a year Jenny was placed in an integrated pre-school. She began to acquire language and other developmental skills at a rapid rate: maneuvering herself on parallel bars, and in her wheelchair, naming her body parts, etc. After one more year Jenny moved back to her natural family with twenty hours of in-home support provided by ENCOR staff.

Jenny is an excellent example of a child moving along a continuum of services for the mentally retarded-medically fragile as indicated in Figure 31.

In the ENCOR region infants and children are no longer admitted to institutions due to medical problems. Those with acute medical needs are treated in generic, neo-natal intensive care units. As acute medical needs are cared for, the children move into the DMU. In communities around the world we would recommend a similar approach.

MEDICAL-DEVELOPMENTAL SERVICES

We have described the history and function of ENCOR's Developmental Maximation Unit. A small percentage of infants and children have sub-acute medical needs that require transitional round-the-clock medical monitoring. This need should also be coupled with intensive developmental programming. As the children's medical needs stabilize, they should them move into more integrative settings.

These more integrative settings consist of three primary options; small, specialized group homes, foster homes, or preferably return to the natural family. Whichever the residential setting, the following factors need to be dealt with:

1. Parent or staff training specify the medical and developmental needs of the particular child.
2. Adaptation of the environment to meet the physical needs of the child. These adaptations include a barrier-free residence, special communication devices, lifting devices, etc.

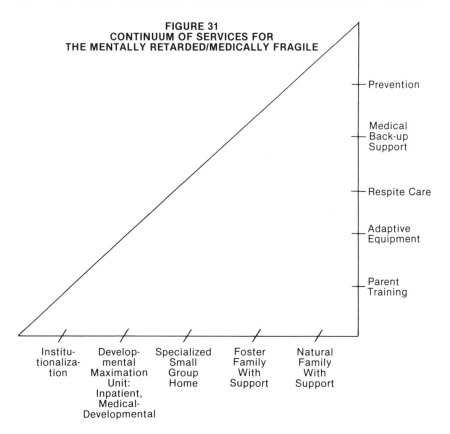

FIGURE 31
CONTINUUM OF SERVICES FOR
THE MENTALLY RETARDED/MEDICALLY FRAGILE

Prevention

Medical Back-up Support

Respite Care

Adaptive Equipment

Parent Training

| Institu-tionaliza-tion | Develop-mental Maximation Unit: Inpatient, Medical-Developmental | Specialized Small Group Home | Foster Family With Support | Natural Family With Support |

3. Respite services for the caregivers, providing specially trained sitters either in the home or out-of-the home.
4. Medical back-up support includes the monitoring of the child's physical condition and any medications, medical consultations, etc.

Jenny moved through such a continuum: institution, DMU, home with support. All mentally retarded-medically fragile children should have the opportunity to receive such supports. (This support is cost-beneficial as is shown in Chapter 11.) The continuum prevents institutionalization; but, more importantly, enables the child's presence and participation in community life.

10 Serving the Mentally Retarded-Mentally Ill

The mentally retarded-mentally ill represent the last group of retarded persons in the United States to move into the mainstreams of family and community life since they present multiple programmatic and environmental challenges. Their needs are often poorly identified and services to meet their needs are few and far between. Professionals often refer them from one agency to another because they fall between the cracks in most service delivery systems.

In this chapter we identify the psychiatric dimensions of mental retardation through an analysis of the needs of 305 mentally retarded-mentally ill individuals and outline the range of programs and services required by this population. Recent studies confirm the findings that 25 to 35% of the mentally retarded population has associated signs and symptoms indicative of mental illness (Chess & Hassibi, 1970; Donoghue & Abbas, 1971; Eaton & Menolascino, 1982; Groden, Domingue, Pueschel, & Deignan, 1982; Menolascino, 1969; Philips & Williams, 1975). This dual diagnosis presents unique clinical and programmatic challenges to professionals in the field of mental retardation and mental health. These challenges are further heightened by the escalating integration of mentally retarded children and adults into the mainstreams of family and community life (Menolascino & McGee, 1981). As retarded persons are served in public schools, group homes, sheltered workshops, and other community-based programs, professionals are confronted with the challenge of serving persons who are not only mentally retarded, but also mentally ill.

THE PSYCHIATRIC DIMENSIONS OF MENTAL RETARDATION

When mental retardation is compounded by allied psychiatric disorders, integration into community life becomes a dual challenge. In order to determine the range of programs and services necessary to meet the needs of the mentally retarded-mentally ill, it is first important to review the types and frequency of psychiatric disorders found in the mentally retarded. Therefore, in the first part of this chapter we report the findings of a recent study of 305 mentally retarded persons with coexisting mental illness. This study was conducted in an acute-care unit at the Nebraska Psychiatric Institute. This unit provides back-up support to Nebraska's community-based mental retardation programs and institutions for the mentally retarded.

From June 1979 through December 1981, 305 persons with a dual diagnosis were evaluated individually by an interdisciplinary team. The study group ranged in age from three to 76 years. Those age five and under represented 1.6% of the study group; age six to ten years comprised 2.6%; age 11 to 15, 8.8%; age 16 to 20, 23.2%; age 21 to 25, 20.6%; age 26 to 30, 10.8%; age 31 to 35, 9%; and over 36, 22.9%. The group was 66% male due to a disproportionately large number of adolescent males. Fo all other age groups, males and females were found in approximately equal numbers. Diagnoses in this sample were based primarily on DSM–III criteria. The types of psychiatric disorders and their frequency are seen in Fig. 32.

The psychiatric disorders in order of frequency were (1) schizophrenic disorders, 29%; (2) organic brain disorders, 19.6%; (3) adjustment reactions, 16.3%; (4) non-specific mental disorders, 13.1%; (5) personality disorders, 10.8%; (6) affective disorders, 6.5%; (7) neurotic disorders, 2.2%; and (8) special symptoms, 1.3%.

Schizophrenia

The 87 patients with schizophrenia included 39 with chronic undifferentiated schizophrenia; seven with schizo-affective schizophrenia; 13 with chronic paranoid schizophrenia; six with catatonic schizophrenia; and 23 with residual schizophrenia. Schizophrenia remains as the most frequently reported type of major mental illness in mentally retarded individuals (Menolascino, 1983).

Psychotic reactions of childhood have presented a major challenge to the clinician since their early recognition as distinct entities by DeSanctis in the early 1900s. Delineation of types of etiologies has been delayed, in part, by the fact that psychotic children frequently function at a mentally retarded level, and early observers believed that all psychotic children "deteriorated." In 1943, "early infantile autism" was described by Kanner (1943). Yet, to la-

FIGURE 32
MENTAL ILLNESS IN THE MENTALLY RETARDED*

Psychiatric Diagnoses	Ages								
	1-5	6-10	11-15	16-20	21-25	26-30	31-35	Over 35	Totals
Organic Brain Disorders									
Organic Brain Syndrome									
—Psychotic Reaction	1			1	7	4		2	15
—Behavioral Reaction		3	11	1	11		7	3	36
Presenile Dementia							3	6	9
									60
Schizophrenic Disorders									
—Catatonic	1			3		1		1	6
—Chronic Paranoid				9				4	13
—Schizo-Affective				1	5		1		7
—Chronic Undiff.				12	4	8	3	12	39
—Residual				5				18	23
									88
Affective Disorders									
—Unipolar Manic Disorder				3	2				5
—Bipolar Affective								2	2
—Depressive Disorder					1	1		1	3
—Unspecified			3	1		2		4	10
									20
Neurotic Disorders									
—Anxiety				1					1
—Depression				1	1		2	2	6
									7
Personality Disorders									
—Schizoid				1	3				4
—Explosive						1	1		2
—Passive Dependent				1		1		2	4
—Narcissistic						2	3	1	6
—Avoidant				1	1			1	3
—Passive Aggressive				3	3		5	2	13
—Unspecified				1					1
									33
Special Symptoms									
—Anorexia Nervosa		1	3						4
									4
Adjustment Reactions									
—Childhood and Adol.	3	2	6	23					34
—Adulthood					6	3	3	4	16
									50
Non-Specific Mental Disorders									
—Pervasive Developmental			1	4	1				6
—Disturbance of Conduct		1	2	4	9	8	2	2	28
—Undersoc.-Aggressive			1		4	1		2	8
									42

N = 305

*A review of retarded patients at NPI: June 1979 through December 1981

bel a child "autistic" presents some formidable problems with regard to diagnostic and treatment considerations. A number of follow-up studies (Menolascino & Eaton, 1967; Rutter & Schopler, 1978), coupled with the rediscovery of the wide variety of primitive behavioral repertoires in the retarded, have tended to mute the earlier clinical enthusiasm concerning the functional psychoses and their inter-relationships to mental retardation.

In this study it was noted that 25 adolescent patients displayed indices of both mental retardation and schizophrenia — the latter having been noted very early in life. For example, the presence of bizarre behavior, persistent withdrawal, echolalic speech, and affective unavailability in early adolescents who had clearly experienced regressive symptomatology from an earlier higher level of functioning, was striking. Three of these adolescents illustrated the superimposition of childhood schizophrenia (i.e., by past history the schizophrenic illness in all three had begun between ages four and six) upon etiologically clear instances of mental retardation (e.g., one had Down's Syndrome, one was post-rubella, and the third had a major cranial malformation as the cause of his mental retardation). Since treatment guidelines are markedly different for youngsters with "autistic" reactions to extremely bewildering extrinsic circumstances, and the combined mental retardation/childhood schizophrenia syndrome noted here, this differential diagnosis is therapeutically significant beyond academic interests.

Adult Schizophrenia and Mental Retardation

Although some clinicians seriously question whether the markedly primitive behaviors noted at certain levels of mental retardation (e.g., severe level with associated poor language evolution) can be separated from schizophrenia, this was not our experience. Significantly, the instances of paranoid schizophrenia were noted in both verbal and nonverbal patients. Included in our sample of the latter were three adults who drew out on paper their "attackers," replete with nonverbal gestures. One such young man would label his separate fingers as the "source" of his common delusions, which he would portray symbolically in crude drawings. Paranoid and catatonic features were the hallmarks of the acute/chronic undifferentiated schizophrenic groups. In the entire group of combined diagnoses of mental retardation and schizophrenia, it was noted that the altered effect responses, hallucinatory phenomena, bizarre rituals, and utilization of interpersonal distancing devices clearly marked the observed behaviors as being in the schizophrenic repertoire.

Organic Brain Syndrome

The diagnosis of an organic brain syndrome (O.B.S.) with a behavioral or psychotic disorder has been descriptively delineated in the previous studies of these disorders in the retarded (Menolascino, 1977). In the present study, criteria for this diagnosis was evidence of an organic brain syndrome by mental status, physical-neurological examinations, and/or personal-clinical history of etiologically significant factors. The diagnosis of *O.B.S. with behavioral reaction* was utilized for the sub-group who displayed inappropriate acting out behaviors against a backdrop of delayed/disorganized personality figures (e.g., emotional lability, impulsivity, frequent tantrums, but no psychotic symptoms). The sub-group with evidence of *O.B.S. and psychotic disorder* presented a different clinical picture than schizophrenia because: (1) the underlying organic brain syndrome signs and symptoms of the disorder were prominent; (2) their out-of-contact behaviors — though the diagnostic hallmark of their presenting clinical picture — were not the type commonly seen in schizophrenia (e.g., no hallucinatory experiences); and (3) their personality structures did not show the progressive involvement of multiple segments of functioning that is characteristic of schizophrenia. Using these critiera, 20% of the study group was found to have O.B.S. with behavioral or psychotic reactions.

Personality Disorders

Personality disorders are characterized by chronically maladaptive patterns of behavior (e.g., antisocial personality, passive-aggressive personality, etc.), which are qualitatively different from psychotic or neurotic disorders (Diagnostic and Statistical Manual of Mental Disorders, Volume III, 1980). Studies reported in the early history of retardation tended indiscriminately to view antisocial behavior as an expected behavioral accompaniment to mental retardation (Barr, 1904). The antisocial personality designation continues to receive much attention, and is frequently over-represented in mildly retarded individuals. It would appear that behavioral problems of an antisocial nature are more frequently seen in this group because the same poverty of interpersonal relationships during childhood that lead to many cases of retardation tend to also lead to impaired object relations and poorly internalized controls (Menolascino & Strider, 1981). Likewise, it leads to reduced frequency of consistent parental/societal expectations and to a higher frequency of poor role models. The diminished coping skills of this group often necessitates their performing deviant acts simply to exist, and reduced judgments makes the acts more ego syntonic. Finally, this group is most likely to be released from institutional settings in young adulthood and to illustrate graphically the effects of institutional detachment on the development of early personality structure.

It is interesting to note that although other personality disorders (e.g, schizoid personality) have been reported in the retarded, we noted this disorder in only four patients. The only other personality disorder in the retarded that has received much attention is the "inadequate personality," even though the application of exact diagnostic criteria would exclude this disorder as a primary diagnosis in mental retardation. In our experience personality disorders occurred in mentally retarded individuals whose behavior was based primarily on extrinsic factors and had no distinct etiological relationship(s) to the symptoms of mental retardation. The presence of personality disorders in 9% of our sample suggests that this group of disorders is not an infrequent accompanying psychiatric handicap for mentally retarded citizens.

Psychoneurotic Disorders

Earlier reviews (Beier, 1964) on this type of mental illness in the retarded suggested a low frequency. Interestingly, these reports suggest that psychoneurotic disorders are more common in individuals in the high-moderate and mild levels of mental retardation and have prompted speculation as to whether the relative complexity of psychoneurotic transaction is beyond the adaptive limits of the more severely retarded. However, recent studies (Menolascino, 1977; May & May, 1979) disputing the concept of incompatability between neuroses and retardation are quite explicit with respect to diagnostic criteria, and attribute the neurotic phenomena to factors associated with atypical developmental patterns in conjunction with disturbed family functioning. For example, psychoneurotic disorders in retarded children clearly link symptoms of anxiety (e.g., fear of failure and insecurity) to exogenous factors such as chronic frustration, unrealistic family expectations, and persistent interpersonal deprivation. These reported findings are not consistent with our experience of noting only seven mentally retarded individuals with psychoneurosis.

Adjustment Reactions of Childhood, Adolescence, or Adulthood

Although this category of psychiatric disorders is perhaps over-utilized in the assessment of the non-retarded, it is only infrequently employed during clinical assessment of mental illness in the retarded population. In this study, one of the highest frequencies of psychiatric disorders was noted to be the adjustment reaction: 16.3% of the total sample. Mentally retarded individuals, by their frequency or organic predisposition to over-reacting to stimuli and limited understanding of social-interpersonal expectations, are highly "at risk" for personality disorganization secondary to minimal interpersonal stress. In our experience, these adjustment reactions are most frequently caused by continuing inappropriate social-adaptive expectations, or unexpected and frequent changes in externally imposed life patterns. Clinically, they respond rapidly to environmental adjustment (when coupled with specific counseling to realign the parental or the residential/educational personnel's unrealistic expectations or goals), and supportive psychotherapy.

As more retarded persons remain in or return to the community, adjustment reaction problems are appearing at a higher frequency than previously noted. Their presence in the community reveals a tendency for some retarded persons to have extreme difficulty in life changes. With the more severely retarded, even changes in classroom or teacher changes, movements from one group home to another, staff turnover, etc., can elicit serious adjustment problems.

THE DUAL DIAGNOSIS

Levels of Mental Retardation

All levels of mental retardation were seen in this study group — from severe-profound mental retardation to mild. While the presence of the previously noted range of psychiatric disorders in the non-retarded population presents multiple clinical and programmatic challenges, these challenges are compounded when occurring in the mentally retarded. Figure 33 depicts the incidence of psychiatric disorders as found in the different levels of retardation in our sample.

Each level of mental retardation presents special challenges in the diagnosis and treatment of the mentally retarded-mentally ill. The study group not only represents the entire range of psychiatric disorders, but also all levels of retardation. Whereas previous studies have focused on institutionalized retarded persons who are generally in the more severe range of retardation, our study represents the entire spectrum of mental retardation.

Severe-Profound Mental Retardation

The severely retarded are characterized by gross central nervous system impairment and a high frequency of multiple handicaps, especially sensory im-

FIGURE 33
LEVELS OF MENTAL RETARDATION:
MENTALLY ILL/MENTALLY RETARDED

LEVELS OF MENTAL RETARDATION	
— Mild	55.7%
— Moderate	25.3%
— Severe/Profound	19.0%

N = 305

pairments and seizure disorders. This population has a high vulnerability to psychiatric disorders (Chess, Horn, & Fernandez, 1971). The moderately retarded likewise present marked vulnerabilities for adequate personality development due to their slower rate of development and their need to problem-solve through concrete approaches. Webster (1971) viewed the personality vulnerabilities of the moderately retarded as stemming from the interpersonal postures that the moderately retarded tend to use in their interpersonal transactions. These encompass selective isolation (benign autism), inflexibility and repetitiousness, passivity, and a simplicity to their emotional life. The mildly retarded present other challenges due to their difficulty in understanding the symbolic abstractions of school work and the complexities of social-adaptive expectations from their family and peer groups.

Besides the vulnerability of the mentally retarded to mental health problems due to the level of mental retardation, other developmental disorders often cause breakdowns in their ability to participate in on-going interpersonal and social transactions. A major allied developmental problem is the inability of retarded persons to process information from the world around them and the inability to express basic needs and emotions. Nearly all of the mentally retarded-mentally ill persons cited in Fig. 33 had severe language and communication disorders, both in terms of receptive and expressive language.

A major cause of the vulnerability of the retarded, especially the more severely retarded, to mental illness is their inability to process information from the world around them. Persons with more severe retardation are often overstimulated by external stimuli and react to this overstimulation through self-abusive, aggressive, or self-stimulatory primitive behaviors. In a sense, these behaviors are forms of communication—nonverbal ways of responding to an otherwise confusing world.

The moderately and mildly retarded present allied challenges in the area of language and communication; however, in a more subtle manner. They typically possess language and are able to verbalize their needs and emotions. Yet, these verbalizations are often deceptive in that they can mask the full depth of their interpersonal and intrapersonal distress.

It is crucial to take into account the impact of these communication disorders in assessing the needs of the mentally retarded-mentally ill. The observed behavioral disorders of the mentally retarded should be considered in light of their likely communication and language disorders.

Another critical factor to consider is the range of allied medical disorders often found in this population. Figure 34 outlines the major allied medical disorders found in the aforementioned study of mentally retarded-mentally ill patients at the Nebraska Psychiatric Institute. Thirty-seven percent had major medical disorders upon admission for treatment.

The major allied medical problem stemmed from seizure activity. Over 22% of the persons studied had on-going seizure disorders ranging from

FIGURE 34
ASSOCIATED MEDICAL AND
DEVELOPMENTAL DISABILITIES

Cerebral Palsy	12
Grand Mal Epilepsy	42
Psychomotor Epilepsy	8
Petit Mal Epilepsy (minor form)	8
Petit Mal Epilepsy (major: myoclonic)	10
Acute Otitis Media	11
Congenital Deafness	8
Diabetes Mellitus	6
Hypothyroidism	8

grand mal to petit mal. These disorders tend to compound and exacerbate the problems inherent in both mental retardation and mental illness, leaving the person in a confused state and incapable of interpersonal and intrapersonal transactions.

Conclusion

The mentally retarded are vulnerable to the entire range of psychiatric disorders. Mental retardation itself in its various levels presents unique problems in terms of the person's ability to process information and respond to and cope with stress. Furthermore, the occurrence of allied medical problems, especially seizure disorders, further compounds the treatment challenges.

Because of the nature of the dual diagnosis, it is necessary to define and provide a continuum of care to meet the chronic and acute needs of the mentally retarded-mentally ill across their lifespan. In the next section of this chapter, we outline such a continuum of programs and services.

A CONTINUUM OF CARE

The mentally retarded-mentally ill present a unique range of psychiatric and developmental needs across their lifespan, as indicated in the previous section. To determine the types of programs and services this population requires, it is helpful to focus on the range of residential and developmental programs that can help the mentally retarded-mentally ill become integrated in the mainstream of community life. A continuum of care must be able to respond to the needs of the mentally retarded-mentally ill at any given point in their lives with whatever programs and services are necessary to maintain them in or return them to the mainstream of family and community life, whether it be direct services such as acute care and specialized group homes, or supportive services such as counseling and case management. Figure 35 depicts a suggested continuum of residential alternatives needed to meet the residential needs of this population.

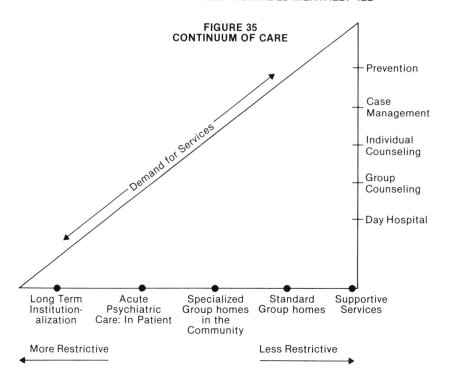

FIGURE 35
CONTINUUM OF CARE

Long-Term Institutionalization

A very small percentage of mentally retarded-mentally ill persons require long-term hospitalization. The primary criterion for such a placement is that the person poses a chronic threat to himself or to others. The data in Fig. 35 reveals six patients who were institutionalized for this reason; specifically, unpredictable, aggressive behaviors and/or self-injurious behaviors, as well as sexually deviant behaviors, such as repeated child molestation. Of the six, the following were the primary reasons; suicide attempts, child molestation, and violently aggressive behaviors. It should be kept in mind that these disorders represent an extremely small percentage of the population, six out of 305 persons.

Besides such person-specific reasons, it must be admitted that institutions play a socio-political role; since it is only recently that communities have started to develop programs and services for the mentally retarded-mentally ill, many communities cannot yet serve this population with extensive, quality services. In the foreseeable future some retarded persons with mental illness will remain institutionalized or will be admitted to institutions.

Whether this population is institutionalized for clinical or socio-political reasons, institutions can play a significant role in meeting their needs through the structure they provide and the preparation of each person for eventual integration into community life. The rate and speed of this integration will depend largely on the development of adequate and appropriate community alternatives.

Acute Psychiatric Care: In-patient Services

A vital issue in the continuum of care is the ability to meet the acute psychiatric needs of the mentally retarded, e.g., treating persons with acute psychiatric symptomatology such as aggressive or self-injurious behaviors, withdrawal, or hallucinatory behaviors. In the proposed continuum this is provided through inpatient, acute psychiatric care services capable of treating psychotic symptomatology such as hyperactivity, self-abusive, aggressive acts, withdrawal, etc. The mentally retarded should have access to acute psychiatric care just as any other citizen. At the same time, this service should be specialized to meet the unique needs of retarded persons.

THE NEBRASKA PSYCHIATRIC INSTITUTE MODEL

An example of an acute care psychiatric service is Nebraska Psychiatric Institute's (NPI) Mental Retardation Unit (Levi, Roberts, & Menolascino, 1979), which serves as Nebraska's primary acute-care facility for the mentally retarded-mentally ill. In 1979, NPI established a six bed inpatient unit to focus on this population. In 1981, NPI expanded its services to the mentally retarded-mentally ill by opening an adjacent specialized unit — increasing the total bed commitment to 15 (out of NPI's 85 bed facility). The primary purpose of this unit is to meet the acute, psychiatric needs of the mentally retarded-mentally ill. A special team of professionals and paraprofessionals was identified to focus treatment on this population and to act as a back-up support.

During the retarded patient's hospitalization in NPI (which lasts an average of 35 days), the primary treatment goal consists of decreasing interfering behaviors to a level wherein each person can be integrated into appropriate community residential, vocational, educational, and leisure activities. There is an intense focus on re-directing and then substituting the presenting abnormal atypical or premature behaviors with appropriate behaviors through a closely scheduled, active, and developmentally-oriented treatment day. Individual psychotherapy, educational therapy, and individualized occupational and recreational therapy are all utilized in conjunction with active family (or alternative caretaker) involvement. Concurrent with this central treatment approach is the judicious utilization of psychoactive medications as a treatment adjunct for initially assisting each person to become more actively engaged in appropriate psychosocial and developmental activities. Rather than focusing unduly on the role of psychoactive medications — a professional posture for which psychiatry has been frequently criticized — the *adjunctive* role of these medications is stressed in the overall treatment approach.

The careful selection, training, and attention to the administration of the programmatic personnel on this special unit is important. Primary professional personnel include: (1) a clinical psychiatrist with a long history of involvement in the psychiatric aspects of mental retardation; (2) a part-time clinical psychopharmacologist; (3) a charge nurse; (4) three shift nurses; (5) a consistent paraprofessional-to-patient staffing with the capacity for one-to-one staffing when necessary (6) an on-staff community liaison person; (7) a part-time social worker, and (8) a part-time psychologist. Specially trained personnel are utilized on a daily scheduled basis, as well as any other necessary resources.

An important aspect of an acute care service is to define its role as a back-up support to other programs and services. This role primarily consists of: (1) acute psychiatric care; (2) crisis intervention; (3) parent training; (4) staff training; (5) program monitoring; (6) medication monitoring; and (7) public education. Though these foci are *not* "new" in the contemporary treatment-management approaches for the mentally ill, they *are* rarely utilized for the mentally retarded-mentally ill population.

Specialized Group Homes

Once a retarded person's acute needs are cared for, transition to community living can be achieved through specialized, community-based group homes. For most persons these homes can be short-term (three to six months); for some they will be long-term (two to three years).

The goal of the specialized group home is the stabilization of the person's behaviors in a community setting and gradual integration into community life. A specialized group home is characterized by:

1. *Structure.* The group home structures the person's day based on his/her current ability to attend to appropriate tasks and interactions. It utilizes the normal flow of the day (self-care and independent living skills) as the mechanism for redirecting and reinforcing the person toward appropriate tasks and interactions.
2. *Staffing Intensity and Flexibility.* The group home provides a staffing pattern sufficient to meet the developmental-behavioral needs of each person. Initially, some persons may require 1:1 staffing. This is provided and then faded down to a 3:1 ratio as soon as possible.
3. *Client Mix.* The group home is careful to match the small group (three to six persons) living together so that the group is as compatible as pos-

sible. Even though all the residents are mentally retarded-mentally ill, the individualized mix of clients avoids inappropriate grouping such as a disproportionate mix of nonverbal clients, acting out clients, self-injurious clients, etc.

4. *Developmental Orientation.* The group home provides a teaching atmosphere. It is recognized that each person, regardless of the severity of the dual diagnosis, is capable of change across time. Each person has an individualized program plan. The initial goal is to gain instructional control over the maladaptive behaviors (e.g., self-abusive, self-stimulatory, aggressive, or avoidant behaviors) through the constant and consistent redirection of those behaviors and the subsequent reinforcement of appropriate behaviors and interactions.

5. *Behavioral Analysis Orientation.* The group home bases itself primarily on the technology of applied behavioral analysis, yet with a special focus on the gaining of appropriate behaviors. Behavioral procedures focus on the acquisition of appropriate behaviors rather than the elimination of maladaptive behaviors.

6. *Balanced Use of Psychoactive Medications.* The group home uses psychoactive medications as an adjunct to developmental-behavioral programming. Medications are only used as a means to initially bring the person's interfering behaviors to the point where developmental programming can take over. As this occurs, medications are then reduced or eliminated.

7. *Comprehensiveness.* The group home is part of a continuum of services that enables movement into less restrictive, less structured residential alternatives, as well as movement into acute care when necessary.

8. *Consistency with Day Program.* The group home functions in coordination with educational and vocational day programs so that each person is ensured of a full developmentally-oriented program. All day programs are outside of the group home.

9. *Stability.* The group home generally is short-term — three to six months. Most clients then move into less structured residential alternatives. However, for some persons, the group home may be a more long-term placement (up to two to three years) in order to provide the stability, the relationship building, and the time which the person needs to acquire the skills necessary to live in a less structured setting.

Other Community-Based Alternatives

Once the mentally retarded-mentally ill person's acute and sub-acute psychiatric needs are controlled and stabilized, a community should be able to respond to his/her needs with a range of less restrictive and less structured alternatives. These take the form of group homes that serve the general retarded population, foster homes, support of the person in his/her natural family, etc. As this movement occurs, the continuum of care should ensure that adequate supportive services exist in the community so that the person's mental health needs are met on an on-going basis. Such supportive services are: (1) day hospitals capable of assisting retarded persons in transition into and maintenance in the mainstream of community life (Fletcher, 1982); (2) individual and group counseling to deal with on-going behavioral-emotional problems (Baron, 1972; Berkovitz & Sugar, 1975; Fletcher, 1982); and (3) case management services to ensure appropriate program planning, coordination, and monitoring (Baucom & Bensberg, 1976).

An emerging trend on the part of mental health programs is the provision of day-hospital services for the mentally retarded-mentally ill. Fletcher (1982) describes one such day treatment program as a specialized treatment program within a community health center. Its goal is to provide an opportunity for mentally ill-mentally retarded adults to participate in an combination of clinical, prevocational, social, and recreational services. This particular day treatment program meets the needs of its clients on a part-time program (one to two days per week) while the clients continue in their vocational and residential community-based mental retardation programs. Support to the clients is provided through a series of structured group activities: group therapy, horticultural therapy, community meetings, music therapy, educational supports, etc. Fletcher (1982) reports measured increases in positive feelings about the self, more involvement in socialization activities, improved impulse control, and more effective problem-solving.

Along with the aforementioned supportive services, it is necessary to have a continuum of educational supportive services, and leisure time services so that the person is fully in family and community life. The residential alternatives need to be in close coordination with the person's public school, sheltered workshops or other vocational placement. Likewise, they need to involve the person as much as possible in the community's social-recreational life.

An Example of the Mentally Retarded-Mentally III in a Comprehensive Community-Based Service System

In Chapter 5 we described the ENCOR system, which serves the general retarded population as well as persons with the dual diagnosis of mental retardation from mild to severe and the entire range of psychiatric disorders. The population includes clients who have been institutionalized and those who have never been institutionalized. ENCOR, like most other community-based service systems, serves the vast majority of the mentally retarded-emotionally disturbed in non-specialized services, for they do not require extraordinary programmatic services and supports. However, a certain percentage require specialized supports and services due to the severity and complexity of their dual diagnosis.

In April 1982, the authors examined the records of the 1,045 ENCOR clients to determine the number of mentally retarded persons who presented significant programmatic challenges. This survey classified ENCOR clients into three levels: (Level 1) clients who presented daily high frequency behavioral management problems, such as the inability to attend to tasks, self-abusive behaviors, aggressive behaviors, hyperactivity, etc.; (Level 2) clients who presented occasional behavioral problems per month; (Level 3) clients who presented behavioral problems on several occasions throughout the year. Eighty-one ENCOR clients within these three levels presented programmatic challenges significant enough to warrant specialized supports and services with respect to type of personnel treating this population, staffing patterns and intensity, need for back-up supports such as special consultants, and the availability of acute psychiatric care services. Figure 36 shows the number of persons with these special needs by level and by service catchment areas (divided into urban or rural areas).

This population of 81 mentally retarded-mentally ill clients within the ENCOR service system is capable of being served in community-based settings, given adequate treatment supports. Figure 36 also displayed the types of residential, educational, and vocational services that these 81 persons receive. They are rather evenly dispersed across the five county urban-rural ENCOR catchment area.

It is important to note that mentally retarded-mentally ill persons of all ages and levels of mental illness can be served in a community-based service system. The 81 persons served in the ENCOR program represent the entire range of psychiatric disorders and present a myriad of programmatic and treatment challenges. Figure 36 outlined the primary symptom clusters and etiologies represented in this identified group.

FIGURE 36
MENTALLY RETARDED/MENTALLY ILL PERSONS REQUIRING
SPECIALIZED SERVICES

Service	Number	Ages				Types of Services				
		0-5	6-21	22-50	51+	School	Vocational Training	Group Home	Foster Home	Family
Urban Areas	55	2	14	34	5	13	42	37	10	8
Rural Areas	26	0	1	24	1	1	25	22	4	0
Total	81	2	15	58	6	14	67	59	14	8

Different programmatic and treatment modalities are based on the intensity and types of behavioral-emotional problems presented. For example, a client who displays high intensity, self-abusive behavior would require a service modality distinct from a mildly retarded person who displayed aggressive behaviors only a few times per year. The self-abusive person might require acute psychiatric care to rapidly decrease such behaviors, followed by a specialized transactional group home setting. The person with occasional aggressive behaviors might only require a highly structured group home setting, with well-trained paraprofessional staff with periodic psychiatric follow-along.

In the ENCOR program the following specific factors aid in serving this challenging population:

1. Acute psychiatric care is available for the small percentage of clients who require it on any given day. Out of the 1,045 mentally retarded persons in ENCOR, two to four persons require acute psychiatric care in a hospital setting for an average of 35 days. This service need is met through the use of generic psychiatric hospitals in the community.
2. Specialized group homes designed to transition persons with sub-acute behavioral needs into less intensive residential settings. These group homes serve no more than six persons. Care is taken to ensure a compatible mixture of persons within each group. Staff is especially trained to deal with the behavioral needs of the residents. Special back-up support is available, as well as follow-along services from professionals in generic agencies in the community.
3. All clients are served in community-based day programs, i.e., public schools and sheltered workshops with necessary supportive services.
4. Practicum training is provided to all paraprofessional staff and/or parents in the area of behavior management as needed. Staffing patterns are higher in these programs (typically one staff for every two clients) until behaviors are brought under control. All staff are regarded as teachers — with the primary responsibility of gaining control over the behaviors through non-aversive techniques.

The types of programs in which these persons participate are the same as those available to all other retarded persons — group homes, public schools, sheltered workshops, etc. Staff is specifically trained to deal with highly aggressive or self-abusive behaviors. Individualized services are well monitored by ENCOR caseworkers and, where necessary, secondary support is called upon, such as special consultative services or hospitalization for acute care. These services typically cost nearly half that of long-term institutionalization, yet provide maximum developmental benefits such as dramatic decreases in maladaptive behaviors, the acquisition of appropriate behaviors and the integration of persons with these special needs into the mainstream of family and community life.

The ENCOR model demonstrates: (1) the mentally retarded-mentally ill can be served in dispersed residential, educational, and vocational settings; (2) there is a need to specialize staff and programs to meet the unique needs of this population; (3) it is important to have a range of services and back-up supports available; (4) initial staffing patterns need to be flexible; and (5) the availability of inpatient, acute psychiatric care is an important dimension in the continuum of care.

TREATMENT ISSUES

Within the framework of the continuum of care, it is important to define a general treatment approach that will enable the mentally retarded-mentally ill to enter into or remain in the mainstream of community life to the maximum extent possible. The general treatment approach recommended for this population encompasses several factors:

1. The professional's posture toward this population;
2. A non-punitive, behavioral orientation;
3. Programmatic flexibility;
4. A total communication approach;
5. Reinforcement techniques;
6. A balanced approach between the use of psychoactive medications and behavioral programming.

Professional Posture

Community programs can adequately, appropriately, and developmentally serve even the most severely involved mentally retarded children and adults. The ENCOR program demonstrates this (Menolascino & McGee, 1981). Services for the dual diagnosis population can be characterized in the following manner: (1) they are concrete, comprehensive, replicable, development-oriented programs; (2) they are ensured across the person's lifespan based on the degree and intensity of services required by each individual; (3) they are small, no more than six persons being housed in any given setting; (4) the various programs and services are dispersed throughout the community in a well-managed service delivery system; and (5) manpower resources are derived from and trained in the local community with adequate medical and psychiatric back-up personnel.

Community-based alternatives must be able to ensure mentally retarded persons and their families that there will be: (1) a variety of community-based less restrictive options utilizing modern treatment and programmatic techniques in small dispersed residential, educational, vocational, and leisure-time services; (2) maximum parental input while still ensuring individual client's rights; (3) ongoing internal and external monitoring of the quality of services; (4) a realistic cost per person for services and assured program financing across time; and (5) prudent risk for all mentally retarded citizens as they live, work, and play in communities, while at the same time safeguarding each person as much as necessary.

Professionals must first review and redefine their posture toward these children and adults—a posture built on developmental hopefulness, gentleness, and warmth. It is helpful for the professional to consider the creation of an *initial* passively dependent (or at least physically tolerant) relationship with each person. More severely retarded persons with severe behavior problems need to develop an initial passively dependent relationship with the professional, which then tends to usher in an increasingly dynamic relationship between them. As this relationship develops, a secondary purpose is sequentially leading the person to a variety of learning readiness opportunities which we term the *threshold of learning*. This initial receptivity to developmental interactions will gradually, but invariably, lead to control over the person's behaviors (self-abuse, aggression, self-stimulation, avoidance) and hence expand opportunities for advanced interactions within ever-increasing circles of interpersonal transactions. The professional needs to develop, in a persistent and stepwise fashion, a sequential (i.e., from obtaining eye contact to attention focusing on tasks) and directional (i.e., from simple to more complex tasks) series of developmental interactions over a six to eight week period. In the beginning, these complex mentally retarded persons tend to "win" most of the interpersonal transactions via obstinancy, refusal to sit, screaming, striking self or others, running away, or indiscriminately throwing objects. The person initially attempts to maintain and even increase the barriers between himself and the interacting professional who represents an intrusion of the chaotic external world. The professional must understand this initial stage of rebellion against "outside" interference, and energetically continue to attempt to engage the person in a series of concrete specific developmental activities. At the same time the professional needs to tolerate—in a passively supportive, but firm professional posture—the initial barrage of heightened inappropriate behaviors. These maladaptive behaviors—rather than representing volitionally destructive or aggressive acts—are the mentally retarded person's basic protective mechanism for coping with a world that has, prior to active treatment intervention, presented itself as quite meaningless and unresponsive. This initial interactive relationship (i.e., making initial meaningful contact) can best be achieved through a constant and sincere display of warmth, tolerance, and uncritical acceptance on the part of the caregiver (Greenspan, 1981).

Behavioral specialists often tend to apply the principles of behavioral analysis in both a lock-step and negative fashion. This population requires flexibility and gentleness in all treatment procedures. In order to maintain the aforementioned positive interpersonal posture and create a dynamic relationship of predictability and trust with the retarded person, aversive behavioral modification techniques should be avoided. Rather than punish this population for behaviors that are not of their own volition, a threefold, gentle technique should be employed when persistently inappropriate behaviors occur: (1) ignore, (2) redirect, and (3) positively reinforce (Stark, Baker, Menousek, & McGee, 1981). All three of these steps are needed simultaneously. For example, while ignoring fidgetiness and concomitant screaming, the professional should re-direct the child by gently taking the person's hand and performing the requested task hand-over-hand with the person. This technique allows the professional an on-going opportunity to positively reinforce the child. This does not mean that professionals solely ignore the maladaptive behaviors. Rather, it means the focus is on the acquisition of appropriate skills and interactions. The person gradually learns that he or she will gain attention (i.e., positive rewards) for appropriate behaviors and interactions and conversely will regularly be ignored for maladaptive behaviors or interactions.

Programmatic Flexibility

The overall posture of uncritical acceptance and use of redirecting techniques must also be reflected in the type of general program in which the child or adult is served. Generally, these persons require six to eight weeks of intensive developmental programming before behavioral control is achieved to the extent necessary to integrate them into less structured, normalizing programs. The mechanism to accomplish this goal is the development of a highly structured program (i.e., utilizing one-to-one staffing for at least 200 minutes per day) for the initial treatment intervention time period (Stark, Baker, Menousek, & McGee, 1981). This intense treatment programming will gain control over the offending behaviors and progressively lead the person to the threshold of learning. Professionals need to divide the person's day into time modules ranging from ten to 30 minutes — depending on the capability of the retarded person to attend. Within these time modules a series of developmental tasks are programmed. These mini-time modules can be fairly normalizing in that they follow the normal flow of the day: self-care skills, academic skills, prevocational skills, communication skills, eating skills, etc. This program structuring becomes the framework for the professional's ability to ignore, redirect, and reinforce the on-going set of behaviors of the complex retarded person.

Another important variable in terms of programmatic flexibility is the control of the physical environment, especially for persons with aggressive or self-abusive behaviors. This is necessary to accommodate the re-directing process in as inconspicuous a manner as possible (Hewitt, 1967). At times it is necessary to gain control in an environment that still permits the person to move in-and-out of the physical space where treatment is occurring.

In the beginning, the responsibility for a maximum degree of structure falls on the professional. There are a number of specific techniques that greatly help in initiating and obtaining treatment goals with this population (Fisher & Zeaman, 1973; Gold, 1972; Horner & Bellamy, 1978; Irvin & Bellamy, 1977), typically requiring that professionals specifically plan all teaching approaches towards obtaining small initial graduations of behavioral control.

The posture and programmatic flexibility will not necessarily lead to the meaningful engagement of the severely mentally retarded child or adult with co-existing mental illness into on-going educational, vocational, residential training programs. Treatment objectives, to be both useful and generalizable (i.e., to their living environments), must consistently focus on dampening (or redirecting) inappropriate behaviors so as to increase the probability that competing desirable behaviors will occur (Stark, et al., 1981). That is, if the professional knows that a person will inconsistently attend to a developmental task, or not attend at all, then the professional needs to arrange the learning environment in such a manner so as increase the probability that the person will attend (Hewitt, 1967). A useful technique is to employ errorless learning (Terrace, 1963; Irvin, 1976). Utilizing this technique for the person with persistent difficulty in performing a task, hence preventing the professional from focusing on reinforcing the acquisition of appropriate skills, the treatment situation may be arranged in such a way so as to decrease the probability of error. Errorless learning can be accomplished by specifically analyzing desired tasks and interactions, then arranging these in a sequential manner and directly providing whatever physical or verbal assistance is necessary to successfully accomplish same (Bellamy, Horner, & Inman, 1979; Crosson, 1967, 1969; Gold, 1973).

Total Communication

A developmental technique that helps professionals gain control over inappropriate behaviors is to teach in silence (Gold, 1980), simultaneously using signs and/or gestures. These children and adults frequently have major primary communication disorders that appear to underlie consequent behavior problems. Communication overstimulation from the *interpersonal* environment often leads to *intrapersonal* confusion. The intrapersonal confusion often becomes compounded and rapidly accelerates into behavioral outbursts. Because of this frequently noted mechanism for initiating personality explosions in these persons, it is helpful to teach *in silence* by the use of gestures, physical prompts, and environmental engineering. As the person becomes accustomed to the required task, verbal input can slowly be introduced. A secondary result of this technique is that it allows the caregiver to use verbal communication only for verbal reinforcements, thereby reducing possible sensory input confusion for the person.

Reinforcement Techniques

The issue of reinforcement for this population is frequently poorly applied by behavioral specialists. Typically, only two options are incorporated: either punish the person for inappropriate behaviors or use primary reinforcement. In our experience, the fist option is harmful and counterproductive and the second is generally unnecessary. It is better to decrease the probability that inappropriate behaviors might occur and direct the person toward appropriate behaviors. There is no reason whatsoever to provoke a child or adult into an escalation of a behavioral outburst in the name of punishment. Indeed, punishment should be eliminated from the repertoire of treatment techniques of any caregiver. The aforementioned technique of ignore, redirect, reinforce is the basic intervention procedure. The end result is that inappropriate behaviors are deflected and the person is continuously redirected toward appropriate behaviors. This treatment approach permits the caregiver to use positive, tactile, and social reinforcement.

Behavioral and Psychoactive Medication Treatment Balance

Another important dimension to the treatment with a dual diagnosis person is the use of psychoactive medication as a tool to assist in leading the person to the threshold of learning (Wilson, 1983). A delicate balance must be struck between the use of psychoactive medications and an ongoing behavioral intervention approach. Both psychoactive medications and behavioral management are essentially neutral tools. As such, either can be used to assist a person to move toward appropriate human engagement or toward human disengagement. They are both subject to abuse. While excellent reviews of the clinical utilization of psychopharmacological agents in mentally ill-mentally retarded persons are available (e.g., Freeman, 1970; Lipman, 1970; Werry & Sprague, 1972), there are relatively few objective studies available. The balance has little to do with an "either-or" posture towards the exclusive use of either psychoactive medication or behavioral management approaches. Instead, the focus should be on a balanced use of both of these approaches — always maintaining the goal of assisting the person to move toward meaningful engagements.

An initial consideration in this professional treatment balance is to briefly examine the clinical rationales for the use of psychoactive medications. The three basic rationales for utilizing medications are: to aid persons (1) who display marked motoric overactivity; (2) who display marked motoric underactivity; and (3) whose overall behavior is slowly (or rapidly) escalating into "out of contact" behaviors (e.g., psychosis).

All of these symptom configurations can produce serious interference with the person's ability to learn or interact appropriately. Putting aside the extensive list of psychiatric syndromes, it is important to objectively analyze the key behaviors that are significantly interfering with the disconnected person's ability to learn and live in normalizing environments. This process involves: (1) pinpointing in objective terms the major current interfering behaviors; (2) measuring and recording their extent and frequency; and (3) arriving at an objective conclusion as to whether or not the observed behaviors are sufficiently disruptive to prevent on-going learning experience or maintenance of the person in the normalizing educational-social-work-recreational routines of community life.

This population requires a true interdisciplinary approach. For example, an adolescent may be hitting, running away, and biting himself at high frequencies. This pattern of behaviors obviously presents many major barriers to the initiation of *any* teaching or training process. Any medication prescribed in a balanced treatment approach should reduce these behaviors sufficiently so that program staff can safely work on the acquisition of appropriate skills and behaviors so that initial behavioral redirection can occur. Thus, the use of psychoactive medications ideally serves the purpose of reducing the inappropriate and disruptive behaviors to a manageable level — just enough to enable the treatment process to take hold and move the disconnected persons towards the threshold of learning.

The initiation of the use of psychotropic medications requires close monitoring by the psychiatrist, with frequent and on-going descriptive input by the programmatic staff. Adjustments relative to the type of medications, dosage, and schedule are made on the basis of on-going relevant programmatic inputs. All concerned persons should understand the basic process involved in this balancing of the use of psychotropic medications with intensive on-going developmental programming. In the balanced treatment regime (i.e., combined utilization of psychoactive medications and behavioral programs), the following basic processes typically occur:

1. *Initiation Phase.* There is noted the gradual effect of the psychoactive medication's dampening of the excessive amounts of inappropriate behaviors to the point where programming efforts can "take hold." This initial effect must be closely and sensitively monitored so as to avoid sedative effects; behavioral availability is the goal, not disorganization or depression of cognitive processes.

2. *Catching-on Phase.* As the initial dampening effect of the psychoactive medication joins forces with the intensive developmental programming (i.e., energetic one-to-one efforts to establish the threshold of learning), the acquisition of appropriate behaviors and skills begins to accelerate, multiplying by their own power; and the inappropriate behaviors begin to decelerate, usually in inverse proportion to the accelerating rate of appropriate learning acquisitions.

3. *Reduction Phase.* Once the second phase begins to stabilize, it is time to focus on the slow reduction and/or elimination of the dosage levels of psychoactive medications utilized in the previous two phases. Concomitantly, intensive developmental programming must continue and extend further into extrinsic interpersonal transactions that can permit the recently acquired behavioral improvement to both stabilize and begin to generalize across a multitude of environments and situations.

Conclusion

In summary, it is clear that persons with the dual diagnosis of mental retardation and mental illness present a persistent challenge to community-based programs and require specialized service models if they are to have their needs met appropriately.

Mentally retarded persons with severe behavioral and emotional problems can be served in community-based settings if a range of educational, vocational, and residential services and supports are available. On the surface the continuum of care for this population appears to be no different in types than those utilized for the mentally retarded population in general. However, they differ in their treatment intensity relative to staffing competency, staffing patterns, and the availability of back-up supports such as acute psychiatric care and follow-along. These concerns must be dealt with in relation to both the quality of services that this population requires as well as how their services impact on other clients in the service delivery system. Once placed in a continuum of care, professionals need to develop a warm, accepting posture towards persons with these needs and apply a range of gentle treatment techniques to ensure optimal integration in community life.

11 The Cost-Benefit Issues in Financing a Community-Based Service System

Besides the ideological aspects of the development and implementation of community-based services, it is the responsibility of professionals and parents in their advocacy roles to develop programs and services that benefit each mentally retarded person in a cost effective manner. The cost of institutional care is typically quite high with very few benefits, if any, to the mentally retarded person. (Gross, 1978; Haring & Hayden, 1981; Conroy, Lemanowicz, Sokol, & Pollack, 1980). In this section we analyze a recent study of the cost-benefit services within ENCOR for services for the mentally retarded-medically fragile (Mazatta, 1976), and case studies of three currently served ENCOR clients with multiple needs.

For the past several years there has been considerable debate of the efficiency of community-based programming vis-a-vis institutionalized programming in the delivery of services to the mentally retarded in general and the multiply handicapped in particular. The substance of this debate has ranged from the moral/ethical questions which attempt to define what exactly are the rights of the individual (as a determinant of which treatment modality is appropriate) to what has been termed the pragmatic question of which modality is most functional in developing the individual to a point where that individual is capable of maintaining a life-style independent of public guardianship or supervision.

The history of research into the theory of which treatment modality provides the optimum cost-benefit pattern is, at best, inconclusive. The primary reason is that comprehensive community systems have existed only since the early 1970's. Studies which have been made have dealt with the issue of community based vs. institutionalized programming. Measures such as employ-

192

ability and recidivism—ex post facto indicators of client progress and failure—have contributed to the present level of understanding of what might be the results of the different treatment modes, but really do not speak to the issue of what in fact is the most effective system. Conley (1973), in his excellent text, *The Economics of Mental Retardation,* states the problem most succinctly:

> Economics is defined as the allocation of scarce resources among competing uses. Any change in well-being, whether by improved health, enhanced security, increased happiness, etc., is relevant to the decision to allocate resources. The problem, however, is how to measure benefits other than earnings, and even if measured, how to compare these non-earnings benefits with costs.

This speaks directly to the issue of how to construct measures that will, through their focus, establish with some degree of confidence the relative effectiveness of one system over another. Can one measure such abstract concepts as happiness and security? Probably not, and so the question remains, how does one determine the most effective means of providing services? Conley has provided us an excellent review of one indicator of success— employability. He analyzes the substantial impact of the employment of the mildly and moderately retarded individual on the ultimate measurement of costs in serving retarded persons in the United States. He has estimated that approximately one-half of the productivity of these individuals results in benefits to the public at large. This benefit is posited on the basis of tax revenue gained through the earnings received (approximately 25% of total income earned) and through the income maintenance costs circumvented (an additional 25% of total income). Using this line of analysis, Braddock (1977) goes on to indicate that for a mildly or moderately retarded person working at a sub-minimum wage of $2.30 per hour, over a forty-year working life, the total positive investment return to society is nearly $650,000. This figure represents taxes returned ($44,840), income maintenance costs avoided ($44,840) and institutional avoidance costs ($560,000). Braddock goes on however, to make an important point regarding these figures. He states that, "As the severity of intellectual disability increases, the economic payback period tends to lengthen, and the potential for an ultimately positive investment return to society diminishes primarily because of employment earning and also: institutional avoidance savings are less likely."

Clear, we may be inclined to say that the system that has the greatest impact on the payback period of its clients is clearly the more desireable one. How do we make this determination, and what are the implications for severely and profoundly retarded individuals, especially those with associated multiple handicaps? Undoubtedly it is not sufficient to simply assume that a normalizing environment will produce the kinds of effects that will result in successful employment for an individual: Though hypothesized, hard empirical examination of this assumption, when coupled with costs, has not been made.

In October 1977, a study was done at the Developmental Maximation Unit (See Chapter 6) of the Eastern Nebraska Community Office of Retardation (Mazatta, 1976). The purpose of the study was to determine the costs associated with serving severely and profoundly retarded, multi-handicapped individuals — a continuum of cost-of-services to these individuals based on the history of their movement from an institutional modality to less segregated residential alternatives in the community and the rate of development that occurs as a result of this treatment continuum.

Eight clients were involved in the study. They were evaluated as severely/ profoundly retarded/multiply handicapped and all but one were non-ambulatory. The clients had no formally developed language abilities. They all had a range of allied medical handicaps, one or more of the following associated disabilities: blindness, hearing loss, or other undetermined sensory dysfunction. Most had other complicating disabilities such as: seizure disorders, scoliosis, genetic malfunctions, hydrocephalisis, etc. The age range of the client population was three to eighteen years. Costs were broken down into three primary categories as follows:

1. *Residential Services.* The Developmental Maximation Unit occupies a discrete wing of a local hospital and had a maximum capacity for ten clients. Residential services at the time of the study were provided at a per diem rate of $10.50 or a maximum annual per client rate of $3,833 (1977). Inclusive of the per diem rate were the following services: room, board, housekeeping and maintenance.

2. *Operational Expenses.* These costs, associated with the provision of day to day medical and support services, included all direct and indirect costs exclusive of those related to residential services. Operational expenses for the fiscal year beginning July 1, 1977, averaged approximately $13,440 per month or an annualized rate of $161,280. The per diem rate derived from this figure was $56 per client.

These two categories provide an over-all cost picture for services provided through the Developmental Maximation Unit. When integrated the following was shown: Gross annual costs were approximately $191,520 and the individual per diem rate was $66.50 per client.

3. A third category of services — education — was not included because, as the Developmental Maximation Unit was originally conceived, these services were provided internally as an adjunct to the aforementioned medical services to form a developmental core. In 1975 this function was transferred to the public schools in response to a legislative mandate in the State of

Nebraska. Of the eight clients living at the Developmental Maximation Unit, seven were participants in full-day education programs. While the costs of the services were not borne by the Eastern Nebraska Community Office of Retardation, they were extremely important for any cost consideration of providing services to this particular type of client.

The annual per client cost of providing educational services through the public schools was approximately $7,213 or $40.07 per day. (The per diem rate was predicated upon a 180-day academic schedule).

This then represented a reasonably accurate picture of costs in the provision of services to the severely/profoundly retarded, multi-handiapped individual at the DMU in 1977. Certainly the prospect of annual per client costs of $24,000 is not calculated to present a convincing argument that community based programs are less costly in terms of resource consumption. What can be said, in a positive way, about this particular treatment modality? It certainly is not, in the classic institutional sense, a maintenance program. As described above, these clients were receiving both comprehensive medical services and a full day of educational services.

In an attempt to determine comparative costs for providing services to these clients (institution, to the DMU, to other alternatives), a total of 61 former DMU clients were analyzed from a cost-service perspective. Of these 61 clients, thirteen were deceased, fifteen had been moved to other programs within ENCOR such as small group homes, twenty-three had returned to their parental homes, two had been placed in foster homes and the remaining eight were the aforementioned clients being served at the DMU at the time of the study.

To illustrate the relationship of client movement toward increasing independence in a less restrictive environment and the costs associated with service delivery, the following hypothetical case is useful: A given client, whom we shall name John, has been transferred from the state institution to the Developmental Maximation Unit. John is a severely retarded, multi-handicapped seven-year-old. The initial evaluations indicate that John's medical involvement, at least as it necessitates DMU placement, will require approximately six months to stabilize, to be followed by transfer to a group home. While his physical well-being has been addressed at the DMU, his behavioral and emotional adjustment is insufficient to permit any greater degree of residential independence. In the group home John is provided intensive training to attain those skills and competencies necessary to adapt to a less restrictive environment. At the conclusion of this training program he is transferred into a well-supported foster home.

What has transpired in the case of John is that as his service needs changed — as his development progressed — his environment progressed with him. Any number of paths could be illustrated that would reveal the alternatives available, each impacting differently on the costs associated with treatment.

In this particular example, the cost continuum for John would be as follows: The per diem rate for services received at the Developmental Maximation Unit, based on average costs at the time of the study, was $66.50. For the six month period that John utilized this service, his total costs amounted to approximately $12,137. The per diem rate for services provided in the group home was $53.04 or $9,680 per year for the additional six months. For the full year of services then the cost amounts to approximately $21,817. Obviously, this configuration of services is quite expensive. However, when we follow into the next fiscal year we find a rather dramatic decrease in costs. Since John remained in the group home for a total of eight months, the first two months of the new fiscal year reflected this still higher per diem rate of $53.04 or a two month cost of $3,227. With the movement to the foster home setting, the per diem rate drops to $24.28 and for the remaining ten month period would amount to $7,387. The aggregate costs then for the second year for services would amount to $10,619. For the succeeding year and incorporating a 9% inflation factor the cost would amount to approximately $9,660.

While the cost data provided above does not convey definitive and necessarily generalizable results, it does indicate a tendency or progression upon which some assumptions can be made with a degree of credibility. In the case illustrated, the time sequencing for each of the residential alternatives represents the normal length of stay experienced for clients entering both the Developmental Maximation Unit and the group home.

Taking the sequenced data just reviewed and incorporating it with data that is known regarding the state institution, it is possible to construct graphically what is essentially a cost differential between the two experiences. Figure 37 illustrates two similar types of movement that might be anticipated within the two environments and the corresponding costs, both independent and cumulative, that are associated with the treatment modes over time. Based on the results of research with ENCOR programs and what is presently available from the institution, it appears that for the severely/profoundly mentally retarded-medically fragile client there is a progressively wider differential between the two delivery systems. Figure 38 illustrates the longitudinal cost flow for services provided under each system, and is predicated on the assumption that the length of stay factors for each service within the two systems is congruent. That is to say, client movement from one service to the next less restrictive service, i.e., client movement from the institution's medical service unit to ENCOR, is held constant with the corresponding movement of our hypothetical ENCOR client discussed earlier. In that example John spent six months at the Developmental Maximation Unit and then

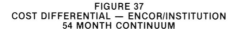

FIGURE 37
COST DIFFERENTIAL — ENCOR/INSTITUTION
54 MONTH CONTINUUM

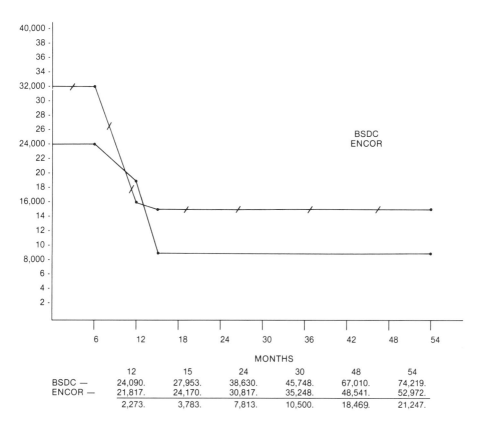

	12	15	24	30	48	54
BSDC —	24,090.	27,953.	38,630.	45,748.	67,010.	74,219.
ENCOR —	21,817.	24,170.	30,817.	35,248.	48,541.	52,972.
	2,273.	3,783.	7,813.	10,500.	18,469.	21,247.

moved to the group home for an additional eight months. Holding the movement patterns between the two systems constant, Figure 37 indicates a cost
imbalance or differential that becomes progressively wider as the client
moves through the continuum. In terms of significant cost events, the differential becomes most disparate from about the 14th month on. Here, the cost
of providing Home Teacher services deviates substantially from that of the
institutional service. At this juncture the increment increase moves from approximately $3,783 to $7,813. Projecting out to the end of the 54 month continuum, the estimated differential between the two systems is slightly over
$21,000.

It is necessary at this juncture, before proceeding to additional cost comparisons, to restate the assumptions that form the base of this comparison.
Earlier we indicated that those costs associated with services provided
through ENCOR were factored annually to compensate for inflationary

FIGURE 38
COST CONTINUUM — THREE ALTERNATIVES
54 MONTHS

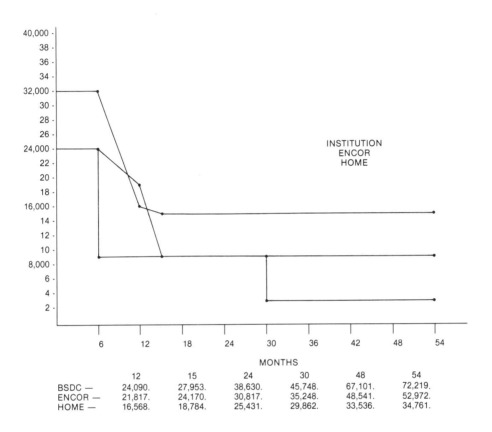

	12	15	24	30	48	54
BSDC —	24,090.	27,953.	38,630.	45,748.	67,101.	72,219.
ENCOR —	21,817.	24,170.	30,817.	35,248.	48,541.	52,972.
HOME —	16,568.	18,784.	25,431.	29,862.	33,536.	34,761.

pressures. The factor utilized was 9% and while this percentage may be open to conjecture, it is suggested that any figure would be, at best, arbitrary. What is important, by way of assumption, is that while the factor was applied against the ENCOR figures, it was not simultaneously utilized in the institutional cost flow. This is explained later.

A second primary assumption already alluded to is the compatibility of the movement between the two systems. The rate of client movement between the two experiences was held constant. Though ample data exists to support the notion that, in fact, a rather significant disparity exists between the rate of client movement in the institution as opposed to the community program, this factor was not incorporated into this example. While this is tantamount to taxing the community program in terms of both future costs (the aforementioned percentage factor) and experienced rate of client movement, it provides a more nearly constant base for the comparison.

Proceeding to Figure 38, a third Continuum of Care element is added to the previous comparison. This element is the Home Care service provided in conjunction with ENCOR and is designed to operate as a support service to clients residing in their natural home. In this service the client and his/her family is provided ancillary services such as transportation, child guidance, etc., in an effort to minimize the difficulties associated with maintaining the client in the least restrictive alternative. As the chart indicates, this alternative provides a rather stark contrast to either the ENCOR or institutional experience.

Figures 39 and 40 provide individual comparisons between the Home Care alternative and either the ENCOR or institutional models. As can be seen from this rather limited analysis, in-home care is a desirable alternative and certainly an important goal direction. A further analysis regarding Fig. 39

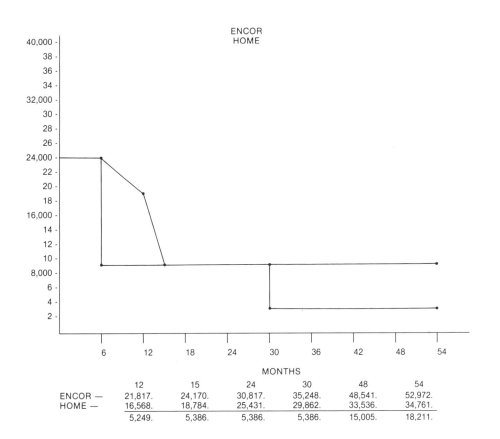

FIGURE 39
COST DIFFERENTIAL — ENCOR/HOME
54 MONTH CONTINUUM

	12	15	24	30	48	54
ENCOR —	21,817.	24,170.	30,817.	35,248.	48,541.	52,972.
HOME —	16,568.	18,784.	25,431.	29,862.	33,536.	34,761.
	5,249.	5,386.	5,386.	5,386.	15,005.	18,211.

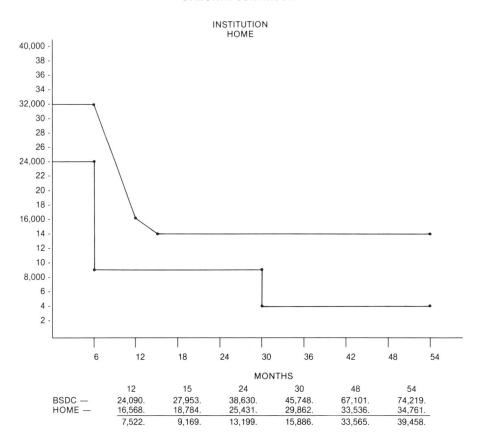

FIGURE 40
COST DIFFERENTIAL — HOME/INSTITUTION
54 MONTH CONTINUUM

INSTITUTION
HOME

MONTHS

	12	15	24	30	48	54
BSDC —	24,090.	27,953.	38,630.	45,748.	67,101.	74,219.
HOME —	16,568.	18,784.	25,431.	29,862.	33,536.	34,761.
	7,522.	9,169.	13,199.	15,886.	33,565.	39,458.

shows that the line of client progress is predicated upon past experience within the ENCOR program. The line of progression is as follows: (1) six months – Developmental Maximation Unit, (2) 24 months – Home Teacher setting, and finally (3) placement in the natural home. Again, this is in concordance with previous experiences in the ENCOR system. Parenthetically, it might be noted that no comparable data was available from the institution.

While the above is a somewhat rudimentary analysis or comparison of the two programs, we believe it represents an essentially accurate picture of variations in longitudinal costs. It does not attempt to take into consideration the more "liquid" nature of the capital investment scheme of community programs, which must be viewed as an asset; nor does it account for those diseconomies associated with state institutions, which can be quite substantial.

Referring back to the historical review of formal Developmental Maximation Unit clients, it should be noted that of the original 61 clients, 23 have returned to their parental homes. The cost implications for such an alternative are quite dramatic and should stand, without question, as one of the goal directions of any system of services to the retarded.

What then are the alternatives for John and other clients like him? As stated earlier, the study referred to regarding residential services in ENCOR does not provide conclusive evidence that in fact community programs are either less expensive or more effective. That it indicates a tendency or progression is evident, and sufficient other research in the field lends support to this notion; but, as expressed earlier, the hard empirical evidence has yet to be obtained.

CASE EXAMPLES

The results of the study conducted by Mazatta (1976) can be capsulized in the cases of three difficult-to-serve ENCOR clients—two severely/profoundly retarded-medically fragile children and one moderately retarded-mentally ill adult. It should be noted that these three case studies represent the most difficult-to-serve persons, a small percentage of the retarded population.

Case One

Jane was originally admitted to ENCOR with the following admission information: "Jane is a 24-day-old baby. She is diagnosed as having hydrocephalus and spina bifida. The brain scan showed 1/16th of an inch of brain tissue. She is epileptic and at the present time extremely medically fragile." Her parents were told that she needed to be institutionalized the rest of her life. Thus, they had made application to the state institution. At the same time ENCOR evaluated the child and Jane's parents decided to admit Jane to the developmental Maximation Unit. Jane's services in the DMA cost approximately $32,000 on an annual basis at that time. Jane spent about three months in the Developmental Maximation Unit without any visits home to her parents. The parents had expressed extreme fears over that period of time about being able to deal with Jane on an on-going basis. During this time period, the staff at the Developmental Maximation Unit and the agency case worker counseled the parents regarding Jane's needs and her program options. At the end of three months at the DMT her medical situation had improved such that it was possible for her to start spending weekends at home. She went home for weekends from the Developmental Maximation Unit for a three month period of time. This period of time was used to encourage the parents that they could take care of their young handicapped daughter. Jane had also, during this period of time, shown significant developmental improvement and was beginning to show developmental delays that were not significantly below her age level. After eight months her parents approached ENCOR and indicated that they were confident of their ability to care for Jane on a regular basis but would like some in-home support from the agency. A three month period of time had occurred in which the parents kept Jane during the week and received weekend respite from the agency. They also received 40 hours a week of in-home support. The annualized costs for Jane's services at this point had decreased to approximately $15,000 a year. After approximately six months, Jane's status was changed so that she now received 20 hours a week of in-home services and periodic respite care. Her current cost of services to the agency is approximately $7,000 per year. It is anticipated that in the near future, the 20 hours a week of in-home services will be able to be withdrawn and that Jane will need to receive only periodic respite services. The cost to the agency of services at that point would be approximately $1,000 per year.

Jane's cost continuum can be summarized as:

1. Prevention of institutionalization – $48,500 per year projected cost;
2. DMU – $32,000 per year;
3. Placement in natural family with maximal support – $15,000 per year;
4. Placement in natural home with moderate support – $7,000 per year;
5. Projected support – $1,000 per year.

Case Two

James first came to the attention of ENCOR staff on a tour of an institutional facility run by the State of Nebraska located in Hastings, NE. James was diagnosed as a profoundly retarded child with severe medical problems. He was approximately 11 years old at the time of our first visit with him. We were told by the staff at the institutional facility that James would never be able to leave the institution and that in fact if he ever did leave, he would undoubtedly die in a very short period of time. Institutional staff informed us that they had also told James' parents that this was just the way life was going to be for James. ENCOR staff were reasonably sure that James could be served in the community and proceeded to develop a community placement plan for him. It should be noted that the average cost of serving James at the time he was in the State of Nebraska institutional facility (1979) was $48,500 per year. Over a period of time, James' parents decided to place him in ENCOR's Developmental Maximation Unit. Both parents and agency staff were given a dire warning that James would die if he were sent to the community. James spent approximately one year in the Developmental Maximation

Unit. During this time, the agency's consulting pediatrician treated James' various medical problems in order to stabilize him. In addition, he received intensive physical and occupational therapy and showed significant improvements in both developmental and physical abilities. During the time that James was in the Developmental Maximation Unit, the annual cost for his services was $32,000 per year. James, at the end of that year, had shown such significant improvment that his individual program planning team recommended placement in a foster home. James was placed in a foster home with weekend respite care in DMU for a year after he left. By 1982, James remained in the foster home without the need to return to the Developmental Maximation Unit for week-end respite care. He is continuing to show significant developmental and physical improvement. The current cost of serving James in a foster placement is approximately $12,000 per year. James' cost continuum can be summarized as:

1. Institution — $48,500 per year;
2. DMU — $32,000 per year;
3. Foster Home — $12,000 per year.

More important than costs, his medical needs are being met while at the same time he is gaining developmental skills.

Case Three

Robert was originally placed in ENCOR from a state institution for the mentally ill. He entered ENCOR at twenty-six years of age after twenty years in a number of different institutions. He was viewed by the institution as an extremely violent and aggressive person who was dangerous both to himself and others. The general view of Robert might be best seen from a psychiatric evaluation that was performed on him at the institution in 1976 starting with the following quote: "Most recently there have been repeated episodes of window breaking and hurting of other patients. This has been dealt with by placing this patient on Haldol, 25 mgs. TID for about a six week period. Also he has been placed in the hospital complex partly for the treatment of physical injuries which he incurred. This seems to be a reinforcing effect. The past few days this patient has been restrained in bed by spread eagling him and he has required practically total care while being thus restrained." The annual cost for his institutional placement was approximately $75,000 per year. Robert was first placed for a four week period of time in the Nebraska Psychiatric Institute for adjustment of his medication levels and for programmatic recommendations for ENCOR staff. After that period, Robert was placed in an ENCOR group home and an ENCOR vocational training facility at a cost of $28,000 per year. During the initial period of time, ENCOR staff had an extremely difficult time dealing with Robert's behaviors. There were frequent periods of aggression — high frequency violence toward staff persons. A behavior program was developed for Robert with the assistance of the Nebraska Psychiatric Institute. The behavioral program was implemented and resulted in significant reductions in Robert's aggressive and violent behavior. Six months after his initial placement in the ENCOR group home, Robert returned to the Nebraska Psychiatric facility for a follow-up visit and readjustment of his medication and new recommended programming. Robert returned to the group home, and has shown a remarkable decrease in behavioral incidents to the point that the agency is now seeing one

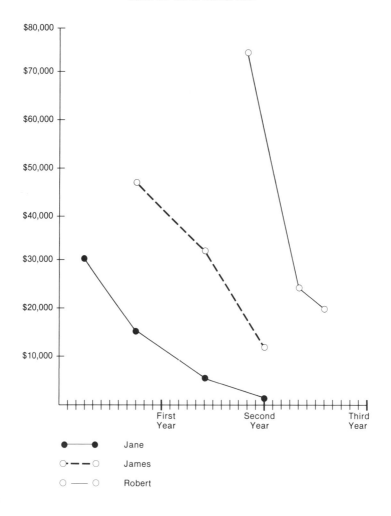

FIGURE 41
COST OF CASE EXAMPLES

behavioral outburst a week and those behavioral outbursts are of an extremely mild nature in comparison to those seen at the time Robert entered the agency. The current annual cost for Robert's services is $28,000 per year. It is projected, based on the current data, that one staff member will be removed from Robert's residence within three months. This will reduce the annual cost for Robert to $20,000 per year.

Robert's cost continuum can be summarized as follows:

1. State institution – $75,000 per year;
2. Specialized and vocational group home placement – $28,000 per year;
3. Projected group home and vocational placement – $20,000 per year.

This cost reduction was accompanied by increased adaptive behaviors – participation in a full day program, improved social interactions, and a concurrent reduction in his violent behaviors.

Figure 41 summarizes these three cases from a cost-service perspective. In each case as the person moves to a more integrated setting, his/her cost of service dramatically decreases and opportunities for learning dramatically increase. Although we do not wish to imply that the cost of community services is always less on a case-by-case basis, it has been ENCOR's experience that costs decrease and benefits increase. Nor do we wish to imply that cost of service should be the fundamental determinant in service provision. Yet, a review of these three extremely difficult-to-serve persons reveals that costs did decrease for them and, more importantly, opportunities for support, individualization, and learning increased.

12

Cost-Efficiency Issues in Serving The Mentally Retarded in Community Settings

INTRODUCTION

Throughout this book we have emphasized the qualitative, beneficial aspects of community-based programs. We have used ENCOR as an example of such a program — a living laboratory of community integration. In the previous chapter we traced the reduction of costs of serving severely retarded-medically fragile persons as they move into integrative alternatives with the benefits inherent therein. While there is a need to build in safeguards to protect the rights of each client served, it is also to ensure that the resources that go into a community-based system are prudently and efficiently spent.

In this chapter we focus on cost-efficiency problems that can beset a community-based program, which mainly involve efficient resource management. There need not be a dichotomy between the cost-benefits of a service system and its cost-efficiency. Yet, unless constant vigilance is maintained, even cost-beneficial programs can inefficiently use public monies.

In the last chapter we cited the cost-beneficial aspects of ENCOR. It is clear that as mentally retarded persons move out of the institution and into an array of community-based alternatives that costs generally decrease while benefits to the person increase. Throughout this book we have stressed the qualitative value of community-based services, the need to move toward maximum integration, and the need for interdependence. We would be remiss if we did not also stress the economics of program administration, the use of public monies in the most efficient way possible, and counterbalance this with the qualitative dimensions of community-based services.

A comprehensive, community-based service system such as ENCOR presents multiple management challenges. Whether a community-based system is large or small, parents and professionals need to be aware of a number of safeguards in the management of community services. A recent report (Touche-Ross, 1983), commission by ENCOR, examined several key management areas in ENCOR in order to determine the agency's management strengths and weaknesses. These areas included: (1) the cost-efficiency and effectiveness of ENCOR's services; (2) the organizational structure of ENCOR; and (3) the cost-effectiveness and efficiency of ENCOR's administrative and support structure. In this chapter we summarize this cost-effectiveness and cost-efficiency study in order to point out the management safeguards that must be built into a community-based service delivery system.

It should be noted that the findings of this study relate directly to ENCOR. However, based on our review of other programs and services in the United States and elsewhere, the findings of the ENCOR study should be helpful in guiding other administrators. It is important to note that, even though nations differ vastly in their priorities and resources, there are cost issues that transcend the availability of resources. Noble (1982) notes:

> Economic costs for rehabilitation programs are the same for both developed and under-developed countries. Their priority and magnitude can differ, as well as their means of service provision. For example, services in rural areas of the world likely have a different focus, depending more on personal assistance—a simpler, less costly system.
>
> The priorities for the utilization of resources differ most notably between economically developed and under-developed areas. In developing countries the urgent necessity for industrial and agricultural development, as well as the development of a basic infrastructure (including sanitation, transportation, communication, and education), can be an obstacle in the provision of social services, especially rehabilitation services. On the other hand, in economically developed nations, the number of social services and the higher salaries paid elevates the costs of rehabilitation services. This increases the cost of meeting the needs of each disabled person (p. 24).

We summarize the Touche-Ross study for the purpose of drawing conclusions applicable or adaptable to all community-based programs for the mentally retarded. ENCOR is now a multi-million dollar agency serving over 1,000 mentally retarded persons. In 1981–82 it had a 7.7 million dollar annual budget. Figure 42 shows that this budget is spent largely in the provision of residential alternatives and secondly in vocational services. Figures 43 and 44 further show that over 80% of these costs are in payroll. If any efficiency is to be brought about in the allocation of finances, it is necessary to concentrate on how these finances are used.

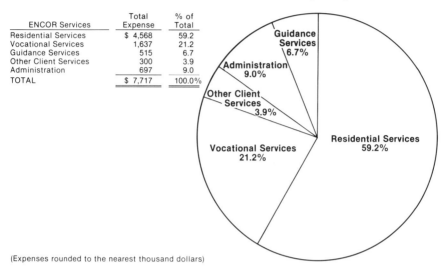

FIGURE 42
ENCOR TOTAL EXPENSE ANALYSIS BY PROGRAM (FY 81/82)

ENCOR Services	Total Expense	% of Total
Residential Services	$ 4,568	59.2
Vocational Services	1,637	21.2
Guidance Services	515	6.7
Other Client Services	300	3.9
Administration	697	9.0
TOTAL	$ 7,717	100.0%

(Expenses rounded to the nearest thousand dollars)

RESIDENTIAL SERVICES

Because the provision of residential services comprises a significant proportion of ENCOR's costs, a more in-depth analysis of these costs and how residential services are administered is warranted. Costs are primarily determined by two factors: (1) the needs of the individual client; and (2) the number of persons served in a particular facility or group of facilities. The cost study did not deal with the issue of the needs of the ENCOR clients and the necessary staffing patterns to meet those needs. This is a qualitative issue. It did, however, analyze the impact of the number of clients served and its effect on per person costs. Figure 45 shows the disparity in costs between various residential models, ranging from the high cost Developmental Maximation Unit (serving severely retarded-medically fragile children) to the low cost semi-independent living options. The study concluded that, with all other variables being equal, the fewer the clients per facility the more costly the service is per client, except for the home-teacher model (in which a client lives in with a family). The latter is the most cost-efficient of the various residential options. In these residential programs more hours of service are received at a lower cost with continuity of personnel because community families are used to providing the alternative rather than an artificial, agency-created and agency-run group home.

At times agency-created group homes are necessary. In these instances size becomes a critical factor relating to cost-efficiency. The study found that the primary reason that ENCOR's group home costs are relatively high is that

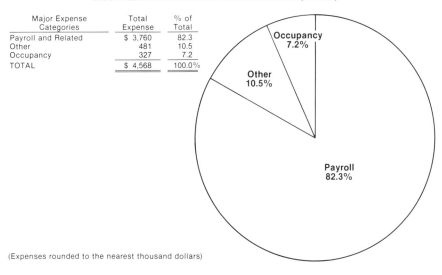

FIGURE 43
ENCOR RESIDENTIAL SERVICES EXPENSE ANALYSIS (FY 81/82)

Major Expense Categories	Total Expense	% of Total
Payroll and Related	$ 3,760	82.3
Other	481	10.5
Occupancy	327	7.2
TOTAL	$ 4,568	100.0%

(Expenses rounded to the nearest thousand dollars)

ENCOR has a very small percentage of group homes for four or more clients. It has 67 persons in "group home" facilities of less than four persons. The study strongly recommended that ENCOR increase the size of its group homes to at least four persons. At the time of the report there were 67 clients in one, two, and three person residential facilities with paid, overnight staff. By increasing the group home size to a four person model, the study concluded that the agency could save as much as $400,000 annually.

Vocational Services

Vocational services represent the second highest cost allocation in ENCOR. (It should be noted that since the mid-seventies ENCOR no longer provides educational services for school-age children since these are now provided by local school districts. For this reason the study did not deal with educational costs.) As in residential services, the number of clients served in a given facility and the staffing needs of the clients served are the variables that most influence the per person cost of services. In ENCOR's six workshops there is an approximate thousand dollar difference in the range of per-person costs from one sheltered workshop to another (see Fig. 46).

Although ENCOR serves a large number of multi-handicapped adults in its sheltered workshops, there seems to be little relationship in per person costs and the number of multi-handicapped adults in a given workshop. A primary factor in cost differences is the cost of the sheltered workshop facility itself. Client needs did not seem to determine higher costs from facility to

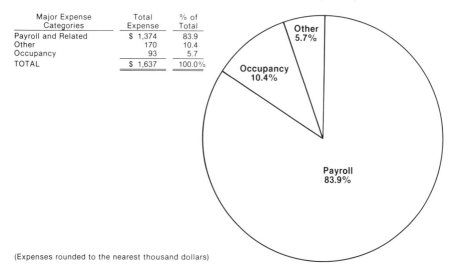

FIGURE 44
ENCOR VOCATIONAL SERVICES EXPENSE ANALYSIS (FY 81/82)

Major Expense Categories	Total Expense	% of Total
Payroll and Related	$ 1,374	83.9
Other	170	10.4
Occupancy	93	5.7
TOTAL	$ 1,637	100.0%

(Expenses rounded to the nearest thousand dollars)

facility. For example, the Central Douglas sheltered workshop serves a disproportionately higher number of multi-handicapped adults than most of the others, yet it has the lowest per person cost. It appears that it is able to serve a mix of mildly and severely involved persons with fewer total staff, and therefore, at a lower per person cost.

MANAGEMENT RECOMMENDATIONS

The Touche-Ross study focused on finding ways to better manage services and preserve programmatic quality. Most of its recommendations emphasized centralizing services, increasing the number of persons served, and minimizing the number of staff hours needed to meet the needs of clients.

1. The study lists several concerns regarding the efficiency of ENCOR's residential services:
   a. ENCOR residences are managed in clusters by a residential manager. The position is responsible for the household management of several facilities, staff scheduling, client financial audits, and a variety of administrative paperwork. Often the residential managers appear to be overworked. Yet, in some instances the residential manager handles the position with relative ease. The difference seems to be the level of responsibility assumed by residential staff working in the particular residences. When "line staff" assume or are given more responsibility

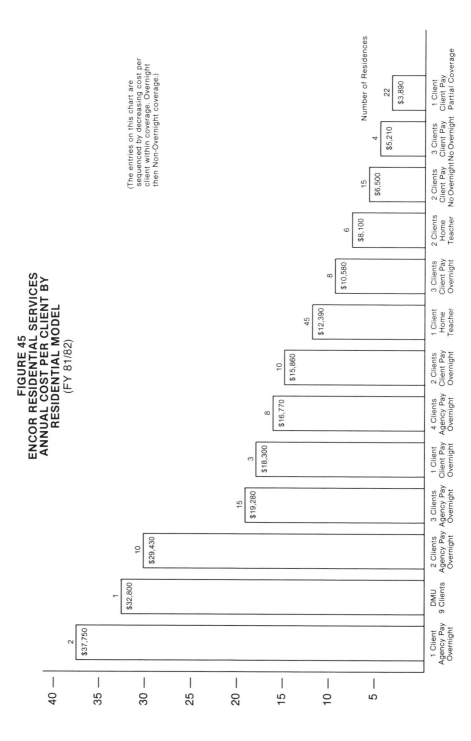

FIGURE 45
ENCOR RESIDENTIAL SERVICES
ANNUAL COST PER CLIENT BY
RESIDENTIAL MODEL
(FY 81/82)

(The entries on this chart are sequenced by decreasing cost per client within coverage. Overnight then Non-Overnight coverage.)

Number of Residences

Model	Number of Residences	Cost
1 Client Agency Pay Overnight	2	$37,750
DMU 9 Clients	1	$32,800
2 Clients Agency Pay Overnight	10	$29,430
3 Clients Agency Pay Overnight	15	$19,280
1 Client Client Pay Overnight	3	$18,300
4 Clients Agency Pay Overnight	8	$16,770
2 Clients Client Pay Overnight	10	$15,860
1 Client Home Teacher	45	$12,390
3 Clients Client Pay Overnight	8	$10,580
2 Clients Home Teacher	6	$8,100
2 Clients Client Pay No Overnight	15	$6,500
3 Clients Client Pay No Overnight	4	$5,210
1 Client Client Pay Partial Coverage	22	$3,890

211

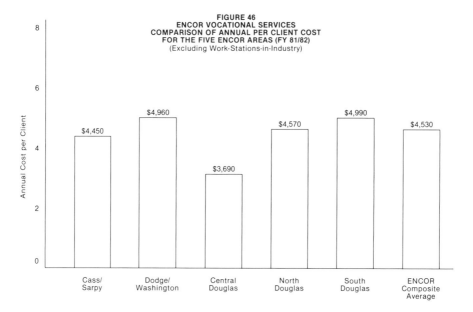

FIGURE 46
ENCOR VOCATIONAL SERVICES
COMPARISON OF ANNUAL PER CLIENT COST
FOR THE FIVE ENCOR AREAS (FY 81/82)
(Excluding Work-Stations-in-Industry)

in the day-to-day operation of the facility, the residential manager is able to pay more attention to staff morale, staff training, and the resolution of problems.

b. The range of residential options provided by ENCOR can be classified into two broad types: group homes and foster homes with home-teachers. The study recommends that group homes should be larger in size. That is, for those who need the structure of a group home, it is more cost-efficient to group four to six compatible clients together rather than support a large number of one, two, and three person "group homes" with paid staff. Qualitatively this means that it is important to group four to six persons together with necessary staffing and supports rather than requiring more staffing for a larger number of facilities. Two examples of this issue are: (1) One ENCOR client (B.P.), a long-term client with violent behaviors, was placed into a one person group home with intense staffing. This was a trial procedure because it had been proven impossible to reduce his violent behaviors in a multi-person group home. He spent 18 months in this one person home. Gradually the intensive staffing was decreased as his violent behaviors decreased. After 18 months he was placed with a foster family with no other children. This allowed his ENCOR cost to decrease from $37,000 per year to approximately $12,000 per year. Prior to this, his institutionalization had cost $72,000 per year. This case example shows how an agency must be flexible to the needs of the individual client and at the same time responsive to cost efficiency. (2) Another

ENCOR client (K.M.), like B.P., had long-term violent behaviors plus more primitive behaviors and severe retardation. He has been living in a one person group home for two years. He had lived in a four bed group home, but was moved because he was injuring other clients in the facility. K.M. could have been moved into a multi-person group home several months ago, but has not been. Two reasons seem to be causing this — staff fear and overprotection. Organizational administrators need to be willing to take the position that once clients show improvement, they should be moved into more efficient settings.

For those who do not require the structure of a group home, the study recommends a wider use of home teachers. It suggests that the home teachers should not be hired as employees of the agency with the inherent cost of "employees" (e.g., taxes and benefits), rather they should be contracted to provide these services.

c. Services for severely retarded medically fragile children currently provided in the Developmental Maximation Unit do not require the use of a hospital setting. The study points out that a hospital environment is not required by the children's needs. The cost of a residential setting in a hospital (the current DMU setting) costs ENCOR $72,000 per year. A group home setting would reduce this cost by approximately $54,000 per year in rent alone. Such a setting would also be less restrictive and more developmentally sound.

2. Regarding vocational services, the study made several cost-efficiency recommendations:

a. A key factor in the provision of vocational services is the number of supportive services necessary to maintain client training opportunities and client movement. The study focused on three of these supports: work-stations-in-industry as a less costly alternative to sheltered workshops, contract procurement, and job placement.

The main issue in each of these factors involved the level at which these supportive services should be managed — at a facility level or a regional level. The study recommends that it is preferable to maintain the development and administration of these services at a regional level, while at the same time involving local sheltered workshop personnel in the development process as much as possible. The study emphasizes the need to keep local staff informed of the status of job placement and contract procurement functions.

Waiting Lists

A constant problem in the administration of all human service agencies is that of being able to provide adequate services to all those in need. Like other community-based mental retardation programs, ENCOR has not been able to develop the number of services necessary to keep up with the demand; thus, there are waiting lists for residential and vocational services. According to the study, there were 34 clients in the ENCOR region awaiting placement in residential services and 99 clients awaiting placement in a sheltered workshop in 1982.

A community-based program is nothing if it does not stretch itself to find ways to meet the needs of all retarded persons in its geo-political region. The study points out a lingering list of close to 100 persons who are in need of residential or vocational services. The right to a free public education means little if upon graduation there is nothing to move into.

Several issues arise out of the waiting list problem: (1) It is important to define ways to identify those who truly need services. (2) If the lack of money is a problem, it is crucial to find new, less costly ways to serve the total population. (3) Money may not be able to be saved; however, it can be used more efficiently. The average cost of serving a person per year can be reduced by serving larger numbers of people. (4) If larger numbers of persons are to be served, the quality of services must be protected.

CONCLUSION

Community-based service systems such as ENCOR need to counterbalance their emphasis on smallness with the efficiency of services. Too often community-based advocates equate a person living alone, with or without staff, as the ultimate goal of normalization. We do not wish to imply that more is better. The efficiency of services implies the need to carefully select residential, vocational, and educational options which foster integration and interdependence. The costs of services in ENCOR are difficult to compare to the costs of serving severely retarded children in Agueda, Portugal. In the community that ENCOR serves, it is presumed that segregated, highly specialized education with its inherent high costs is necessary, whereas in Agueda the children are placed in regular classrooms at a minimal cost. Both benefits and efficiency are determined in different parts of the world at different points in their history.

In Chapter 1 we stressed the need to focus on community options that nurture interdependence. "Smallness" is an important variable in the development of interdependent communities. Advocates can learn from the insights of studies such as the Touche-Ross report, which we have summarized in this chapter. For example, it is difficult to rationalize a "group home" with one or two persons. It is reasonable to assume that one or two other compatible persons could be placed in such a group home, thereby reducing the costs on a per person basis. Another example is the Developmental Maximization Unit where a group home could be used instead of a hospital setting with a $52,000 savings in rental costs.

If community-based programs are to survive, they must be ready to critically question how they are using public monies and be willing to blend service quality with service efficiency.

Throughout this book we have focused on the generalizability of the ENCOR model to all community-based programs and services for the mentally retarded. Although the ENCOR example represents but one agency in an industrialized nation, with the concomitant financial resources available, it is still possible to draw organizational lessons from the ENCOR model which transcend political, economic and geographical differences. Most of these challenges will differ in proportionality and specificity, but the organizational principles transcend time and place.

1. A community-based service agency must be able to eventually meet the residential, vocational, and educational needs of all mentally retarded persons in its geo-political area. ENCOR's waiting list can be substantially reduced by increasing the number of persons served in facilities that are deemed to be "full." It must be kept in mind that 80% of all mentally retarded persons are mildly retarded and, thus, do not require massive staffing — 80% of the cost of the provision of services. If there is space available, the person should be served.

2. A community-based service system needs to develop a case management system sensitive enough to know not just individual needs, but also the systemic needs of the total client population. In ENCOR it is obvious that there are several group homes in which one or two other persons could be served. Yet, there has been no coordinated effort to track where and when openings are available. Community-based programs must be willing to efficiently manage all of their resources in order to maximize the use of those resources for the broadest number of persons possible.

3. A large community-based service system tends to overbureaucratize itself with specialization. It is important to recognize that what most retarded persons need is some structure to their lives in relation to where they live, work, go to school, and play. Most staff in these settings are paraprofessionals, who if they were given guidance, could manage specific programs and services well. Paraprofessionals should be given the opportunity to exert leadership in group homes and workshops. Back-up staff (e.g., psychologists and therapists) should transfer their expertise to the paraprofessional staff.

4. As community-based service systems grow in resources and size (number of clients served and the number of staff employed), there is a dichotomy between the provision of services at the community level and the need to cen-

tralize services into a system. In ENCOR this has meant dividing the system into sub-areas which can be more responsive to local needs and at the same time centralizing region-wide functions for the sake of efficiency (e.g., contract procurement for several sheltered workshops).

5. Cost-efficiency needs to be counterblanced with cost-benefits. There is a line at which the client receives the highest programmatic benefit at the most efficient cost. If the agency goes on either side of that line then the total client population suffers. Often the agency does not know when this balance is reached. A major management challenge is to determine this line.

6. A community-based service system needs to assume programmatic responsibility for all retarded persons in its geo-political area. Management-wise, this means that the agency should serve a mix of disabilities rather than starting with the more mildly involved. This enables the agency to build in the resources needed to serve the total mix of clients. Too often deinstitutionalization serves only the "easy" clients. The community is then not able to develop the technology needed to serve more challenging clients. For example, many community-based programs refuse to serve more severely retarded persons. ENCOR has the capacity to serve a large percentage of severely disabled persons because it has purposefully served a mix of retarded persons since its inception. Community programs that do not build this capacity into their system will be faced with the prospect of developing programs and services for the severely retarded with little background or experience.

7. A community-based service system should focus some of its resources on the prevention of secondary handicapping conditions. As community programs are preventing institutionalization, likewise a community program can prevent more serious handicapping conditions by having prevention-based services built into the system such as: in-home support services, parent training, respite services, outpatient psychiatric services, etc.

8. A community-based program needs to place a high priority on hiring and training middle management staff. For example, the Touche-Ross study stated that where a residential manager was doing well, the residences in his/her control were doing well. It is middle-management that assumes the responsibility for the expenditures of money, community interfaces, data for long-range planning, and quality control.

9. Client movement through the system into less restrictive alternatives demands a sensitive and responsive management system. As in the two cases cited earlier in this chapter, one client was moved out of a one person group home with all due speed, the other has lingered in an exceptionally costly alternative. In other instances, clients are moved out of the system without the necessary supports to meet their on-going needs. Any system needs to be responsive to the placement of each individual in a setting which meets the

person's needs. As these are met, the system should move the person into more efficient services.

10. The most important aspect is that if resources are not used wisely it is likely that clients are not well served. Community-based programs need to nurture a self-discipline in all that they do. The original idea behind the small ENCOR facilities was to move persons into the least restrictive setting. Without self-discipline and critical questioning on the part of agency staff, this in some cases has resulted in financial waste and at times client decay.

Parents and professionals who advocate for community-based programs need to be sensitive and responsive to the wide allocation of resources. In this chapter we have attempted to point out some of ENCOR's administrative weaknesses. Hopefully, this will help all advocates do a better job of meeting the needs of all mentally retarded persons.

13 Staff Training and Development

Community-based services for the mentally retarded are bringing about new health-care manpower needs. It becomes obvious that, given these rapidly expanding treatment approaches, new educational and training strategies for developing manpower pools of para-professionals, professionals, and parents need to be developed.

Until recently the professional field focused on medical syndromes, sensory and perceptual assessments, and the finer nuances of standardized global intelligence tests. Categorization and descriptive classifications have given way to focusing on adaptive behavior measures; the impact of normalization and the developmental model, and the utilization of behavior analysis and, most importantly, *how* to therapeutically intervene to enhance the growth of retarded citizens through prescriptive teaching. Bricker (1970) succinctly states this basic shift in strategy as follows, "I wish to affirm my belief in the importance of the nervous system and to indicate a conviction that a host of events can do damage to it and to its functioning. However, only the failure of a perfectly valid, perfectly reliable, perfectly efficient program of training will convince me that the identification of the deficit is sufficient reason to stop trying to educate the child." (p. 20)

The focus of current models of service provision for the severely retarded include these essential concepts of service, which in turn impact on personnel preparation:

1. *Care giving* has been greatly enhanced by behavioral analysis approaches to teaching of self-help skills and the interruption/redirection of stereotyped behaviors. Herein, the terms, stimulus, re-

218

sponse, reinforcement schedules, initiation, and generalization have been wielded into a powerful treatment posture (Bijou, 1979).

2. *Training* has been enriched by the contributions of discrimination learning theory, transfer of learning paradigms, language stimulation (especially programs which embrace a behavioral orientation to verbal/non-verbal tasks), and vocational skills.

3. *Social ecology* with its clear findings that the physical and social-interpersonal environments wherein the retarded citizen finds himself must be environments which fully support the ongoing caregiving and teaching efforts.

A major bond linking community-based programs together is their manpower approach. These programs have the following characteristics in common:

1. Each must have *appropriate back-up consultation services,* whether this might be medical, psychiatric, industrial engineering, etc.

2. Each must have *administrative leadership supportive of the principles of normalization and the developmental model,* a leadership which is able to translate modern technology into programmatic actions.

3. Each must have line *staff (paraprofessionals) trained in their respective field,* but also *able to translate those skills into developmental programs.*

4. Each must utilize *paraprofessional staff* for the large majority of the "programming" as well as *maximum parental involvement.*

5. Each must be able to *rapidly train* new staff because each is designed as a replicable program.

Figure 47 demonstrates the wide range of professionals and paraprofessionals who are involved in mentally retarded person's lives at any given point in time in community programs.

More than 80% of the personnel who come in contact with mentally retarded persons in service programs are paraprofessionals (NIMR, 1972). Many of these professions are relatively new, and many universities or technical colleges have not yet responded to these manpower needs. Much work must be done to develop skills for this type of personnel (e.g., general behavioral development skills). Lastly, the tremendous role that parents and family play in the development of the child must be underscored! Enhanced parenting skills and ongoing in-home support services can expand the parent-family role.

An overview of a manpower preparation model which focuses on the educational/training preparation needed to meet the needs of severely retarded and/or mentally retarded-emotionally disturbed persons in

FIGURE 47
RANGE OF NEEDED PARAPROFESSIONALS AND PROFESSIONALS

community-based programs is presented in Fig. 48. This model covers the entire range of needs of mentally retarded persons and the personnel required to meet these needs, from routine to the most complex. It should be noted as the needs become more complex, the level of specialization becomes greater, but the number of retarded individuals involved becomes less. The large percentage of mental health and medical needs can be prevented or, when present, be appropriately cared for by well-prepared parents and paraprofessionals. As the needs become more complex, the need for sensitive and well trained community health and medical professionals becomes obvious.

THE RELATIONSHIP OF PERSONNEL AND SERVICES

As mentioned earlier, the resolution of the mental health and medical needs of mentally retarded persons and their families is complex and will only occur with time. It will require the development of both programs and personnel, since there is an inevitable relationship between these two factors.

In the past, mentally retarded persons who were concurrently medically fragile and/or emotionally disturbed, were likely institutionalized or unserved. These non-options required little more than custodial care workers and, accordingly, precious little attention to personnel preparation. Today, however, the situation is substantially different. Modern, community-based service alternatives demonstrate that even the most severely involved mentally retarded persons can have their needs met in the community.

As the various services and appropriate personnel evolve over the next decade, there will increasingly arise the issue of the locus of responsibility for the delivery of services to mentally retarded citizens. A suggested format for the relationship between levels of service needed and the locus of responsibility for services and manpower preparations is illustrated in Figure 49.

It should be noted that the large majority of mentally retarded persons (Level 1) have routine medical and mental health needs. This group should be able to have their needs met through the general mental retardation service system, given adequately trained and sensitive staff. Acute medical and mental health needs (Level 2) should be met by an ongoing interface between the mental retardation and mental health-medical systems, with mental retardation professionals assuming the responsibility for the provision of adequate services. In Level 3, mentally retarded persons with chronic mental illness and medical needs should be under the care and responsibility of appropriately trained and sensitive mental retardation professionals with appropriate back-up staff. In summary, the large majority of mentally retarded persons should have their needs met through the general mental retardation delivery system, with appropriate interfaces with the mental health/medical systems providing the necessary services for the smaller numbers of more complex retarded persons who need highly specialized services.

FIGURE 48
PROPOSED MANPOWER MODEL FOR EDUCATION AND TRAINING
OF PARAPROFESSIONALS AND PROFESSIONALS

		Graduate and Post-graduate Educational Level
	Undergraduate and Graduate Educational Level	Psychologists Psychiatrists Educators Social Workers etc.
Secondary Schools, Technical College and Undergraduate Level of Education	Program Managers Program Planners Teachers Therapists Psychologists Social Workers	
Parents Houseparents Aides		
Families — paraprofessional level 80%	MH-MR Graduate Level 15%	MH-MR Post Graduate Level 5%
Community and Technical College Resources	University Resources	University and UAF Resources

FIGURE 49
SERVICE NEEDS AND LOCUS OF RESPONSIBILITY

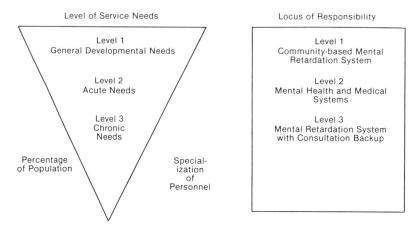

Level of Service Needs   Locus of Responsibility

Level 1
General Developmental Needs

Level 2
Acute Needs

Level 3
Chronic
Needs

Percentage
of Population

Special-
ization
of
Personnel

Level 1
Community-based Mental
Retardation System

Level 2
Mental Health and Medical
Systems

Level 3
Mental Retardation System
with Consultation Backup

CONCLUSION

The day when the needs of mentally retarded citizens are being cared for primarily through institutionalization is, in our opinion, slowly coming to an end. Today's retarded citizens — of all levels of severity — should be living with their families and/or in their communities. This modern challenge brings with it the need for adequately prepared personnel in all communities across the world (i.e., parents, paraprofessionals, and professionals).

The manpower model described here will require the adoption of new ideologies by some. It will also require an interface between programs, community-technical colleges, and universities. It will require linkages between the mental retardation and/or developmental disability systems and the mental health and medical systems. The current challenges in this area are compelling reasons for preparing the manpower pool necessary to appropriately serve the most severely handicapped of our retarded fellow citizens.

IV FUTURE DIRECTIONS

14

Perspectives on Provision of Community Services to Individuals with Mental Retardation

INTRODUCTION

We have reviewed a range of issues relative to the participation of all retarded persons in family and community life. We have emphasized the importance of parent associations in the evolution of integrative programs and services. We have outlined the types of programs and services that need to be developed in communities around the world and have described one such community-based program—ENCOR. We have emphasized the challenge of serving the mentally retarded-mentally ill and the mentally retarded-medically fragile.

Communities and nations that choose to embark on this journey toward interdependence will be confronted with a number of basic and challenging issues as these children and adults are placed in well-supported natural homes, surrogate homes, or group homes and as they enter integrated schools, the work force, and community life.

The basic issues that parent associations need to gradually reach consensus on are: (1) the meaning and acceptance of the developmental assumption; (2) the application of the principle of normalization and the evolution of concrete instrumentalities to ensure the severely retarded person's integration in the community and at the same time to ensure that each person's needs will be met; (3) the development of new teaching strategies based on gentle postures, and (4) the movement toward the interdependence of all persons. These issues are especially important for the more severely retarded for it is more difficult to see this growth and development and it is more complex to support them in community life. The resolution of these differences will enable parents and professionals to envision the presence and participation of all persons in community life. We will review these issues from three perspectives: ideological, technological, and the movement toward interdependence.

IDEOLOGICAL PERSPECTIVES

The Developmental Model

The major ideological thrust of the 1980s is twofold (1) to understand the meaning of the developmental model vis-a-vis the severely mentally retarded and (2) to determine the degree to which the normalization principle should be applied to this population. One cannot be understood without the other. The principle of normalization has its origins in the assumption that all mentally retarded persons are developmental beings; that all are full human beings. If not, it would not make sense to provide normalizing services, settings, and conditions for them.

The developmental model (Wolfensberger, 1972; Menolascino, 1977, Roos, 1979) as we know it today has been interpreted to mean that all mentally retarded persons are capable of human development at their own rate and with varying degrees of plasticity across their lifespans. The developmental model had its origins in early studies of embryological anatomy in the 18th and 19th centuries. In the 18th century it was quite popular to hold that every germ cell contained the potential of an organism of its own kind—fully formed—and that developmental growth consisted primarily of its coming into being with sequential increases in size. This preformationist view paved the way for the slow acceptance of the idea of evolution in the 19th century. For example, from the evolutionary ideas of Darwin, Francis Galton concluded that mental development, like anatomical maturation, was predetermined by heredity. William Wilhelm Stern (1914) conceived the idea of dividing mental age by chronological age to obtain the intelligence quotient, and the concept of fixed intelligence as being totally consistent with the concept of evolution became widely accepted. It was not until the work of scientists such as Jean Piaget (1950) that there arose theories which helped explain the effects of differing external environments on human development. For example, Piaget helped explain how such effects come about through the adaptive changes taking place in developing organisms as they accommodate their abilities and understandings to normal and evermore demanding external circumstances (Hunt, 1961). However, even today we are confronted with the two historical extremes in viewing the mechanisms of human development: (1) There are those who conceive of development as a global unfolding process completely predetermined by the genotype. That is, each infant and child develops as a whole from the moment of conception through an automatic process of unfolding behavior primarily directed by the predetermined ongoing anatomical maturation. (2) Conversely, others emphasize an almost unlimited influence of exterior learning experiences upon the developmental process. They explain human development as a process of connecting early motor or sensory actions with an ever-changing array of new external stimuli, and the subsequent chaining of stimulus-response units into larger systems of psychobiological responses to the physical and interpersonal worlds.

Rather than accepting either one of these dichotomous positions, it would be preferable to define the mentally retarded person as one whose cognitive functions are impaired, but whose potential for human development is unknown — that is, whose development is an open book and highly dependent upon *both* internal factors as well as external factors. In brief, the impact of exterior environment interior state upon the individual can be described in terms of the person's ability to learn to interact adaptively with the world around him.

The issue of human development is not only an intrinsic phenomenon, but also an extrinsic phenomenon. It is relatively easy to clarify the potential for human development from an extrinsic perspective. There is much data available to indicate that a child or adult who has not had adequate and appropriate environmental conditions is going to be retarded when compared with children raised in a nurturing environment (Dennis, 1960; Hunt, Mohandessi, Ghodssi, Akiyama, 1976). This is especially obvious when we look at twin studies that have compared similarly endowed mentally retarded persons in institutions to their counterparts in community-based programs (Conroy et al., 1980; Menolascino & McGee, 1981).

What *is* human development for this population? For the mentally retarded-medically fragile person and the mentally retarded-mentally ill person, we are often times confronted with someone who lacks almost all basic skills. For example, the profoundly retarded-medically fragile person often lacks even basic reflex motions: It therefore becomes necessary to define developmental goals such as sucking, eye tracking, grasping, etc., (Menolascino & Pearson, 1974). Likewise, the severely retarded person with severe emotional problems, often challenges us to define human development vis-a-vis such development barriers as highly self-abusive aggressive, or markedly avoidant (i.e., "autistic") behaviors. Whether the person presents medical or behavioral barriers, along with severe mental retardation, we are confronted with the dilemma of what constitutes human development as well as the degree to which the environment can be adapted to be supportive or enhancing of those intrinsic developmental skills which do exist.

Just as programs around the world in the last three decades have redefined what learning milestones are for the mild and moderately retarded, so in future years we will have to define what learning milestones might be for those with severe profound mental retardation and allied medical and behavioral needs. We also must define more exactly the impact of a number of extrinsic variables so that these can be taken into consideration in our definition of human development. These extrinsic variables can relate to the person himself, to previous learning opportunities, and to external environmental factors. Relative to the person himself, such factors as age, size, allied medical problems, allied psychiatric problems, level of mental retardation, degree of receptive and expressive language all impact on how well we interact developmentally with the person. Relative to previous learning alternatives we must take into consideration the intensity of past developmental programming, the quality and intensity of staffing, the consistency of programming, and programmatic perseverance and flexibility. Relative to environmental factors we must take into consideration the quality of past and current environments, the opportunities for developmental growth, opportunities for bonding with caregivers, and the consistency and structure of programming within the daily living environments.

Prevention and Cure

Recent advances in both biomedical and behavioral sciences have improved, and will continue to improve, our ability to prevent and even "cure" or reverse the condition of mental retardation. Such advances only strengthen the developmental assumption that all mentally retarded individuals are capable of learning and growing, which is a significant shift away from the fait accompli view of this disability.

Research and prevention efforts have dramatically decreased the incidence particularly of the more severe levels of handicapping conditions. We are already noting enhanced prevention of mental retardation from (1) regionalized comprehensive prenatal care centers; (2) the prevention of prenatal and postnatal infections, such as rubella and bacterial meningitis, which involve the central nervous system; (3) enhanced early diagnostic techniques such as amniocentesis, and increasingly effective treatment *in utero* of chromosomal and metabolic diseases; (4) the prevention of both external (e.g., lead and mercury) and internal (e.g., Rh incompatibility) intoxication sources; and (e) increasing intervention into the recurring sets of early childhood experiences which so adversely effect developmental potentials, such as negative psychosocial learning environments and child abuse.

Beyond its impact on the incidence of mental retardation, these instances of successful prevention approaches have lifted the previously hopeless cloud from these conditions ("You can't fight the genes . . .") and have had significant impact on public attitudes and policy. For example, elucidation of the cause of Rh factor blood incompatibility led to a rational approach to its prevention via the use of Rho-GAM to desensitize the Rh (−) mother. Currently, a number of localities require that the Rh type be recorded on marriage license registries of known Rh (−) mothers, and have programs for the distribution of Rho-GAM.

We envision a marked increase in further prevention efforts at the primary, secondary, and tertiary levels, further reducing incidence rates. These efforts will strongly influence the number and types of programs, such as residential services, and service systems that will be necessary in the future. We expect a decreased time lag between the generation of new research findings and their direct and indirect translation into programs. An interesting current innovation involves the use of the advanced technology of the space program in the creation of micromechanical equipment to establish individualized prosthetic environments for severely retarded and multiply handicapped citizens. In the future, we shall see a marked increase in these technological interventions into the developmental history of the severely handicapped individual. In brief, current-future research efforts are focusing on expanding the technological base on which we can devise increasingly more successful preventive and/or treatment intervention approaches. It should be noted that this current-future focus on prevention and allied early intervention efforts have become national goals in many nations: England, France, Sweden, Denmark, and the United States.

Beyond prevention, we are moving toward the actual cure of mental retardation. While the word cure often smacks of quackery when applied to significantly handicapped persons such as the severely retarded, yet, significant gains in curative approaches to primary, secondary, and tertiary cure:

1. Cure for a few, e.g., Murphy's disease, PKU, hypothyroidism, craniostenosis, etc.
2. Treatment for many, e.g., control of seizures, visual and auditory services, motor prostheses, psychotherapy and psychoactive pharmacological agents for managing allied emotional and personality problems, etc.
3. Habilitation for all, e.g., maximizing intellectual, social adaptive, and vocational potential via specific educational, social-recreational, vocational, and residential programs.

Furthermore, we have for some time now been very effective in obtaining "partial" cures, such as the alleviation, minimization and/or control of many of the frequent accompanying symptoms that hinder the retarded citizen's ultimate developmental progress. In other words, the alleviation of secondary symptoms such as effective seizure management has served to minimize the level of the handicap. For example, some of our mildly retarded citizens have, with special help, been able to function in the non-retarded range.

Currently, burgeoning basic and applied research efforts promise realistic payoffs in the very near future. Included in these future approaches to cure are: (1) recent work which shows that the enzyme errors in some of the inborn errors of metabolism can be reversed by cultured and implanted skin fragments, e.g., fibroblasts in glycoprotein disorders; (2) current animal research which clearly illustrates that neuronal regeneration in the spinal column and brain is possible; (3) continuing research on an increasing number of psychopharmacological agents with memory and/or learning enhancement characteristics; (4) recent attempts to reduce the RNA turnover rate in "extra" chromosome disorders such as Down's Syndrome; and (5) using amniocentesis to confirm prenatal signs of neural tube defects, and rather than recommend abortion as a "treatment," use of intrauterine surgery on the fetus to correct lesions such as a meningomyelocele. Rather than get lost in the swirling debates as to what constitutes cure, it seems clear that the future will increasingly see the use of very early fetus-infant-child intervention techniques to cure the "incurable."

The developmental assumption is the basic ideological force in the movement toward the interdependence of all persons. In previous chapters we demonstrated how even the most severely retarded can be in the mainstream of family and community life. Our brief discussion of preventive and curative approaches gives new meaning and hope to the developmental assumption.

NORMALIZATION

Accepting the intrinsic-extrinsic challenges of the developmental model, we can more appropriately consider the meaning and interpretation of the principle of normalization (Wolfensberger, 1972; Nirje, 1969; Menolascino, 1977) for the most severely retarded. For these persons whose capacities for learning are often substantially limited, the principle of normalization has to be translated into the types of environmental and prosthetic supports which they require: It's not simply a constricted two-choice dichotomy of either: (1) insisting on the same conditions for all mentally retarded persons as are available to non-handicapped individuals, or (2) developing village-like subcommunities across the world and completely segregating them in such environments for the "deviants." We should avoid the semantic arguments of those pseudo-intellectuals who examine the word normalization from their theoretical perspective (Bachrach, 1980; Perr, 1978; Throne, 1979) without any basis in reality. Rather the focus of our advocacy efforts must be on the individual needs of every severely retarded, multiply handicapped citizen. The principle of normalization must be defined not only in terms of educational, vocational, residential, and social-recreational placements, but also in terms of the types of programs and supports which the person needs in order to maintain himself or herself in family and home community environments.

It should be noted that the principle of normalization does not mean that we are going to expect and/or make the mentally retarded person "normal." This incorrect interpretation assumes that we cannot or will not focus, to whatever degree necessary, on the programmatic, prosthetic, and environmental supports and adaptations which the individual retarded person needs in order to function within the normal environments of our homes, communities, and the generic supports therein.

On the other hand, "normal-or-nothing" advocates need to recognize the entire constellation of factors which swirl around the individual severely retarded person and his allied complex developmental needs: They blindly insist that the principle of normalization can fully be applied to all mentally retarded persons in the same manner without regard to each person's uniqueness. They have focused on integration without considering the programmatic and societal changes which must concurrently occur in order to attain these just goals; for example, the role of parents and the family in the placement process, the assurances for programmatic and placement stability and consistency, the quality and intensity of manpower available to meet the individual needs of every severely retarded person, the past experiences of the mentally retarded person and his family vs. the service delivery system, as well as allied medical and psychiatric factors which come to bear on the ongoing physical, emotional, and developmental status of these severely retarded persons. Many pro-normalization advocates tend to disregard the need for assuring both the retarded person and his family that all of these factors (which are basic instrumentalities for the accomplishment of true integration) *will* be taken into consideration and dealt with consistently.

There should be some assurances of stable and ongoing funding of programs, services, and supports which the individual mentally retarded person might require. Issues such as, "What will happen to my son (or daughter) after we die?" need to be dealt with and resolved by pro-normalization advocates in their local communities (Menolascino, 1974). The President's Commission on Mental Health (1978) has stated that professionals often miscast parents and their demands for services as manifestations of displaced hostility or even as psychopathology arising out of chronic sorrow. Normalization advocates need to understand the concerns and needs of the family constellation if they are to advocate for the mentally retarded individual.

The Integration Corollary

A major corollary of both the developmental model and normalization principle is the issue of integration (Wolfensberger, 1972). Advocacy of physical and social integration of mentally retarded persons into community life does not mean that the mentally retarded person should be denied the types of special services and supports that he or she needs. As in the principle of normalization, the concept of integration does not mean, nor should it mean, "dumping" the mentally retarded person into the community—the school, the home, industry, or social-recreational activities.

Simply placing a mentally retarded person in the mainstream of family and community life and leaving the person and his family with no resources *is* dumping. It denies, often cruelly and destructively, the programmatic and societal supports that all severely retarded persons require (Jaslow & Spagna, 1977).

We must admit that a certain percentage of deinstitutionalization has resulted in dumping, rather than the placement of mentally retarded persons into community-based service systems to meet their needs (Mayeda & Sutter, 1981). On the other hand, segregation should not be allowed simply because a person happens to be mentally retarded. It must be recognized that for integration to occur adequate supports need to be provided for each individual mentally retarded person.

In individual cases integration might mean the preparation of classroom teachers and non-handicapped children to accept and respond to mentally retarded classmates (Morra, 1979). It may mean that a particular child needs a teacher aide to help him in the normal classroom setting, or perhaps a barrier-free environment.

Moving away from the dichotomy of segregation vs. integration, the global ideological challenge inherent in the developmental model, the principle of normalization—and the corollary of integration—should focus on a movement toward interdependence; that is, "differentness" being accepted, specialized supports being given where necessary, independence available where possible, and services ensured across the mentally retarded person's lifespan to whatever degree is needed at any given point in time.

Normalizing the Mentally Retarded Adult

It is a logical conclusion, based on the principle of normalization, that most mentally retarded adults should and can participate in and benefit from the world of work (Wolfensberger, 1967; Gold, 1973; Bellamy, Horner, & Inman, 1979). There has perhaps been too much emphasis on the cultural appropriateness phenomenon. It would perhaps be more productive to focus on the mentally retarded person's participation in the world of work, not so much because of economic gains, but rather because participation in the world of work is an excellent *vehicle* for involving the mentally retarded person in the mainstream of life, although it is obvious that community-based programs must ensure a range of social recreational activities outside of the world of work (Birenbaum & Re, 1979). This active participation in itself is a powerful developmental activity for the retarded person. It also serves to heighten the awareness of the lay public to the contributive aspects of the mentally retarded person to society.

However, it cannot be denied that there is a very small percentage of retarded persons who cannot actually benefit from this type of "culturally appropriate" activity. For example, in ENCOR there are less than 10 mentally retarded adults out of more than 1,000 clients who are in "prevocational" programs, rather than vocational programs, due to their multiple developmental, behavioral, or medical needs. Those who cannot participate in the mainstream of the world of work, even with support, should not be degraded and simply left to fend for themselves. Professionals must develop and actively support work training programs, and social-recreational programs for these individuals (especially those with allied medical or behavioral challenges), whose total participation in the world of work is temporarily precluded. Therefore, it behooves parent-professional advocates to establish creative, integrative, developmental, and enjoyable activities and services to help this subpopulation of the retarded to participate in the mainstreams of daily community life as much as possible.

TECHNOLOGICAL PERSPECTIVES

With the gradual resolution of the aforementioned ideological and treatment issues, the next major challenge will be to define a new teaching posture toward the most severely retarded. There is not so much a lack of teaching and treatment technology, but a lack of a teaching and treatment philosophy. In Chapter 10 we reviewed a series of teaching treatment techniques based on a gentle, tolerant, caring relationship with the severely retarded person.

Beyond medical and psychiatric diagnoses, it is crucial to understand the nature of the problems of the most severely retarded. Most often, the etiology of their developmental needs can be traced to extreme difficulties in processing and expressing information within the world around them. The basic developmental needs can be traced back to modes of primitive communication. When a severely retarded person is displaying maladaptive behaviors (such as hitting, biting, scratching, screaming, spinning, and feces smearing), in the majority of the cases it is fair to describe these behaviors as primitive modes of communication. In attempting to understand the etiology of these behaviors, we should interpret them as the person's most powerful way, and sometimes only way, of expressing his/her needs and understanding of the world. In most instances severely and profoundly retarded persons have no language or, at best, minimal language. As they grow from infancy to childhood they learn to express themselves and to gain attention through a repertoire of such behaviors. Conversely, these maladaptive behaviors most often tend to be punished, resulting in increased frequency of the behaviors the punishment was intended to decrease.

To develop a gentle posture, it is crucial that we understand the nature of behavioral problems in the severely-profoundly retarded. This population is generally characterized by multiple developmental needs. The impact of impairments of the central nervous system in these children must be understood. Metaphorically, persons with severe-profound mental retardation process information from the world around them into their central nervous system in one of two ways: (1) The information that enters into their central nervous system is overstimulating. They are not able to separate out the multiple stimuli entering into them — sounds, visual stimuli, auditory stimuli, olfactory stimuli, and tactile stimuli. It is as if a lightening storm is created in the central nervous system through overstimulation caused by the entrance of these stimuli. The end result in this case is often acting-out behaviors or refusal to respond. (2) External stimuli enter into the central nervous system slowly or are not processed in the same manner as in normal children. In this case parents and teachers often respond negatively to the child, though the child has "not understood" the information presented.

Given the above, it is not surprising that these persons develop a repertoire of behaviors as responses to impairments of their central nervous systems. These behaviors are the range of aggressive, self-abusive, self-stimulatory, and avoidant behaviors so often the focus of punishment-based programmatic interventions.

These same children and adults are also often characterized by multiple handicapping conditions such as the various forms and types of epilepsy and cerebral palsy, and disabilities related to sight and hearing, as well as a number of other medically-based disabilities that further compound the teaching-treatment challenge.

Parents and professionals will need to merge a behavioral approach which focuses on the development of human interactions and bonding with a humanistic approach which focuses on the interdependence between the severely retarded person and the caregiver. Figure 50 summarizes the components of this gentle posture:

1. *Affection* needs to be purposefully integrated into the teaching-treatment process. We have already reviewed a number of gentle teaching techniques in Chapter 10. These techniques need to be coupled with a focus on gentle verbal and tactile interactions.
2. *Tolerance* needs to be purposefully integrated into the teaching-treatment process. Many severely retarded persons possess a high degree of medical and/or psychiatric problems that without tolerance, often serve as barriers in the teaching-treatment process.
3. *Instructional control* needs to be gained before any further developmental gains can be made. This is achieved through maximizing opportunities for positive consequences, especially positive interactions. This

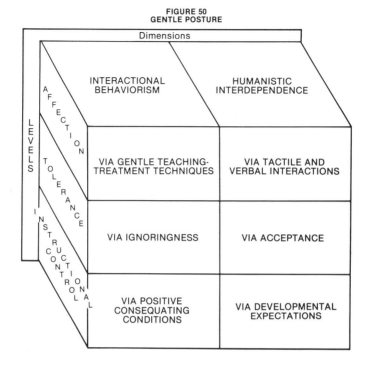

FIGURE 50
GENTLE POSTURE

necessitates high developmental expectations and the initial use of developmental tasks to gain instructional control.

COMPUTER TECHNOLOGY

For the past 20 years, researchers have convincingly demonstrated that mentally retarded individuals can be taught highly complex work skills when afforded systematic training and appropriate supervision to maintain satisfactory production. Today and in the future, the use of telecommunication systems have opened up major options for mentally retarded individuals in both information acquisition and information sharing. The concept of in-home terminals and computers using both audio and visual input and output systems could create new job opportunities, recreational activities, and learning environments for those individuals with limited ability and mobility. Electrode switches and alternate communication mechanisms can be designed to aid in environmental manipulation. New medical and aerospace technology such as the use of the laser has been demonstrated to be successful in a variety of fields. As mentioned earlier in this chapter, breakthroughs in the biomedical field will allow us via computer technology to place many high-speed devices in the body and brain which will trace a wide range of bio-logical reactions. Such devices can improve one's overall health, the ability to learn, remember and communicate with one's environment. For example, the Association for Retarded Citizens has undertaken a new biotechnology pro-ject in cooperation with the IBM Corporation and other aerospace industries in developing a total technological environment where individuals with cog-nitive and physical deficits can maximize their full potential.

Microcomputer terminals can be designed to aid in training and the provi-sion of activities in daily living, employment opportunities and recreational activities. Computer programs can be designed to reinforce behaviors and use prompt training and re-training activities at home and at work. Research in this area ranges from the use of the microcomputer as a behavioral micro-scope to monitoring and interacting with infant development in order to teach specific behavioral movements based upon contingent responses of the infant. In such instances the microcomputer functions as a learning prosthe-sis for the retarded individual. With the computer we will be able to utilize the concepts of immediate positive reinforcement, learning and relearning in such a way that the cost will be considerably low and less labor-intensive. The microcomputer will allow individuals with physical and cognitive limitations to improve motor skills in such a way that they could be amplified to interact with the world around them.

From a service perspective, the storage and rapid retrieval capacity of com-puters has just begun to be used in the total delivery service system. The coordination of community-based service systems utilizing the computer as a case management resource will ensure fewer procedural bureaucratic failures in the delivery of comprehensive services. Programs can be evaluated by using data available in the central storage area or planning for the future in determining an appropriate resource for an entire population.

INTERDEPENDENCE PERSPECTIVE

To move toward the interdependence of all persons it is important to resolve two issues: (1) the rights of the retarded person versus parental rights and (2) whether retarded persons have special rights because of their special needs.

Parents Rights vs. The Rights of the Mentally Retarded Citizen

The dichotomy of parents' rights versus their mentally retarded sons' or daughters' rights is a most heated issue, one that most often comes to a ques-tion of who has the final say over the placement of a mentally retarded person in an institution, in a segregated classroom, in a sheltered employment setting, and so on. While this issue has primarily been viewed in legal terms, in fact, legalistic principles often do not help to clarify the relationship between parents and child.

The 1970's focused on the rights of mentally retarded persons because up to this time they had been virtually considered as non-persons. Thus, today we are confronted with the other side of the existential dilemma — the rights of the parents of the mentally retarded and the juxtaposition of these rights with those of the mentally retarded.

This dilemma must be resolved for it is clear that parents are the strongest voice of the mentally retarded. Without their concern and advocacy the mentally retarded will be lost in a shallow sea of transient advocacy. Parents are the only group with a natural, lifelong concern for the mentally retarded.

A major existential dilemma confronted by parents of the mentally retarded concerns the question of deinstitutionalization. Although we pointed out that comprehensive, community-based programs are possible and demonstratable, it is still a fact that many communities have not yet created comprehensive, community-based alternatives to institutions. Thus, in most places when a professional recommends community placement the parent is placed in a quandry. The institution has almost assuredly guaranteed to the parents that the child/adult would have a clean, secure, protected place across his lifespan, an environment which although not normalizing, at least would give the perception and feeling of security. Now the professional wants the parents to place the child/adult in a community program that is likely poorly funded, with no history, and likely not part of a comprehensive, developmentally intense, and publicly monitored system. Too many mentally retarded persons have been dumped out of institutions rather than placed in comprehensive, community-based service systems.

Turnbull, Ellis, Boggs, Brooks, & Biklen (1981) described the current legalistic approach in the United States to parents' rights versus children's rights as the interposition of legal considerations between the natural relationships of parents with their children. This legal wall views the parents as inherently untrustworthy rather than generally loyal, trustworthy and steadfast allies of their mentally retarded son and daughters.

The relationship and bond between parents of mentally retarded persons and the mentally retarded themselves needs to be clearly defined. Rather than merely a matter of dependence versus independence, the issue is how much "protection" (support) the individual mentally retarded person requires in a given situation and the nature of the ongoing relationship between the parent and the mentally retarded person. Parents, professionals, and the mentally retarded themselves need to focus on making decisions in a "best fit" manner. Depending upon the situation, we need to take into consideration a number of factors such as: the needs of the mentally retarded person, the relationship and bond of the parent to the child across time, the need for programmatic stability, the pursuit of the maximum degree of interdependence. The final solution of this existential problem should be the clarification of the concept of interdependence. All people depend upon one another. The question is how much and to what degree at any given point in time. The end result of normalization should not be the independence of the mentally retarded person in society, but the maximum degree of interdependence for all persons — mentally retarded or not.

Special Rights for Persons with Special Needs

On opposite sides of this issue are those advocates who hold that: (1) mentally retarded persons by the very nature of their mental retardation should have special rights regardless of the costs involved in implementing those rights and (2) those who hold that this is not normalizing and that if we advocate for equal protection and treatment we cannot advocate for "special privileges."

It is functionally established in many communities that mentally retarded persons do have the same basic rights as any other citizens. The problem is that in order to acquire, maintain, or establish these rights it is often necessary to give special supports to the mentally retarded person. For example, the right to go to a regular school might mean that the bathroom in the school might have to be made accessible to meet the needs of a multiply handicapped-mentally retarded child. Should the cost of this "right" be borne by the taxpayer?

A reasonable posture towards this dichotomous position would be to focus on the needs of the individual mentally retarded person from the perspective of what costs are legitimate and reasonable in the acquisition of such mainstreaming opportunities.

It could legitimately be questioned that any of the supports and services which we deem necessary are only necessary because there has been built up a human service industrial complex around the mentally retarded population.

An analysis of the creative services of poorer communities (such as Agueda, Portugal) would give us clues as to how to meet rights without creating a human service industry. This analysis would lead us to the very nature of interdependence and community living. The question is not whether or not mentally retarded persons should have equal rights with all other citizens. This fact has been well established. Rather, the question is what types of reasonable supports should be made available to mentally retarded citizens in order to equalize their citizenship with others. We need to recognize that individualized supports which establish a certain equality do not signify special rights. Rather they represent the provision of equal opportunity to the person who has special needs.

Economically poorer countries confront this dilemma. For example, in Spain where severely mentally retarded children do not have a functional right to a free public education, advocates are often confronted with this challenge. Thirty-percent of their nondisabled children do not attend school for lack of teachers and school buildings. How can we advocate that all mentally retarded persons should go to school? Spanish advocates reply:

1. All children should have the right to attend school, including the most severely mentally retarded. Advocates of all children regardless of need must agree with this.
2. When resources are limited, then all advocates need to recognize their interdependence and work in solidarity. Injustice done to one is injustice done to all. It is obvious that for the severely mentally retarded the "survival of the fittest" posture to human life will leave them abandoned. A capitalistic approach to human rights will not meet the basic human needs and rights of the mentally retarded. The road to community participation for the severely mentally retarded is not illuminated by the glow of total individual independence. Many of these citizens do not even have boot straps to lift themselves up. For equal rights special supports must be given. Without such supports there can be no rights.

Therefore, we do not advocate for special rights, but for the basic rights for all persons to live and grow in the mainstream of community life with whatever supports the person might require. In such a manner, all persons will truly be treated as equal.

CONCLUSION

The issues we have dealt with go to the very essence of the advocacy movement. The original thrusts of the 1960's and 1970's were built more on matters of the heart than of the mind. We collectively felt that it was good and just to embrace the concepts of normalization and the developmental model. We had seen and heard of these working in the Scandanavian countries (Kugel & Shearer, 1976). We were horrified by the purgatory of institutions (Blatt & Kaplan, 1966). We moved to bring out retarded citizen home. We were dismayed that mentally retarded citizens had no rights.

Today we are confronted with the same issues as yesterday, but in often more subtle and divisive forms. We must analyze these issues, look for programs which symbolize normalization, the developmental model, and the establishment of equal rights, especially for the more severely mentally retarded. By the year 2,000 we should look back and see that these issues and their resolutions were more of the heart than of the mind. We should see all children learning to live together — the essence of interdependence.

We have attempted to review the global and specific aspects of mental retardation — from the roots of change to basic issues which will confront us in the future. The challenges of today rest in our hearts' responses to the basic quest for interdependence.

References

Alioa, G. Assessment of the complexity of the least restrictive environment doctrine of Public Law 94–142. In L. Morra (Ed.), *LRE: Developing criteria for the evaluation of the least restrictive environment provision.* Philadelphia, PA: Research for Better Schools, Inc., 1979.

Anderson, O. W. *Blue Cross since 1929: Accountability and the public trust.* New York, NY: Ballinger, 1975.

Association for Retarded Citizens-United States (ARC-US). *Issues related to services for mentally retarded persons: A preliminary issue discussion paper.* Arlington, TX: ARC-US, 1981.

Bachrach, L. L. Is the least restrictive environment always the best? Sociological and semantic implications. *Hospital and Community Psychiatry,* 1980, *31* (2), 97–103.

Bank-Mikkelsen, N. E. Denmark. In R. B. Kugel & A. Shearer (Eds.), *Changing patterns in residential services for the mentally retarded.* Washington, DC, President's Committee on Mental Retardation: U.S. Government Printing Office, 1976.

Barker, R., & Associates. *Habitats, environments, and human behavior: Studies in ecological psychology and eco-behavioral science.* San Francisco, CA: Jossey-Bass, Inc., 1978.

Baron, F. N. Group therapy improves mental retardate behavior. *Hospital and Community Psychiatry,* 1972, *23,* 7–11.

Barr, W. *Mental defectives: Their history, treatment and training.* Philadelphia, PA: Blakiston's Son & Co., 1904.

Baucom, L. D., & Bensberg, G. J. *Advocacy systems for persons with severe disabilities. Context, components, and resources.* Lubbock, TX: Texas Tech University, 1976.

Behavior Today – The Professionals. Newsletter, August 13, 1979, Volume 10, #31.

Beier, D. Behavioral disturbances in the mentally retarded. In H. A. Stevens & R. Heber (Eds.), *Mental retardation: A review of research.* Chicago, IL: Chicago University Press, 1964.

Bellamy, G. T., Horner, R. H., & Inman, D. P. *Vocational Habilitation of Severely Retarded Adults: A Direct Service Technology.* Baltimore, MD: University Park Press, 1979.

Berkovitz, I. H., & Sugar, M. *Indications and contraindications for adolescents in group and family therapy.* New York, NY: Brunner/Mazel, 1975.

Berkson, G., & Landesman-Dwyer, S. Behavioral research on severe and profound mental retardation (1955–1974). *American Journal of Mental Deficiency,* 1977, *91,* 428–454.

241

Bijou, S. *Developmental needs of the retarded.* Presentation at, Briding the Gap Conference. Atlanta, GA: National Association for Retarded Citizens, 1979.

Biklen, D. *The community imperative: A refutation of all arguments in support of institutionalizing anybody because of mental retardation.* Syracuse, NY: Center on Human Policy, 1979.

Biklen, D. *The community imperative.* Syracuse, NY: Center on Human Policy, 1980.

Biklen, D. The least restrictive environment: Its application to education. In G. B. Melton (Ed.), *Child and youth service and the law.* New York, NY: Haworth Press, 1982 (in press).

Birenbaum, A., & Re, M. A. Resettling mental retarded adults in the community — almost four years later. *American Journal of Mental Deficiency,* 1979, *83* (4), 323–329.

Blatt, B. *Souls in extremis: An anthology on victims and victimizers.* Boston, MA: Allyn and Bacon, 1963.

Blatt, B., & Kaplan, F. *Christmas in purgatory.* Boston, MA: Allyn and Bacon, 1966.

Bogdan, R., & Taylor, S. The judged, not the judges: An insider's view of mental retardation. *American Psychologist,* 1976, *31* (1), 47–52.

Braddock, D. *A national deinstitutionalization study,* State Government, Vol. 50, No. 4. Lexington, KY: Council of State Governments, Autumn 1977.

Bricker, W. A. Identifying behavioral deficits. *American Journal of Mental Deficiency,* 1970, *75* (16), 120–128.

Brown, L., Branston, M. B., Hamre-Nietupski, A., Johnson, F., Wilcox, B., & Grunewald, L. A rationale for comprehensive longitudinal interactions between severely handicapped students and other citizens. *AAESPH Review,* 1979, *4* (1), 3–14.

Cantilli, E. J., Schmelzer, J. L., & the Staff Division of Information, Administration on Aging. *Transportation and Aging, Selected Issues.* Based on Proceedings of the Interdisciplinary Workshop on Transportation and Aging, Washington, DC, May 24–26, 1970. (DHEW Publication Number SRS 72-20232). Washington, DC: U.S. Government Printing Office, 1971.

Cavara, P. *Experiencia de Parma.* Paper presented at the First International Symposium on Cerebral Palsy. Seville, 1979.

Chemarin, Y. & Desroy, J. Centros de ayuda por el trabajo. *Siglo Cero,* 1980, *69* (May-June), 40–45.

Chess, S., & Hassibi, S. Behavior deviations in mentally retarded children. *Journal of the American Academy of Child Psychiatry,* 1970, *9* (2), 282–297.

Chess, S., Horn, S., & Fernandez, P. *Psychiatric disorders of children with congenital rubella.* New York, NY: Brunner/Mazel, 1971.

Conferencia Episcopal de Latina America. *Terceira Conferencia Geral Do Episcopado Latino-American.* Puebla, Mexico: Conselho Episcopal Latino-Americana, 1978.

Conley, R. *The Economics of mental retardation.* Baltimore: Johns Hopkins University Press, 1973.

Conroy, J. W., Lemanowicz, J. S., Sokol, L., & Pollack, M. *Development of seventeen former Pennhurst residents who are now in community living arrangements in Montgomery County. Pennhurst study-brief: Report #1.* Philadelphia, PA: Temple University, October 1980.

Cook, P. F., Dahl, P. R., & Gale, M. A. *Vocational training and placement of the severely handicapped vocational opportunities.* Palo Alto, CA: U.S. Office of Education, The American Institutes for Research in the Behavioral Sciences, 1977.

Cook, R. E. The free choice principle in the care of the mentally retarded. In R. Kugel & W. Wolfensberger (Eds.), *Changing patterns in residential services for the mentally retarded.* Washington, DC, President's Committee on Mental Retardation: U.S. Government Printing Office, 1970.

Crossen, J. E. *The experimental analysis of vocational behavior in severely retarded males* (Final Report, Grant No. OEG32-47-0230-6024). Washington, DC: U.S. Department of Health, Education, and Welfare, 1967.

Crossen, J. E. The functional analysis of behavior. A technology for special education practices. *Mental Retardation,* 1969, *7* (4), 15–19.

Daniels, D. N. The community mental health center in the rural area: Is the present model appropriate? *American Journal of Psychiatry,* 1967, *124.3,* (Supplement, Oct.), 32–37.

Delbecq, A., & Van deVen, A. A group process model for Problem I certification and program planning. *Journal of Applied Behavioral Science,* 1971, *7* (4), 466–492.

Delbecq, A., Van deVen, A., & Gustafson, D. *Group Techniques for Program Planning: A Guide to Nominal Group and Delphi Processes.* Glenville, IL: Scott Forsment, 1975.

Dennis, W. Causes of retardation among institutional children. *Iran Journal of Genetic Psychology,* 1960, *96,* 47–59.

Diagnostic and Statistical Manual of Mental Disorders, Volume III (DSM-III). Washington, DC: American Psychiatric Association, 1980.

Djukanovic, V. The Democratic Republic of North Vietnam. In B. S. Hetzel (Ed.), *Basic health care in developing countries.* Oxford: Oxford University Press, 1978.

Donoghue, E. C., & Abbas, K. A. Unstable behavior in severely subnormal children. *Developmental Medicine and Child Neurology,* 1971, *13,* 512–519.

Dupont, A. Proceedings of the Sixth Delaware Conference on the Handicapped Child. Wilmington, DE: 1968.

Dybwad, G. *Exodus from pandemonium: A reformation of residential treatment for the mentally retarded.* Seattle, WA: Special Child Publications, 1967.

Dybwad, G. A Society Without Institutions. Presentation to the Residential Alternatives Symposium, University of Hartford, December 1978 (unpublished).

Eastern Nebraska Community Office of Retardation (ENCOR). *Action Plan.* Omaha, NE: ENCOR, 1979.

Eaton, L. & Menolascino, F. Psychiatric disorders in the mentally retarded: Types, problems, and challenges. *American Journal of Psychiatry,* 1982, *139* (10), 1297–1303.

Edgerton, R. B. & Bercovici, S. M. The cloak of competence: Years later. *American Journal of Mental Deficiency,* 1976, *80,* 485–497.

Ellis, N. R., Balla, D., Estes, O., Hollis, J., Isaacson, R., Orlando, R., Palk, B. E., Warren, S. A., & Siegel, P. S. Wyatt v. Hardin C.A. 3195-N. U.S. District Court, Middle District of Alabama, October 18, 1978 (Memorandum of Balla, et al.).

Enthoven, A. The systems analysis approach. In A. Henrichs & S. Taylor (Eds.), *Program budgeting and benefit-cost analysis.* Palisades, CA: Goodyear Publishing Co., 1969.

Ferleger, D., & Boyd, A. Anti-institutionalization: The promise of the Pennhurst case. *Stanford Law Review,* April 1979, 3.

Fisher, M., & Zeaman, D. An attention-retention theory or retardate discrimination learning. In N. Ellis (Ed.), *The international review of research in mental retardation, Vol. 6.* New York, NY: Academic Press, 1973.

Flavier, J. M. Rural reconstruction. In B. S. Hetzel (Ed.), *Basic health care in developing countries.* Oxford: Oxford University Press, 1978.

Fletcher, R. J. *A Model Day Treatment Service for the Mentally Retarded-Mentally Ill.* Kingston, NY: Beacon House, 1982 (unpublished manuscript).

Flint, B. *The child and the institution.* Toronto: University of Toronto Press, 1966.

Forrester, J. *Urban dynamics.* Cambridge, MA: M.I.T. Press, 1972.

Freeman, R. D. Psychopharmacology and the retarded child. In F. Menolascino (Ed.), *Psychiatric approaches to mental retardation.* New York, NY: Basic Books, 1970.

Freire, P. Cultural action, a dialectical analysis. *Centro intercultural de documentacion,* 1970.

Galloway, C. *Philosophical and service design implications: A review of sheltered workshops and related programs.* State of California, Department of Rehabilitation, 1979.

Gilhool, T. *Habilitation of developmentally disabled persons in a small group setting versus a large group institutional setting.* Philadelphia, PA: PILCOR, 1978.

Goffman, E. *Asylums.* New York, NY: Doubleday, 1961.

Gold, M. W. Stimulus factors in skill training of retarded adolescents on a complex assembly task: Acquisition, transfer, and retention. *American Journal of Mental Deficiency,* 1972, *76,* 517–526.

Gold, M. W. Research on the vocational habilitation of the retarded: The present, the future. In N. R. Ellis (Ed.), *International review of research in mental retardation, Vol. 6.* New York, NY: Academic Press, 1973.

Gold, M. W. *Research on the vocational habilitation of the retarded: The present and the future.* Urbana, IL: Children's Research Center, 1979 (unpublished).

Gold, M. W. *Try another way training manual.* Champaign-Urbana, IL: Mark Gold and Associates, 1980.

Goldfried, M., & Merboum, M. *Behavior change through self-control.* New York, NY: Holt, Rinehart and Winston, 1973.

Gollay, E. Friedman, R., Wyngardner, M., & Kurtz, N. *Coming back.* Cambridge, MA: Abt Press, 1978.

Goodfellow, R. *Group homes: One alternative.* Syracuse, NY: Human Policy Press, 1974.

Goodyear, D. L., Bitter, J. A., & Micek, L. A. Rehabilitation service for rural, rural-urban and urban clients. *Rehabilitation Counseling Bulletin,* 1973, *17* (2), 92–99.

Greenspan, S. *A Unifying framework for educating caregivers about discipline.* Omaha, NE: Boys Town Center for the Study of Youth Development, 1981.

Groden, G., Domingue, D., Pueschel, S., & Deignan, L. Behavioral/emotional problems in mentally retarded children and youth. *Psychological Reports* 1982, *51,* 143–146.

Gross, A. *The use of cost effectiveness analysis in deciding on alternative living arrangments for the retarded.* Fourth Annual Conference of the International Association for the Mentally Deficient, 1978 (unpublished document).

Grunewald, K. National patterns: Sweden. In R. Kugel & A. Shearer (Eds.), *Changing patterns in residential services for the mentally retarded.* Washington, DC, President's Committee on Mental Retardation: U.S. Government Printing Office, 1976.

Grunzberg, H. C. The hospital as a normalizing training environment. *Journal of Mental Subnormality,* 1970, *16,* 71–83.

Gustafson, D., Shukla, R., Delbecq, A., & Walster, W. A comparative study of differences or subjective likelihood estimates made by individuals, interacting groups, delphi groups, and nominal groups. *Organizational Behavior and Human Performance,* 1973, *9,* 280–291.

Halderman v. Pennhurst, No. 74-1345 (E.D. Pa. 1977). State School and Hospital, 466F. Supp. 1295, U.S. Third Circuit Court of Appeals (1978).

Haring, N., & Hayden, A. *Effectiveness and cost-efficiency of early intervention with handicapped children.* Seattle, WA: University of Washington, 1981 (unpublished document).

Harris, R., & Harris, C. *A new perspective on the psychological effects of environmental barriers.* Washington, DC, President's Committee on Employment of the Handicapped: U.S. Government Printing Office, 1976.

Hassinger, E. W. Pathways of rural people to health services In E. W. Hassinger & L. R. Whiting (Eds.), *Rural health services: Organization, delivery, and use.* Ames, IA: Iowa State University Press, 1976.

Hatch, J., & Erpp, J. A. Consumer involvement in the delivery of health services. In E. W. Hassinger & L. R. Whiting (Eds.), *Rural health services: Organization, delivery and use.* Ames, IA: Iowa State University Press, 1976.

Hewitt, F. M. Educational engineering with emotionally disturbed children. *Exceptional Children,* 1967, *33,* 459–467.

Hitzing, W. Hoffman, K., Killenbeck, M., Loop, B., Neil, K., & Wood, J. *Deinstitutionalization: Recommendations to region VII DD office.* Omaha, NE: The Center for the Development of Community Alternative Service Systems, 1977.

Hoben, M. Toward integration in the mainstream. *Exceptional Children,* 1980, *46* (2), 100–105.

Horacek v. Exon, Civil No. 79-L-299, U.S. District Court, District of Nebraska, Plan of Implementation. Nebraska Mental Retardatio Panel, November 1978.

Horner, R. H., & Bellamy, G. T. A conceptual analysis of vocational training with the severely retarded. In M. Snell (Ed.), *Systematic instruction of the moderately, severely, and profoundly handicapped.* Columbus, OH: Charles E. Merrill, 1978.

Human Services Coordination Alliance. *Service coordination: An introduction to the Louisville system.* Louisville, KY: United Way Classification Project, 1977.

Hunt, J., McV. *Intelligence and experience.* New York, NY: Ronald Press, 1961.

Hunt, J., McV., Mohandessi, K., Ghodssi, M., & Akiyama, M. The psychological development of orphanage-reared infants' interventions with outcomes (Tehran). *Genetic Psychological Monograph,* 1976, *94,* 177–221.

Hyman, H. *Health planning: A systematic approach.* Rockville, MD: Aspen Systems Corp., 1975.

International League of Societies for the Mentally Handicapped (ILSMH). *The child with retardation today — The adult of tomorrow.* R. Perske (Ed.), 1979.

Irvin, L. K. General utility of easy-to-hard discrimination training procedures with the severely retarded. *Education and Training of the Mentally Retarded,* 1976, *11* (3), 247–250.

Irvin, L. K., & Bellamy, G. T. Manipulation of stimulus featured in vocational skill training of the severely retarded: Relative efficacy. *American Journal of Mental Deficiency,* 1977, *81,* 486–491.

Jaslow, R., & Spagna, M. Gaps in a comprehensive system of services for the mentally retarded. *Mental Retardation,* 1977, *13,* 6–9.

Kanner, L. Autistic disturbances of affective contact. *Nervous Child,* 1943, *2,* 217–250.

King, M. *Medical care in developing countries.* Oxford: Oxford University Press, 1966.

Koenig, C. H. *Charting the future course of behavior.* Lawrence, KS: School of Education, University of Kansas, 1972 (unpublished).

Kral, P., Crowther, E., Edwards, M., Howie, S., Morrill, D., Stacey, E., Svoboda, D., Wood, J., & Girardeau, F. *A study of Title XIX impact potential for service to the developmentally disabled of Kansas.* Kansas State Developmental Disabilities Planning Council, 1978.

Kugel, R., Shearer, A. *Changing patterns in residential services for the mentally retarded.* Washington, DC, President's Committee on Mental Retardation: U.S. Government Printing Office, 1976.

Kugel, R., & Wolfensberger, W. *Changing patterns in residential services for the mentally retarded.* Washington, DC: U.S. Government Printing Office, 1969.

Kushlick, A. Wessec, England. In R. Kugel & A. Shearer (Eds.), *Changing patterns in residential services for the mentally retarded.* Washington, DC, President's Committee on Mental Retardation: U.S. Government Printing Office, 1976.

Leland, H. Book review of *The family papers: A return to Purgatory,* B. Blatt, A. Ozolins, & J. McNally (Eds.), *American Journal of Mental Deficiency,* 1981, *85,* 438–439.

Levi, C. A., Roberts, D. B., & Menolascino, F. J. Providing psychiatric services for clients of community-based mental retardation programs. *Hospital and community psychiatry,* 1979, *30,* 383–384.

Lindsley, O. R. Direct measurement and prosthesis of retarded behavior. *Journal of Education,* 1964, *147,* 62–81.

Lipman, R. S. The use of psychopharmacological agents in residential facilities for the retarded. In F. J. Menolascino (Ed.), *Psychiatric approaches to mental retardation.* New York, NY: Basic Books, 1970.

Lynch, K. P., Kiernan, W. E., & Stark, J. A. *Prevocational and Vocational Education for Special Needs Youth: A Blueprint for the 1980s.* Baltimore, MD: Paul H. Brookes, 1982.

Manes, S. W. *Funding resources.* 1976 National Forum on Residential Services. Arlington, TX:

National Association for Retarded Citizens, Research and Demonstration Institute, 1976.

May, J., & May, J. *Overview of emotional disturbances in mentally retarded individuals.* Presentation at, Annual Convention of the National Association for Retarded Citizens, Atlanta, GA, 1979.

Mayeda, T., & Sutter, P. *Deinstitutionalization: Phase II.* Pomona, CA: UCLA Neuropsychiatric Institute Research Group, 1981.

Mazatta, L. *Cost-effectiveness in serving medically fragile children.* Omaha, NE: University of Nebraska Medical Center, 1976 (unpublished).

McGee, J. *The needs of autistic persons and their families.* Omaha, NE: Nebraska Chapter on the National Society for Autistic Children, 1979.

McGee, J., & deLorenzo, E. *Como estabelescer prioridades en la elaboracion de programas assistenciales.* Primer Seminario Nacional Sobre Ninez, Juventud y Familia, Montevideo, 1976.

McGee, J., & Hitzing, W. *Comprehensive systems.* 1976 National Forum on Residential Services. Arlington, TX: National Association for Retarded Citizens, Research and Demonstration Institute, 1976.

McGee, J., & Hitzing, W. *The continuum of residential services: A critical analysis.* Proceedings of the Symposium on Residential Services. Arlington, TX: National Association for Retarded Citizens, 1978.

McGee, J., & Menolascino, F. *Life goals for persons with severe disabilities: A structural analysis. Viewpoints in teaching and learning.* Bloomington, IN: School of Education, University of Indiana, Vol. 57, No. 1, 1981.

McGee, J., & Pearson, P. Personal preparation to meet the mental health needs of the mentally retarded and their families. In F. Menolascino (Ed.), *Bridging the gap: Mental health needs of mentally retarded persons.* New York, NY: Wiley, 1981.

Menolascino, F. J. Emotional disturbances in mentally retarded children. *American Journal of Psychiatry,* 1969, *126,* 54–62.

Menolascino, F. Understanding parents of the retarded — A crisis model for helping them cope more effectively. In F. Menolascino & P. Pearson (Eds.), *Beyond the limits: Innovations in services for the severely and profoundly retarded.* Seattle, WA: Special Child Publications, 1974.

Menolascino, F. J. *Challenges in mental retardation: Progressive ideology and services.* New York: Human Sciences Press, 1977.

Menolascino, F. J. *Schizophrenia in the mentally retarded: A comparative study of thioridazine and thiothixene in retarded and non-retarded schizophrenic adults.* New York, NY: Impact Med. Comm., 1983.

Menolascino, F. J., & Eaton, L. Psychoses of childhood: A five year follow-up study and experiences in a mental retardation clinic. *American Journal of Mental Deficiency,* 1967, *72,* 370–380.

Menolascino, F. J., & Egger, M. L. *Medical Dimensions of Mental Retardation.* Lincoln, NY: University of Nebraska Press, 1978.

Menolascino, F., & McGee, J. The new institutions: Last ditch arguments. *Mental Retardation,* 1981, *19* (5), 215–220.

Menolascino, F. J., Neman, R., & Stark, J. A. *Curative aspects of mental retardation: Biomedical and behavioral advances.* Baltimore, MD: Paul H. Brookes, 1983.

Menolascino, F., & Pearson, P. *Beyond the limits: Innovations in services for the severely and profoundly retarded.* Seattle, WA: Special Child Publications, 1974.

Menolascino, F. J., & Strider, F. Advances in the prevention and treatment of mental retardation. In S. Arieti (Ed.), *American handbook of psychiatry, 7th Ed.* New York, NY: Basic Books, 1981.

Mitler, P. *Frontiers of knowledge in mental retardation, Vol. 1.* Baltimore, MD: University Park Press, 1980.

Morra, L. *Developing Criteria for the Evaluation of the Least Restrictive Environment Criterion.* Philadelphia, PA: Research for Better Schools, 1979.

Nagi, S., McBeoom, W., & Collette J. Work employment and the disabled. *American Journal of Economics and Sociology,* 1972, *31* (1), 21-34.

National Association for Retarded Citizens (NARC). *Teacher preparation and certification.* Arlington, TX: NARC, 1973.

National Congress of Organizations of the Physically Handicapped. Testimony of the National Congress of Organizations of the Physically Handicapped for the Oversight Hearings before the Senate Subcommittee on the Handicapped, of the Committee on Labor and Welfare, with Respect to the Rehabilitation Act of 1973, as Amended. Washington, DC, 1976.

National Institute on Mental Retardation (NIMR). *A national manpower model.* Toronto: NIMR, 1972.

National Institute on Mental Retardation. *Residential services: Community housing options for handicapped people.* Toronto: NIMR, 1975.

Nebraska Department of Education. *Benefitting the handicapped children of Nebraska.* Omaha, NE: Meyer Children's Rehabilitation Institute, 1977.

Nirje, B. The normalization principle and its human management implications. In R. B. Kugel & W. Wolfensberger (Eds.), *Changing patterns in residential services for the mentally retarded.* Washington, DC, President's Committee on Mental Retardation: U.S. Government Printing Office, 1969.

Noble, V. The economia de la minusvalia. *Siglo Cera,* Nov.-Dec. 1982, *84,* 18-50.

Olshansky, S. Changing vocational behavior through normalization. In W. Wolfensberger (Ed.), *Normalization: The principle of normalization in human services.* Toronto, Canada: National Institute on Mental Retardation, 1972.

Packard, K., & Laveck, B. *Public attitudes.* Washington, DC, President's Committee on Mental Retardation: U.S. Government Printing Office, 1976.

Park, L. D. Barriers to normality for the handicapped adult in the United States. *Rehabilitation Literature,* 1975, *36* (4), 108-111.

Perlman, L. G. (Ed.). *Legal barriers and stigma as it effects employment of persons with epilepsy.* Washington, DC: Comprehensive Vocational Rehabilitation for Severely Disabled Persons Conference, 1975.

Perr, M. The most beneficial alternative: A counter point to the least restrictive alternative. *VI Bulletin of American Academy of Psychiatry and the Law,* 1978, 4.

Perry, B. G. Transportation and communication as components of rural health care delivery. In E. W. Hassinger & L. R. Whiting (Eds.), *Rural health services: organization, delivery and use.* Ames, IA: Iowa State University Press, 1976.

Perske, R. *New directions for parents of persons who are retarded.* New York, NY: Abingdon Press, 1973.

Philips, I., & Williams, N. Psychopathology and mental retardation: A study of 100 mentally retarded children. *American Journal of Psychiatry,* 1975, *132,* 1265-1271.

Piaget, J. *Psychology of intelligence.* (Trans. Malcom Piercy & D. E. Berlyn.) London: Routledge & Kegan Paul, Ltd., 1950.

President's Commission on Mental Health. *Report of the Liaison Task Panel on Mental Retardation, Vol. 11.* Washington, DC: U.S. Government Printing Office, 1978.

President's Committee on Mental Retardation. *Mental retardation: Century of decision.* Washington, DC: U.S. Government Printing Office, 1976.

President's Committee on Mental Retardation. *The leading edge. Service programs that work.* Washington, DC: U.S. Government Printing Office, 1978.

Radford, A. J. Village-based mental health and medical care resources. In B. S. Hetzel (Ed.), *Basic health care in developing countries.* Oxford: Oxford University Press, 1978.

Reeder, C. W. *Activities of the regional rehabilitation research institute on attitudinal, legal, and recreational barriers.* Washington, DC: Comprehensive Vocational Rehabilitation for Severely Disabled Persons Conference, 1975.

Ross, P. Custodial care for the "sub-trainable": Revisiting an old myth. *Law and Psychological Review,* 1979, *1,* 1–14.

Rosen, A. *The evaluation of hostels. New prospects for retarded citizens.* London: National Society for Mentally Handicapped Children, 1976.

Rothman, D. J. Can de-institutionalization succeed? *New York University Education Quarterly,* 1979, Fall, 16–22.

Rutter M., & Schopler, E. *Autism: A reappraisal of concepts and treatment.* New York, NY: Plenum Press, 1978.

Scheerenberger, R. *A History of Mental Retardation.* Baltimore, MD: Paul H. Brookes, 1983.

Seminario Internacional sobre Empleo Protegido, Conclusion. *Siglo Cero,* 1980, *69,* 16–19.

Servicio Internacional del Informacion sobre el Deficiente Subnormal. *Vivienda y convivencia del subnormal.* A. Fierro (Ed.). San Sebastian: Servicio Internacional del Informacion sobre I Subnormal, 1978.

Servicio Internacional del Informacion sobre Subnormales. *Subnormales Profundos: Curso de Actualizacion* J. Eguia (Ed.). San Sebastian: Servicio Internacional del Informacion sobre Subnormales, 1975.

Shontz, F. *Naturalism and the behavioral-ecological point of view.* Paper presented at, 47th Annual Session of the American Congress of Rehabilitation Medicine. New York, August 19, 1970.

Shumacher, E. F. *Small is beautiful.* New York, NY: Harper & Row, 1973.

Sigelman, C. K. *Group homes for the mentally retarded.* Lubbock, TX: Texas Research and Training Center in Mental Retardation, 1973.

Skarnulis, E. *Residential services for the mentally retarded.* Omaha, NE: Eastern Nebraska Community Office of Retardation, 1976.

Skarnulis, E. Presentation at the Iowa Association for Retarded Citizens, 1977 (unpublished).

Skinner, B. F. *Science and human behavior.* New York, NY: Macmillan, 1953.

Smith, D. *Obstacles.* Report of the Special Committee on the Disabled and the Handicapped. Ottowa: Canada House of Commons, 1981.

Spencer, J. *Final Report — Regional Planning Program for Prevocational Services to Deaf/Blind Children.* Dallas, TX: South Central Regional Center for Deaf/Blind Children, Callier, Center, 1974.

Stark, J. *An evaluation of a semi-programmed self-modification technique designed to improve self-control with groups of emotionally disturbed adolescents.* Lincoln, NE: University of Nebraska, 1973 (Unpublished doctoral dissertation).

Stark, J. An evaluation of a semi-programmed self-modification techniques designed to improve self-control with groups of emotionally disturbed adolescents. In Brighan (Ed.), *Behavioral analysis in education: Self-control and reading.* Dubuque, IA: Kendall Hunt, 1976.

Stark, J., Baker, D., Menousek, P., & McGee, J. A functional approach to the vocational training of mentally retarded/behaviorally involved adolescents and adults. In F. Menolascino & J. Stark (Eds.), *Mental illness in the mentally retarded.* Balitmore, MD: Paul H. Brookes Publishing, 1981.

Stenner, R. *Social and economic conditions of the mentally retarded in selected countries.* United Nations Department of Economic and Social Affairs, Brussels, Belgium, 1976.

Stern, W. *The psychological methods of testing intelligence.* (G.M. Whipple, Transl.). Baltimore, MD: Warwicks York, 1914.

Stufflebeam, D. *Educational evaluation and decision making.* Bloomington, IN: Phi Delta Kappa, 1971.

Taylor, S. *The custodians: Attendants and their work at state institutions for the mentally retarded.* Ann Arbor, MI: University Microfilm, 1977.

Taylor, S. *Making integration work: Strategies for educating students with severe disabilities in regular schools.* Syracuse, NY: Syracuse University, 1981.

Terrace, H. S. Discrimination learning with and without "errors." *Journal of the Experimental Analysis of Behavior,* 1963, *6* (1), 1–27.

Thompson, M. M. *Housing and handicapped people.* Washington, DC, President's Committee on Mental Retardation: U.S. Government Printing Office, 1976.

Throne, J. Deinstitutionalization: Too wide a swath. *Mental Retardation,* 1979, *77,* 171.

Tizard, J. *Community services for the mentally handicapped.* London: Oxford University Press, 1969.

Toledo, M. *Integration in Spain.* Presentation at, International Conference on Cerebral Palsy, Washington, DC, 1981.

Touche-Ross and Company. *Cost Study of the Community-based Mental Retardation Regions and the Beatrice State Developmental Center.* Lincoln, NE: Department of Public Institutions, 1980.

Touche-Ross and Company. *A report on ENCOR services.* Omaha, NE: Touche-Ross and Company, 1983 (unpublished report).

Turnbull, H. R., Ellis, J. W., Boggs, E. M., Brooks, P. O., & Biklen, D. *The Least Restrictive Alternatives: Principles and Practices.* Washington, DC: American Association on Mental Deficiency, 1981.

Turoff, M. The design of a policy Delphi. *Technological Forecasting and Social Change,* 1970, *2,* 17–34.

United Nations. *Declaration on the Rights of Mentally Retarded Persons.* New York, NY: United Nations General Assembly, 2027th Plenary Meeting, 1971.

U.S. Department of Health, Education, and Welfare. *Long range projection for the provision of comprehensive services to individuals.* Washington, DC: Office for Handicapped Individuals, 1975a.

U.S. Department of Health, Education, and Welfare. *Mental retardation: The known and unknown* (OHD 76–21008). Washington, DC: U.S. Government Printing Office, 1975b.

U.S. Department of Health, Education, and Welfare. *Returning the mentally disabled to the community: Government needs to do more* (HRD–76–152). Washington, DC: U.S. Government Printing Office, 1977.

U.S. Department of Health, Education, and Welfare. *Health – United States Public Health Service* (PHS–78–1232). Washington, DC: U.S. Government Printing Office, 1978.

U.S. Department of Housing and Urban Development. *Interim Report: Barrier Free Access to the Man-Made Environment – A Review of Current Literature.* Washington, DC: U.S. Government Printing Office, 1975.

Urban Institute. *Study of Federal policies related to the disabled.* Washington, DC, Department of Health, Education, and Welfare: U.S. Government Printing Office, 1975.

Vail, D. J. Mental health and mental retardation programmes in rural America. *British Journal of Social Psychiatry and Community Health,* 1972–73, *6* (3), 170–186.

VanVechter, D., Pliss, I., & Barry, M. B. Housing and transportation: Twin barriers to independence. *Rehabilitation Literature,* 1976, *37,* 202–207, 221.

Vincent, N. New equipment opportunities for disabled of Los Angeles. *American Rehabilitation,* 1977, Nov.-Dec., 18–23.

Voces, A. Integration escolar. *Federacion Espanhola de Associaciones Pro Subnormales,* 1981, 188 (Madrid).

Walker, J. A. What about the homebound. *Journal of Rehabilitation,* 1973, Mar.-April, 21–22, 41.

Webster, T. B. Unique aspects of emotional development in mentally retarded children. In F. J. Menolascino (Ed.), *Psychiatric approaches to mental retardation.* New York, NY: Basic Books, 1971.

Wehman, P. *Competitive employment: New horizons for severely disabled individuals.* Baltimore, MD: Paul H. Brookes Publishing Co., 1981.

Weiss, C. H. *Evaluating action programs; Readings in social action and education.* Boston, MA: Allyn & Bacon, 1972.

Werry, J. S., & Sprague, R. L. Methylphenidate and haloperidol in children. *Archives of General Psychiatry,* 1972, *32,* 720–795.

Willowbrook Panel. *Willowbrook Community Placement Plan.* New York, NY: Willowbrook Master's Office, 1976.

Wilson, J. Psychopharmacological agents in mental retardation: Issues and challenges. In F. Menolascino & B. McCann (Eds.), *Briding the gap: Mental health needs of mentally retarded persons.* Baltimore, MD: University Park Press, 1983.

Wolfensberger, W. Vocational preparation and occupation. In A. Baumeister (Ed.), *Mental retardation.* Chicago, IL: Aldine Press, 1967.

Wolfensberger, W. The origin and nature of our institutional models. In R. Kugel & W. Wolfensberger (Eds.), *Changing patterns in residential services for the mentally retarded.* Washington, DC, President's Committee on Mental Retardation: U.S. Government Printing Office, 1969.

Wolfensberger, W. *The principle of normalization in human services.* Toronto: National Institute on Mental Retardation, 1972.

Wolfensberger, W., Clark, J., & Menolascino, F. J. *The report of the Nebraska citizens study committee on mental retardation.* Omaha, NE: Greater Omaha Association for Retarded Citizens, 1969.

Wolfensberger, W., Grandy, B., Flynn, R., & Johnson, T. *Environmental Barriers to Habilitation of Mentally Handicapped Individuals,* 1974 (unpublished manuscript).

Zarfas, D. E. Moving toward the normalcy principle in a large government operated facility for the mentally retarded. *Journal of Mental Subnormality,* 1970, *16,* 84–92.

Author Index

Numbers in *italic* denote pages with complete bibliographic information.

Subject Index